Ultimate Nuxt.js for Full-Stack Web Applications

Build Production-Grade Server-Side Rendering (SSR) and Static-Site Generated (SSG) Vue.js Applications Using Nuxt.js, Node.js, and Composition API

Lau Tiam Kok

www.orangeava.com

First published: January 2024

Published by: Orange Education Pvt Ltd, AVA™

Address: 9, Daryaganj, Delhi, 110002

ISBN: 978-81-96815-14-1

www.orangeava.com

Dedicated To

My beloved late parents, whom I will meet again, someday

About the Author

Lau Tiam Kok, aka Lau Thiam Kok, is a cross-disciplinary full-stack web developer and designer born in Penang, Malaysia. He holds a Bachelor of Applied Arts degree from the University Malaysia Sarawak and an MSc in Digital Futures from the Institute of Digital Art and Technology, University of Plymouth, UK. With over 10 years of freelancing, he has collaborated with various individuals, institutions, and companies. Lau works with designers or independently, from designing layouts to coding the frontend and server-side programs to produce responsive and modern websites.

In the past, he also worked collaboratively on air-quality monitoring projects. As a data analyst, he used R, openair, Shiny, MongoDB, RethinkDB, Express.js, Koa.js, Socket.IO, and Nuxt to create data analysis web apps and real-time IoT data platforms. Currently, his focus is on web development using WordPress, PHP, JavaScript, Vue.js, Nuxt, Vite, Node.js native modules such as HTTP, and utility-first CSS such as Tailwind CSS.

About the Technical Reviewer

Rohit Bahekar, a highly proficient Vue.js Developer hailing from India, brings over 7 years of steadfast dedication to the design and deployment of tailored, highly responsive web applications and e-commerce solutions. Possessing an in-depth mastery of Vue.js, Nuxt.js, Vuex, Pinia, HTML, JS, and CSS, he demonstrates proficiency in a wide array of tools and technologies, including Express.js, Node.js, Git, MySQL, MongoDB, SQLite, Jest, Selenium, AWS, GitHub Actions, and Terraform.

With a substantial impact on distinguished organizations such as Virtuoso, Linkfire, and VSH Solutions, his professional journey comprises roles such as FrontEnd Engineer and Software Engineer. His contributions are palpable in accomplishments such as the optimization of ad units, enhancement of code quality, and resolution of intricate product issues. Rohit's commitment to excellence is underscored by his academic foundation, which includes holding a Bachelor of Engineering in Computer Science and Engineering. Beyond his technical acumen, Rohit's achievements encompass the publication of a Chrome extension, the development of a screen recording feature, and the receipt of multiple Employee of the Month accolades. In addition to his accomplishments, Rohit's pivotal involvement in the design and implementation of novel features across multiple projects, all while serves as a mentor to expedite the growth of new team members.

Acknowledgements

I would like to express my gratitude to Orange AVA for providing me with the opportunity to write this book and share my knowledge with a wider audience. My thanks extend to the editorial team for their unwavering support and patience throughout the journey of writing this book. I am grateful to the graphics team for their contribution to the production of this book. Additionally, I want to thank the technical reviewers and external editors for their significant contributions to improving this book tremendously. Last but not least, heartfelt thanks to my family and friends for their support and love. Without the contribution of all these people in this journey of writing, this book would have been impossible.

Preface

Ultimate Nuxt.js for Full-Stack Web Applications aims to help you build Vue SSR and SSG apps by using the Composition API and Nuxt 3+, along with other Nuxt-related libraries and high-level frameworks, such as Windi CSS, Less CSS preprocessor, and WordPress. Throughout this book, you will learn to structure directories for Nuxt projects, build your Nuxt app with pages, layouts, routing, and components, and write stores, middleware, composables, and utility functions (a.k.a. "utilities"). You will learn to manage data in MongoDB, MariaDB/MySQL, RethinkDB, and Redis for your Nuxt apps. Furthermore, you will discover how to manage these databases internally in your Nuxt project with Nitro and externally outside Nuxt with the Node.js HTTP API. Additionally, you will create a shopping cart system using Pinia, cookies, and Redis; build a GraphQL layer to manage data; generate static pages with WordPress; deploy your Nuxt apps, and last but not least, you will explore other options to build Vue SSR and SSG apps and take your Nuxt journey further.

Ultimate Nuxt.js for Full-Stack Web Applications is the successor of *Hands-on Nuxt.js Web Development* (https://lauthiamkok.net/origins/digital/hands-on-nuxtjs-web-development), both authored by the same author. If you have already learned Nuxt from its predecessor, which is based on Nuxt 2, and would like to upgrade to Nuxt 3+ and update the old NPM packages, frameworks, and tools, this book is your resource. Whether you are coming from its predecessor or starting anew, you still can pick up and make use of *Ultimate Nuxt.js for Full-Stack Web Applications* independently. Like its predecessor, this book emphasizes using Nuxt to connect and communicate with other Node.js and PHP applications remotely, such as Node.js HTTP applications, WordPress, and GraphQL servers. This approach allows you to maintain your Nuxt.js applications as "thin" as possible while leveraging modern server-side technologies and applications. *Ultimate Nuxt.js for Full-Stack Web Applications* is more focused on this idea than its predecessor by removing basic topics, knowledge, skills, and old technologies. Notwithstanding, you may find similarities in the core idea, some example apps, and minor text between these two books.

Chapter 1

Get to know types of apps and find out where Nuxt falls in line with. Start a Nuxt project with Nuxi (Nuxt scaffolding tool). Explore Nuxt's project structure, such as the `/server/` and `/public/` directories. Learn how to customize your Nuxt app with the `nuxt.config` file.

Chapter 2

Create static and dynamic pages, as well as static and dynamic routes in Nuxt apps. Design static and dynamic page layouts with the `definePageMeta` and `setPageLayout` Nuxt APIs, along with the `NuxtLayout` Nuxt component. Develop auto-import composables (both top-level and nested) and utilities. Establish client-only and server-only plugins. Install plugins using the `nuxt.config` file. Generate auto-import plugins with the `provide` plugin helper. Create globally executed functions to run automatically when the route changes are manually applied, and create named middleware to be manually applied on specific pages.

Chapter 3

Serve public and static assets, such as images and fonts, in Nuxt projects. Use Windi CSS as a UI framework for Nuxt apps and create responsive layouts with Windi CSS. Write CSS using Less as the CSS preprocessor in your Vue apps. Serve dynamic assets using composables in the `<template>` block.

Chapter 4

Fetch data from remote APIs using the `useFetch` Nuxt API. Handle HTTP errors (for example, 404 and 500 errors) with the `showError` Nuxt API and the `error.vue` file for unknown routes, internal server errors, and JavaScript default errors during development and runtime.

Chapter 5

Create global states with the `useState` Nuxt API to be shared between the server and client across components and pages. Manipulate global states from specific pages. Build a counter and a shopping cart system with Pinia. Establish a client-server data-persistent store with the `useCookie` Nuxt API. Create a client-server data-persistent store with `localStorage` and Redis.

Chapter 6

Create Nuxt's built-in API layers, API routes, and API calls with server middleware, server plugins, and server utilities. Store and manage data with Nitro's default in-memory data storage. Integrate the MongoDB database internally in the Nuxt apps. Use the Nuxt Content module and Markdown documents as your database in Nuxt apps.

Chapter 7

Create Hot Module Replacement (HMR) Node.js apps with Vite, Node.js HTTP API, and `find-my-way` HTTP router. Create an HMR Node.js app with MySQL database and MongoDB database. Enable CORS in HMR Node.js apps for integrating with your Nuxt app. Create a real-time Nuxt app with RethinkDB and manage your app data with the RethinkDB database, Socket.IO, and the HMR Node.js app.

Chapter 8

Create a custom REST API with WordPress and Carbon Fields (a WordPress custom fields library) to serve data for your Nuxt app. Create custom fields with Carbon Fields for managing the SEO and Open Graph meta information dynamically for your Nuxt app. Develop a framework-agnostic PHP app that complies with PHP Standards Recommendations (PSR) to serve data for your Nuxt app.

Chapter 9

Introduce GraphQL and its benefits. Create HMR GraphQL apps with GraphQL Tools, Node.js HTTP API, MongoDB, and WordPress for your Nuxt app. Fetch data from GraphQL servers using GraphQL queries in your Nuxt apps.

Chapter 10

Create static-generated (SSG) sites with Nuxt and WordPress. Fetch data and stream assets from WordPress into your Nuxt project for making SSG sites. Take your Nuxt app further with testing, deployment, other Nuxt modules, such as Nuxt GTA and Nuxt-Auth, and other Nuxt APIs, such as composable APIs, utilities APIs, and component APIs. Explore options, such as using Quasar, Gridsome, and Vite SSR alone or Vite SSR plugins, for building Vue SSR and SSG apps.

Downloading the code bundles and colored images

Please follow the links or scan the QR codes to download the ***Code Bundles and Images*** of the book:

https://github.com/ava-orange-education/Ultimate-Nuxt.js-for-Full-Stack-Web-Applications

The code bundles and images of the book are also hosted on ***https://rebrand.ly/5cb440***

In case there's an update to the code, it will be updated on the existing GitHub repository.

Errata

We take immense pride in our work at **Orange Education Pvt Ltd,** and follow best practices to ensure the accuracy of our content to provide an indulging reading experience to our subscribers. Our readers are our mirrors, and we use their inputs to reflect and improve upon human errors, if any, that may have occurred during the publishing processes involved. To let us maintain the quality and help us reach out to any readers who might be having difficulties due to any unforeseen errors, please write to us at :

errata@orangeava.com

Your support, suggestions, and feedback are highly appreciated.

DID YOU KNOW

Did you know that Orange Education Pvt Ltd offers eBook versions of every book published, with PDF and ePub files available? You can upgrade to the eBook version at **www.orangeava.com** and as a print book customer, you are entitled to a discount on the eBook copy. Get in touch with us at: **info@orangeava.com** for more details.

At **www.orangeava.com**, you can also read a collection of free technical articles, sign up for a range of free newsletters, and receive exclusive discounts and offers on AVA™ Books and eBooks.

PIRACY

If you come across any illegal copies of our works in any form on the internet, we would be grateful if you would provide us with the location address or website name. Please contact us at **info@orangeava.com** with a link to the material.

ARE YOU INTERESTED IN AUTHORING WITH US?

If there is a topic that you have expertise in, and you are interested in either writing or contributing to a book, please write to us at **business@orangeava.com**. We are on a journey to help developers and tech professionals to gain insights on the present technological advancements and innovations happening across the globe and build a community that believes Knowledge is best acquired by sharing and learning with others. Please reach out to us to learn what our audience demands and how you can be part of this educational reform. We also welcome ideas from tech experts and help them build learning and development content for their domains.

REVIEWS

Please leave a review. Once you have read and used this book, why not leave a review on the site that you purchased it from? Potential readers can then see and use your unbiased opinion to make purchase decisions. We at Orange Education would love to know what you think about our products, and our authors can learn from your feedback. Thank you!

For more information about Orange Education, please visit **www.orangeava.com**.

Table of Contents

CHAPTER 1

Introducing Advanced Nuxt Web Development

Introduction

Welcome to *Chapter 1*. In this first chapter, you will learn about the different types of apps and where Nuxt falls in. You will start by creating a minimal Nuxt project with Nuxi (Nuxt scaffolding tool), explore Nuxt project structure, such as the `` `/public/` `` and `` `/server/` `` directories, and discover the reserved directories and files in Nuxt, such as `` `.env` ``, `` `composables` ``, `` `plugins` ``, `` `utils` ``, and so on. In addition, you will learn to customize your Nuxt app with the `**nuxt.config**` file.

Structure

The topics that will be covered in this chapter are as follows:

- Knowing Nuxt and Starting Nuxt Projects
- Understanding the Nuxt Project Directory Structure
- Making Custom Configurations in Nuxt Projects

Knowing Nuxt and Starting Nuxt Projects

Nuxt is a higher-level Vue framework in Node.js web development for creating Vue apps that can be server-side rendering apps (SSR) or static-generated apps

(SSG, which stands for "Static Site Generation"). Even though Nuxt apps can be deployed as SSG apps, the full power of Nuxt lies in its server-side rendering (SSR) for building universal apps.

A universal app is merely a JavaScript code that can be executed on the client and server sides. However, if you wish to develop a classic (or traditional) SPA, which runs on the client side only, you can use vanilla Vue instead. If you are interested in building a low-level Vue SPA, as well as a low-level Vue SSR app, check out [*Advanced Vue.js Web Development*](https://github.com/lautiamkok/Advanced-Vue.js-Web-Development) by the same author of this book.

Notwithstanding, before creating any app with Nuxt or Vue, you should know the different types of apps and which Nuxt falls in line with. You also should know what this book uses Nuxt for which can take you to endless backend possibilities and integrations with Nuxt. So, let's look into the various app types in the following section.

Types of Apps

The web apps we have and see today are quite different from those decades ago. The options and solutions in those days were scarce. But they are blooming in recent years. Whether they are called **applications** or **apps**, they are the same. However, let's call them "apps" throughout the book, and we can categorize them as follows:

- **Traditional Server-side Rendered App (SSR)**

Server-side rendering is the approach of delivering the data and HTML to the browser on the client side of your screen. It was the most common and only way approach when the web industry just emerged. In traditional SSR apps (they were also called "dynamic websites" in the past), every request requires a page re-rendered anew from the server to the browser. This reloads all the scripts, styles, and templates once more on every request you send to the server. Reloading and re-rendering do not sound compelling and are not elegant at all. Hence, it gave birth to single-page apps (SPAs).

- **Traditional Single-page App (SPA)**

SPAs are client-side rendered apps that render content, which include templates, in the browser by using JavaScript, without having to reload the entire app when navigating to new pages. Following is an example of a SPA that you would get on your browser when requesting it from the server:

```html
<!DOCTYPE html>
<html>
<head>
  <meta charset="utf-8">
  <title>Vue App</title>
</head>
<body>
  <div id="app"></div>
  <script src="https://unpkg.com/vue/dist/vue.js"
type="text/javascript"></script>
  <script src="/path/to/app.js"type="text/javascript"></script>
</body>
</html>
```

The preceding app contains only bare-bones HTML, with a container, **`<div>`**, having only **app** as its ID and nothing else inside it. The content of your apps, such as text, images, headings, paragraphs, and other **`<div>`** blocks that structure your page, will be loaded through JavaScript on runtime. However, traditional SPAs have a poor performance on the search engine because the SPA content that is loaded via JavaScript mostly cannot be executed by the crawlers. This gave rise to universal server-side rendered (SSR) apps.

- **Universal Server-side Rendered App (SSR)**

As you can see from the previous app categories, both traditional SSR apps and SPAs have their drawbacks. There are things to lose in SPAs: slower performance on the initial load and not being able to be crawled by search engines. On the other hand, traditional SSR apps are faster on the initial load and undoubtedly great for SEO. However, the development experience and user experience in traditional SSR apps are not as good and exciting as SPAs. So, ideally, both traditional SSR apps and SPAs can be balanced for user experience and performance. This is where universal server-side rendering (SSR) comes into play.

Universal SSR apps are developed in JavaScript with Node.js. They offer a solution for the flaws of traditional SSR apps and traditional SPAs. Universal SSR apps, just like traditional SSR apps, are loaded on the server side first when they are requested. Their pages are rendered on the server side before being sent to the browser, and then they will switch to run on the client side for the rest of their lifespans unless you refresh the browser, and their life cycles will restart anew.

However, building a universal SSR app from scratch can be time-consuming. Hence, frameworks such as Nuxt have risen in popularity these days. In addition, running universal SSR apps requires a Node.js server, which can be a setback for some businesses because **Node.js** servers are usually expensive. This is where static-generated apps (SSG) come in.

- **Static-generated App (SSG)**

SSG apps are static apps (or sites) that consist of static pages, which are generated by a static site generator and stored as static HTML pages. You then can upload the entire static site to a static hosting server that doesn't require any server-side support. Frameworks like Nuxt and Gridsome generate static pages out of the box from the app that you develop in them. For example, Nuxt generates HTML pages from each of your routes into a `dist` folder during the generate-build step, as follows:

````
```bash
-| dist/
----| favicon.ico
----| index.html
----| 200.html
----| 404.html
----| _payload.json
----| about/
------| index.html
------| _payload.json
----| contact/
------| index.html
------| _payload.json
----| _nuxt/
------| index.c028b9e6.js
------| contact.e4e929f1.js
------| R0000166.17f4c9d5.jpg
------| R0001844.96a4176f.jpg
------| ...
```
````

So, when a static app is initially loaded on the browser, you will always get the full content (text, images, meta info, and so on) immediately, no matter which route you are requesting. Then the app will perform like a traditional SPA for the rest of its lifespans unless you refresh the browser, and its life cycle will restart anew. However, since no server-side support for static-generated apps, there will be no real-time rendering from the server.

Nuxt as Universal SSR Apps and SSG Apps

From the categories in the preceding section, you probably have figured that Nuxt is a framework for building universal SSR apps and static-generated apps. Let's take a look a bit deeper into Nuxt and how this book uses these types of applications with other web technologies.

Years ago, we used server-side scripting languages like PHP to create traditional SSR apps, along with template engines such as Twig (https://twig.symfony.com/) to render the view for our apps. However, this has posed a tight coupling risk. With the emergence of universal SSR Frameworks such as Nuxt, perhaps we can harness their power to decouple the view from the server-side scripting for good. We can have two server-side apps run concurrently: a Node.js HTTP app and a Nuxt SSR app. The Node.js HTTP app (which can be Express, Koa, or any other app) is used to handle the backend data management, while Nuxt is used to consume the API and handle the view. Let's call the Node.js HTTP app as a "backend" app and Nuxt as a "frontend" app. Then, we can see that they complement each other seamlessly.

Even though we can manage the data in the same Nuxt app, doing so can lead us back to the tight coupling risk and other risks such as making our app harder to maintain and debug when the app grows larger and relies on various data-managing software on the server side. So, we should keep our Nuxt app as "thin" as possible by lifting the burden of data management from it. What's more – we can use WordPress, a PHP app, or any non-JavaScript app as the backend app to manage the data for our Nuxt app!

This separation approach also works perfectly when using Nuxt as an SSG app. During the static generation process, Nuxt can crawl the links in your Nuxt app to generate dynamic routes and save their data from the remote API as `` `_payload.json` `` files inside the `` `/dist/` `` folder. These payloads, much like the ones you can see in the example of a static app in the previous section on the SSG app category, are then used to serve as the data that was originally pulled from the remote API. With that, you are not calling the API anymore when serving the static site publicly, which keeps your API secure and private from the public.

Starting Nuxt Projects

You can create your Nuxt projects with `` `npx` `` quickly and easily in the following steps:

1. Use `npx` to install a fresh Nuxt project with a project name:

   ```
   $ npx nuxi@latest init <project-name>
   ```

2. Pick **npm** when you are prompted to pick a package manager as follows:

   ```
   > Which package manager would you like to use?
   ● npm
   o pnpm
   o yarn
   o bun
   ```

3. Change your directory to your project to install the project dependencies:

   ```
   $ npm install
   $ npm run dev
   ```

4. Start the development process:

   ```
   $ npm run dev
   ```

5. Check your Nuxt app out on your browser at `localhost:3000`.

Now you have a minimal Nuxt 3 project installed, and you can start developing your app into a more complicated and advanced one. However, before developing your minimal Nuxt app further, you should learn about the project structure provided during installation, as well as the Nuxt directory structure that consists of reserved directories and files, which you will encounter throughout this book. Let's get to it in the next section!

Exploring the Nuxt Project Directory Structure

When developing a new app, you will always need a directory structure to organize your source files into groups and categories for better future maintenance.

Getting a directory structure that can be mutually agreed upon and followed by all your fellow developers is challenging. This is where frameworks like Nuxt come into play. While Nuxt is not just a framework for directory structures, in this topic, we will look into the directory structure in Nuxt that you and your co-developers can agree on and develop your app without conflicting and arguing over the directory structure in the long term. So, let's find out!

Exploring the Project Structure

After creating the project with Nuxt, if you take a look inside the project directory, it provides us with a minimal structure as follows:

```
├── package.json
├── tsconfig.json
├── nuxt.config.ts
├── app.vue
├── .gitignore
├── .nuxt
│   └── ...
├── node_modules
│   └── ...
├── public
│   └── favicon.ico
└── server
    └── tsconfig.json
```

From this basic structure, you can build and grow your app in the root directory. For example, at some point later, you would add more directories in it such as **`pages`**, **`layouts`**, **`components`**, and **`stores`** directories. For the time being, let's discover the role of the following **highlighted** directories and files that are pre-installed by Nuxt for you:

- **The `package.json` File**

The **`package.json`** file is used to contain the dependencies and (command) scripts of your app. You get the following default scripts and dependencies in this file by default:

```bash
// package.json
{
  "name": "nuxt-app",
  "private": true,
```

```
  "type": "module",
  "scripts": {
    "build": "nuxt build",
    "dev": "nuxt dev",
    "generate": "nuxt generate",
    "preview": "nuxt preview",
    "postinstall": "nuxt prepare"
  },
  "devDependencies": {
    "@nuxt/devtools": "latest",
    "nuxt": "^3.8.0",
    "vue": "^3.3.7",
    "vue-router": "^4.2.5"
  }
}
```

- **The `nuxt.config.ts` File**

The **`nuxt.config.ts`** file is used to configure your Nuxt app. You should see the following options (or properties) by default when you open this file:

```js
// nuxt.config.ts
export default defineNuxtConfig({
  devtools: { enabled: true }
})
```

For more information on configuring your Nuxt app with **`nuxt.config.ts`**, please visit https://nuxt.com/docs/api/configuration/nuxt-config. We will come back to this **`nuxt.config.ts`** file again for configuring your Nuxt app in the next section.

- **The `/public/` Directory**

The **`/public/`** directory is used to serve assets that you don't want to be compiled during the build process or cannot be compiled, such as favicon files. This directory contains a **`favicon.ico`** file by default when installing your project with Nuxt. You can create a **`static`** sub-directory to keep these files, and they will simply be copied during the build. All files in this directory are mapped to the server root directly, making them accessible under the root URL directly. For example, **`/public/static/1.jpg`** is mapped as **`/static/1.jpg`**, so you can access it on your browser as follows:

```
http://localhost:3000/static/1.jpg
```

Also, you can access it in the **`<template>`** block on any component or page. For example:

```html
// pages/about.vue
<template>
  <img scr="/static/1.jpg" />
</template>
```

- **The `/server/` Directory**

The **`/server/`** directory is used to create and register APIs internally inside the Nuxt project for your Nuxt app. Files inside the following sub-directories are scanned automatically to register APIs with HMR support:

```
server
├── api
│   └── ...
├── routes
│   └── ...
└── middleware
    └── ...
```

In each file, you must use a **`defineEventHandler`** or **`eventHandler`** (alias) to define a default function, and then export it with a response data in JSON. For example:

```js
// server/api/greet.ts
export default defineEventHandler(event => {
  return {
    great: 'Hello World'
  }
})
```

After that, you can call the preceding API in the `<script>` block on any component and page. For example:

```js
// pages/index.vue
<script setup>
const { data } = await useFetch('/api/greet')
</script>
```

We will look into this directory again and use it to create local APIs to manage data for our Nuxt apps in *Chapter 6, Managing Data with Nitro Server Engine in Nuxt*. For more information about this directory, please visit https://nuxt.com/docs/guide/directory-structure/server.

The preceding directories and files will be used throughout this book in the upcoming chapters. If you wish to find out the role of other directories and files included with the project installation but not covered in this section or this book, please visit https://nuxt.com/docs/guide/directory-structure. For now, let's discover the reserved directories and files in Nuxt in the following section.

Discovering the Reserved Directories and Files

From the preceding basic project structure, you can add the following reserved directories and files in your Nuxt project whenever you need them to provide solutions in building your Nuxt app:

```bash
├── package.json
├── tsconfig.json
├── babel.config.js
├── nuxt.config.ts
├── app.vue
├── ...
├── .env
├── assets
│   └── ...
├── components
│   └── ...
├── composables
│   └── ...
├── content
```

```
│   └── ...
├── layouts
│   └── ...
├── middleware
│   └── ...
├── modules
│   └── ...
├── pages
│   └── ...
├── plugins
│   └── ...
└── utils
    └── ...
```

We will use some of the preceding directories and files often in the upcoming chapters. For the time being, let's discover the role of the following highlighted reserved directories and files:

- The **`.env`** File

The **`.env`** file is used to add your custom environment variables the **`dev`**, **`build`**, and **`generate`** time. They are automatically loaded at these modes and can be accessed in **`/nuxt.config.ts`** and in modules. For example:

```
// .env
API_BASE_URL=https://dummyjson.com
```

Then the preceding environment variable can be accessed in **`/nuxt.config.ts`**:

```js
// nuxt.config.ts
export default defineNuxtConfig({
  runtimeConfig: {
    public: {
      apiBaseUrl: process.env.API_BASE_URL
          }
    }
  }
})
```

After that, you can access it anywhere throughout your app. For example:

```js
// pages/cart.vue
<script setup>
const runtimeConfig = useRuntimeConfig()
const { data, error } = await useFetch(`/products/?limit=10`, {
  baseURL: runtimeConfig.public['apiBaseUrl']
})
</script>
```

- **The `/assets/` Directory**

The **`/assets/`** directory is used to add the assets of your project, such as images, fonts, and style sheets (Less, Stylus, or Sass files), which you want to be compiled during the build process. For example, you may have a Less file, as follows:

```css
// assets/styles.less
@width: 10px;
@height: @width + 10px;

header {
  width: @width;
  height: @height;
}
```

Nuxt will compile the preceding code into the following CSS for your app during the build process:

```css
header {
  width: 10px;
  height: 20px;
}
```

- **The `/components/` Directory**

The **`/components/`** directory is used to add Vue components. You should keep small and reusable components in this directory. You can even create nested components in this directory. For example:

```

components
└── foo
    └── bar.vue
```

Then, you will get the name of the preceding component that is based on its directory and filename as follows:

```html
<FooBar />
```

- **The `/composables/` Directory**

The **`/composables/`** directory is used to add Vue composable functions (also known as "composables"). They should be reusable and self-contained. Each composable file should contain one single composable only. For example:

```js
// composables/use-foo.ts
export default () => {
  return 'bar'
}
```

After that, you can use the composable in the **`<script>`** block on any component and page. For example:

```js
// pages/index.vue
<script setup>
const bar = useFoo()
</script>
```

Also, you can use it in the **`<template>`** block on any component or page. For example:

````
```html
// pages/about.vue
<template>
  <p>
    {{ useFoo() }}
  </p>
</template>
```
````

Nuxt comes with tons of built-in composables, such as **`useRuntimeConfig`** and **`useFetch`**, which you have seen in the **`.env`** directory in the preceding sections. You can check out the rest of Nuxt composables at https://nuxt.com/docs/api/composables.

- **The `/layouts/` Directory**

The **`/layouts/`** directory is used to add reusable layouts for your app. They are enabled only by adding a **`<NuxtLayout>`** component in **`/app.vue`**. For example:

````
```html
// app.ts
<template>
  <NuxtLayout>
    <h1>
      Layouts and Pages
    </h1>
    ...
  </NuxtLayout>
</template>
```
````

And you might have a default layout created in the **`/layouts/`** directory as follows:

````
```html
// layouts/default.vue
<template>
  <div>
    <p>
      default
````
````

```
    </p>
    <slot />
  </div>
</template>
```

The preceding layout will be loaded into the **`app.ts`** file as follows:

```html
<div>
  <p>
    default
  </p>
  <h1>
    Layouts and Pages
  </h1>
  ...
</div>
```

- **The `/middleware/` Directory**

The **`/middleware/`** directory is used to add middleware for executing code before navigating to a route of your app. In other words, they are **route middleware**. You must use **`defineNuxtRouteMiddleware`** to create a middleware. For example:

```js
// middleware/auth.ts
export default defineNuxtRouteMiddleware((to, from) => {
  const user = useAuth()
  if (!user.value) {
    return navigateTo('/login')
  }
})
```

And then you can manually apply preceding middleware on any route/ page. For example:

```js
// pages/profile.ts
<script setup>
definePageMeta({
  middleware: 'auth'
```

```
})
</script>
```

The preceding middleware is executed only when navigating to **`/profile`**, before entering this route and rendering the page. This can be useful if you want to perform user authentication before granting access to this page.

- **The `/pages/` Directory**

The **`/pages/`** directory is used to add routes and pages for your app. A **`<NuxtPage>`** component is required to display the pages in this directory. For example:

```html
// app.ts
<template>
  <div>
    <NuxtPage />
  </div>
</template>
```

And you might have a page added in the **`/pages/`** directory as follows:

```html
// pages/contact.vue
<template>
  <p>
    How to contact me...
  </p>
</template>
```

Then, you can access the preceding page on your browser as follows:

```
http://localhost:3000/contact
```

- **The `/plugins/` Directory**

The **`/plugins/`** directory is used to add Vue plugins to your app. You must use a **`defineNuxtPlugin`** Nuxt utility function with a **`provide`** key to create a plugin. For example, a plugin that runs on both the client and server sides:

```js
// plugins/foo.ts
export default defineNuxtPlugin(nuxtApp => {
  return {
    provide: {
      greet: (name: string) => `Greeting, ${name}!`
    }
  }
})
```

Then, you can call the preceding when you want to use them in the **`<script>`** block as follows:

```js
// pages/index.vue
<script setup>
const { $greet } = useNuxtApp()
console.log($greet('Matt'))
</script>
```

You can also use it in the **`<template>`** block on any component or page. For example:

```html
// pages/profile.vue
<template>
  <p>
    {{ $greet('Marlene') }}
  </p>
</template>
```

- **The `/utils/` Directory**

The **`/utils/`** directory is used to add your own utility functions (also called "utilities") that can be used across your app. Just like composables, utilities should be reusable and self-contained. Each utility file should contain only one single utility function. For example, a utility that checks if a string is a JSON string or not:

````
```js
// utils/is-json.ts
export default str => {
  try {
    JSON.parse(str)
  } catch (e) {
    return false
  }
  return true
}
```
````

After that, you can use the utility in the **`<script>`** block or anywhere. For example:

````
```js
// pages/index.vue
<script setup>
const string = '{"name":"John", "age":30, "car":null}'
console.log(isJson(string)) // true
</script>
```
````

Also, you can use it in the **`<template>`** block on any component or page. For example:

````
```html
// pages/about.vue
<template>
  <p>
    {{ isJson('hello world') }} // false
  </p>
</template>
```
````

Like composables, Nuxt comes with tons of built-in utilities that you have seen in the preceding directories, such as **`defineNuxtRouteMiddleware`**, **`navigateTo`**, **`definePageMeta`**, and **`defineNuxtPlugin`**. You can check out the rest of Nuxt utilities at https://nuxt.com/docs/api/utils.

The preceding directories and files are the ones we will use throughout the book. We will look into them again and use them in the upcoming chapters. Some of them will be used more often than others. It is worth knowing that files added to these directories are auto-imported. This means you can use them directly in the **`<script>`** or **`<template>`** block without manually importing them with the JavaScript **`import`** statement. If you wish to check out the remaining directories and files not covered in this section or this book, please visit https://nuxt.com/docs/guide/directory-structure. For now, let's discover the configuration in Nuxt projects in the next section.

Making Custom Configurations in Nuxt Projects

By default, you can start your Nuxt project and run the Nuxt app immediately without any further configuration. However, you may need to extend the default configuration, such as adding Nuxt modules, registering plugins, and so on. Basically, you only need the **`nuxt.config.ts`** file to configure your Nuxt project. You just need to pass your preferences through the Nuxt configuration options in this file. So, let's discover some of the configuration options!

Discovering Configuration Options in `nuxt.config.ts`

After installing a fresh project with Nuxt, you should get a **`nuxt.config.ts`** file inside your project folder. If you open this **`nuxt.config.ts`** file, you should see the following configuration option:

```js
// nuxt.config.ts
export default defineNuxtConfig({
  devtools: { enabled: true }
})
```

The **`devtools`** option is one of the Nuxt configuration options that you can use to specifically customize your Nuxt app. There are tons of configuration options available that you can use to customize or extend Nuxt to suit your requirements, such as **`alias`**, **`app`**, **`build`**, and so on. You don't need to know or use all of them, but let's get familiar with some of the following **highlighted** options:

- **The `devtools` Option**

Nuxt comes with a Nuxt DevTools module, which is enabled by default, regardless of whether you have this option enabled in **`/nuxt.config.ts`** or not.

This tool gives you insights about your app during development and is useful for debugging your app. However, if you want to turn it off during development, you can set a `false` value to the `devtools` option:

```js
// nuxt.config.ts
export default defineNuxtConfig({
  devtools: { enabled: false }
})
```

For more information about this Nuxt DevTools module, please visit https://devtools.nuxt.com/.

- **The `app.head` Option**

The `app.head` option is used to set a default `<head>` tag on every page of your app, which includes `<title>`, `<meta>`, `<script>`, `<link>`, and so on. For example:

```js
// nuxt.config.ts
export default defineNuxtConfig({
  app: {
    head: {
      title: 'Advanced Nuxt.js Web Development',
      meta: [
        { name: 'viewport', content: 'width=device-width,
initial-scale=1' },
        { name: 'description', content: 'Build SSR & SSG Vue apps
with Nuxt and Composition API' },
        { name: 'keywords', content: 'Vue, Nuxt, SSR' }
      ],
      script: [
        {
          src: 'https://cdnjs.cloudflare.com/ajax/libs/lodash.
js/4.17.21/lodash.min.js',
          type: 'text/javascript'
        },

        {
          innerHTML: `
            document.addEventListener("DOMContentLoaded", function
() {
              const numbers = [1, 2, 3, 4]
              const shuffle = _.shuffle(numbers)
              console.log(shuffle)
```

````
            })
          `,
          type: 'text/javascript',
          body: true
        },
      ],
      link: [
        { rel: 'stylesheet', href: 'https://fonts.googleapis.com/css2?family=Open+Sans' },
        { rel: 'icon', href: '/favicon.svg', type: 'image/x-icon' }
      ],
      style: [
        { children: 'html, body { font-family: "Open Sans", sans-serif }', type: 'text/css' }
      ],
      noscript: [
        { children: 'JavaScript is required to run this site. Please enable it on your browser.' }
      ]
    }
  },
})
```
````

The preceding configuration will produce the following tags inside the `` `<head>` `` on every page:

````
```html
<head>
  <meta name="viewport" content="width=device-width, initial-scale=1">
  <title>Advanced Nuxt.js Web Development</title>
  <meta name="description" content="Build SSR &amp; SSG Vue apps with Nuxt and Composition API">
  <meta name="keywords" content="Vue, Nuxt, SSR">
  <link rel="stylesheet" href="https://fonts.googleapis.com/css2?family=Open+Sans">
  <link rel="icon" href="/favicon.svg" type="image/x-icon">
  <style type="text/css">html, body { font-family: "Open Sans", sans-serif }</style>
  <script src="https://cdnjs.cloudflare.com/ajax/libs/lodash.js/4.17.21/lodash.min.js" type="text/javascript"></script>
  <noscript>JavaScript is required to run this site. Please enable it on your browser.</noscript>
  ...
````

```html
</head>
```

On the other hand, the script that you have the `body` key set to `true` will be appended inside the `<body>` tag as follows:

```html
<body>
  ...
  <script type="text/javascript">
    document.addEventListener("DOMContentLoaded", function () {
      const numbers = [1, 2, 3, 4]
      const shuffle = _.shuffle(numbers)
      console.log(shuffle)
    })
  </script>
</body>
```

Note that the styles and scripts you set in this `app.head` option are not compiled during the build. They will be processed as they are in this option. However, it is better to compile your code for production unless you have to set them in this option. You will learn how to develop your styles and scripts that are compiled during development and build in the upcoming chapters.

- **The `css` Option**

The `css` option is used to set the global styles of your app. You can use the extension of your CSS pre-processor in this option, and Nuxt will compile the code automatically during development and build – as long as you have the required loader of your pre-processor installed in your project. For example:

```js
// nuxt.config.ts
export default defineNuxtConfig({
  css: [
    '@/assets/styles/css/font-face.css',
    '@/assets/styles/css/main.css',
    '@/assets/styles/less/main.less',
  ]
})
```

- **The `devServer.port` Option**

The **`devServer.port`** option is used to change the listening port of the development server of your app. The default port is **`3000`** in Nuxt, but if you ever need to use a different port during development, you can set it in this option. For example:

```js
// nuxt.config.ts
export default defineNuxtConfig({
  devServer: {
    port: 5173
  }
})
```

Now your app is running on **`localhost:5173`** for development. However, Nuxt will still use the **`3000`** port for production. So, if you need to change that too, you can use a **`.env.production`** in your project root as follows:

```
// .env.production
HOST=localhost
PORT=4173
```

Only with the preceding configuration in the **`.env.production`** file, your production app is then running on **`localhost:4173`**.

- **The `dir` Option**

The **`dir`** option is used to customize the name of the default directories that are used by Nuxt. Unless you need to, it is better to keep them as they are by default, as follows:

```js
// nuxt.config.ts
export default defineNuxtConfig({
  dir: {
    assets: 'assets',
    layouts: 'layouts',
    middleware: 'middleware',
    modules: 'modules',
    pages: 'pages',
```

````
    plugins: 'plugins',
    public: 'public',
    static: 'public'
  }
})
```
````

- **The `imports` Option**

The `imports` option is used to add your custom directories for Nuxt to auto-import the files that you put in them. The default directories in this option are `composables` and `utils` only. So, if you have a **stores** directory at some point and want the files in this directory to be auto-imported, then you can set them here. For example:

````
```js
// nuxt.config.ts
export default defineNuxtConfig({
  imports: {
    dirs: ['stores']
  }
})
```
````

With the preceding configuration, Nuxt can now auto-import files from the `/stores/` directory, as well as the files from the `composables` and `utils` directories. Note that setting additional auto-import directories in this option will not override the default directories (`composables` and `utils`).

- **The `modules` Option**

The `modules` option is used to install Nuxt modules to extend Nuxt's core functionality for your app. There are tons of Nuxt modules developed by the Nuxt team and community that you can integrate into your app. For example:

````
```js
// nuxt.config.ts
export default defineNuxtConfig({
  modules: [
    'nuxt-windicss',
  ],
})
```
````
````

- **The `plugins` Option**

The `plugins` option is used to manually install un-scanned plugins in the `/plugins/` directory. Nuxt only scans and registers the top-level plugins in the `/plugins/` directory automatically for you. However, if you have nested plugins, Nuxt will ignore them. So, you can use this option to register them. For example:

```js
// nuxt.config.ts
export default defineNuxtConfig({
  plugins: [
    '~/plugins/fooz/fooz-1.ts', // both client & server
    { src: '~/plugins/fooz/fooz-1.ts' }, // both client & server
    { src: '~/plugins/fooz/fooz-1.ts', mode: 'client' }, // only on client side
    { src: '~/plugins/fooz/fooz-1.ts', mode: 'server' } // only on server side
  ]
})
```

- **The `runtimeConfig` Option**

The `runtimeConfig` option is used to pass environment variables across your app. It can be used to keep private information from being accessed by public users, such as API tokens/ keys, which should be kept available on the server-side only. However, the information that is set in the `public` key is not only available on the server-side but also exposed to the client-side. For example:

```js
// nuxt.config.ts
export default defineNuxtConfig({
  runtimeConfig: {
    apiKey: 'ghp_mRxDcmE0a4Pri',
    public: {
       appBaseURL: 'http://localhost:3000',
       apiBaseURL: 'http://localhost:4000'
    }
  }
})
```

The preceding configuration will produce the following information on your browser:

````
```html
<body>
  ...
  <script>
    window.__NUXT__={};window.__NUXT__.config={public:
{appBaseURL:"http://localhost:3000",apiBaseURL:"http://
localhost:4000"},app:{baseURL:"/",buildAssetsDir:"/_nuxt/",cdnURL:""}}
  </script>
</body>
```
````

Notice that the information of **`appBaseURL`** and **`apiBaseURL`** can be traced in the **`window`** object, but the information of **`apiKey`** is not printed in the **`window`** object.

- **The `srcDir` Option**

The **`srcDir`** option is used to change the source directory of your app. The source directory of your app is set to the project root by default in Nuxt, but you can change that if you prefer to set it to a specific folder. For example:

````
```js
// nuxt.config.ts
export default defineNuxtConfig({
  srcDir: 'src/'
})
```
````

With the preceding configuration, Nuxt will change the load path of the source directory to **`/src`**, and you can develop your app on this directory structure as follows:

````
```
├── package.json
├── tsconfig.json
├── nuxt.config.ts
├── node_modules
├── public
└── src
    ├── app.vue
    ├── error.vue
````
````

```
├── assets
├── components
├── composables
├── content
├── layouts
├── middleware
├── modules
├── pages
├── plugins
└── utils
```

The preceding configuration options are the basic and common options that you need to know to kick off a Nuxt project and to go through this book. We will look into some of these configuration options again in the upcoming chapters. Note that Nuxt is actually pre-configured to suit most of the project scenarios that you would encounter, so you don't really need to configure it much. Nonetheless, if you wish to check out the remaining configuration options not covered in this section or this book, or if you need some specific configuration to suit your needs, please visit https://nuxt.com/docs/api/nuxt-config. For now, let's start creating pages, layouts, composables, plugins, utilities, and middleware in your Nuxt projects in the next chapter.

You can find the example app for this topic in **`/1.nuxt/1.essentials/1.config/`** in the GitHub repository of this course.

Conclusion

Well done! You have managed to complete the first chapter of your journey into Nuxt. In this chapter, you have learned that Nuxt apps fall in line with the categories of SSR and SSG apps among the other types of apps. You have installed a minimal Nuxt project and dipped into the Nuxt directory structure. Also, you have learned the role of some highlighted directories and files, such as **`nuxt.config.ts`**, **`.env`**, **`pages`**, **`composables`**, and so on. Lastly, you have learned about configuring and extending your Nuxt project with **`nuxt.config.ts`** and explored some of the highlighted configuration options, such as **`devtools`**, **`app.head`**, **`css`**, **`plugins`**, **`runtimeConfig`**, and so on.

In the next chapter, you will create static and dynamic pages as well as static and dynamic routes in Nuxt. You will learn to create plugins for client-side only, server-side only, and both. In addition, you will create global and local middleware to be applied globally and manually on specific pages. Lastly, you will learn to create composables and utilities. So, stay tuned!

CHAPTER 2

Creating Pages, Layouts, Composables, Plugins, Utilities, and Middleware

Introduction

Welcome to *Chapter* 2. In this chapter, you will create static and dynamic pages and static and dynamic routes in Nuxt apps; static and dynamic layouts with **`definePageMeta`**, **`setPageLayout`**, **`NuxtLayout`**, and middleware; plugins (top-level and nested) with **`defineNuxtPlugin`**, **`provide`**, and **`nuxt.config.ts`** for client-side only, server-side only, and both; global and named middleware with **`defineNuxtRouteMiddleware`**, **`defineNuxtPlugin`**, and **`addRouteMiddleware`** to be applied manually on specific pages and globally; composables (top-level and nested) and utilities with **`export`**, **`export`**, **`default`**, and **`defineNuxtPlugin`**.

Structure

The topics that will be covered in this chapter are as follows:

- Creating Static and Dynamic Routes
- Creating Static and Dynamic Layouts
- Creating Plugins and Middleware
- Creating Composables and Utilities

Creating Static and Dynamic Routes

A page is just a Vue component in nature. It is a parent component that can consist of smaller components. But for the sake of separation of concerns, this type of parent components are called *pages* and stored in the **`pages`** directory. While the smaller components are kept in the **`/components/`** directory. There is no strict rule that you must do this in a Vue app. But in Nuxt, it is a structure that you should follow to make your Nuxt apps more manageable. So, in a complex Nuxt app, you might have the following pages that you need to create in the **`/pages/`** directory:

```
pages
├── index.vue
├── about.vue
├── blog.vue
│   ├── post-1.vue
│   ├── post-2.vue
│   └── ...
├── shop.vue
│   ├── product-1.vue
│   ├── product-2.vue
│   └── ...
└── contact.vue
```

And you would want to access these pages on operating routes, for example:

```
/
/about
/contact
/blog
/blog/post-1
/shop/product-1
```

You cannot achieve that on Vue itself. You will need a Vue plugin, **Vue Router**, https://router.vuejs.org/, to help you to access your pages via these routes. Vue Router allows you to create robust routes for navigating between pages in a single-page application (SPA) without having to refresh the page. Nuxt comes with Vue Router pre-installed so you don't have to install it like in a Vue app. So let's discover how you can use it to create and handle routes for us. We will first begin by creating simple routes to serve our pages. So, in the coming sections, you will discover how to use this plugin to create simple to dynamic routes, as well as handle unknown routes.

Creating Simple Routes and Pages

Simple routes are created by simply adding arbitrary and fixed names to your route list. Each name is prefixed with a `/` and each route is just a JavaScript object, for example:

````
```js
[
  { path: '/' },
  { path: '/about' }
]
```
````

In a Vue app, you will need to map these routes manually to the designated components:

````
```js
[
  { path: '/', component: HomeComponent },
  { path: '/about', component: AboutComponent }
]
```
````

You then can access them on the browser address just as you set them in the route list:

````
```
/
/about
```
````

In Nuxt, routes are auto-generated and mapped to the components automatically for you. So let's follow the following steps to create these simple routes and see how Nuxt does the magic in your Nuxt app:

1. Create a new directory called **`pages`** in the project root directory with the following pages (Vue components):

```
pages
├── index.vue
└── about.vue
```

Note that the **`index.vue`** page will be the home page of your Nuxt app.

2. Add some basic content on each page as follows:

- The **`home`** page:

```
// pages/index.vue
<template>
  <p>
    Hello World!
  </p>
</template>
```

- The **`about`** page,

```
// pages/about.vue
<template>
  <p>
    Hello About!
  </p>
</template>
```

3. Create a dummy data that contains the app's navigation items in the **`app.vue`** component:

```js
// App.vue
<script setup>
const menu = [
  {
    title: 'Home',
```

````
      path: '/'
    },
    {
      title: 'About',
      path: '/about'
    },
    {
      title: 'Shop',
      path: '/shop'
    },
    {
      title: 'Blog',
      path: '/blog'
    }
  ]
</script>
```
````

We will create the pages and routes for the blog and shop in the coming sections.

4. Display the navigation data in the **`<template>`** block via the **`v-for`** loop and display the page content via a **`<NuxtPage>`** component:

````
```html
// App.vue
<template>
  <h1>
    Layouts and Pages
  </h1>
  <ul v-if="menu">
    <li v-for="(item, index) in menu">
      <NuxtLink :to="item.path">
        {{ item.title }}
      </NuxtLink>
    </li>
  </ul>
  <NuxtPage />
</template>
```
````

- The **`<NuxtPage>`** component is a built-in component that comes with Nuxt and it is used to display the page that corresponds to the requested URL. It is just a wrapper around the **`RouterView`** component from Vue Router. For more information about this component, please visit https://nuxt.com/docs/api/components/nuxt-page#nuxtpage.
````

- The `<NuxtLink>` component is used to create links, the `<a>` elements, for Vue Router to change the URL and load the page without reloading the entire document. It is just a replacement component for the `<RouterLink>` component from Vue Router. For more information about this component, please visit https://nuxt.com/docs/api/components/nuxt-link#nuxtlink.

5. Run the app on the `dev` environment:

```
$ npm run dev
```

You should see the `home` page is loaded at `localhost:3000` with the site menu that you just created. If you navigate to `localhost:3000/about`, you should see the `about` page. Notice that the requested page is loaded into the `<NuxtPage>` component without reloading the navigation and the `app.vue` component. The `router-link-active` and `router-link-exact-active` classes are added to the `<a>` element when it is clicked. For more information about these two classes, please visit https://next.router.vuejs.org/api.

You can also create sub-routes and sub-pages by organizing `.vue` files into different folders and then they will be mapped automatically into your route list. For example, you can create the main page of your shop (`/pages/shop.vue`) and a sub-folder that contains a list of your product pages as follows:

```
pages
├── shop.vue
└── shop
    ├── product-1.vue
    ├── product-2.vue
    └── ...
```

Nuxt will map the preceding pages and generate routes for you out of the box as follows:

```
/shop
/shop/product-1
/shop/product-2
```

However, manually creating the sub-routes like this is repetitive and difficult to manage in the long term. Imagine, you have hundreds or thousands of products that are stored dynamically in a remote database, it is not good to have to create routes for them manually. So, simple routes should not be used for cases like this. This type of route is good for top-level pages, such as **`/about`**, **`/contact`**, and **`/posts`**. If you have multiple sub-pages in each of these top-level pages and they will increase dynamically over time, then you should use dynamic routes to handle the routes for these sub-pages. So, let's find out how you can create dynamic routes and pages in the next section.

Creating Dynamic Routes and Pages

A dynamic route is a route that is denoted with a **`:`** (colon) pattern, such as **`:id`**,**`:username`**,**`:slug`**, and so on. This dynamic segment is called **`param`** (short for the parameter) in Vue Router and they will be stored in **`$route.params`** the **`$route`** object. You then can access this parameter from **`$route.param`** in your components and pages, for example, **`$route.params.id`**.

So if you create a **`/shop/:slug`** dynamic route, URLs like **`/shop/product-1`** and **`/shop/product-2`** will both match and map to this route. And the value of their parameters (**`slug`**) will be exposed as **`this.$route.params.slug`** in every component. Once again, in Nuxt, these dynamic routes are auto-generated and mapped to the dynamic components automatically for you. So let's find out how you can create dynamic routes and pages in a Nuxt app in the following steps:

1. Create a **`shop`** sub-folder with an **`index.vue`** page and a **`[slug].vue`** page in the **`/pages/`** directory as follows:

```
pages
└── shop
    ├── index.vue
    └── [slug].vue
```

The **`[slug].vue`** page will be the single product page that will change its content dynamically whenever its dynamic route is matched. It is not a mandatory rule in developing Vue apps that you must use square brackets for dynamic pages. But in Nuxt apps, you should use square brackets for dynamic pages to distinguish them from simple pages.

2. Create a dummy static data that contains the shop navigation items on the `shop` page in `/pages/shop/index.vue`:

````
```js
// pages/shop/index.vue
<script setup>
const menu = [
  {
    title: ‘Product 1’,
    path: ‘/shop/product-1’
  },
  {
    title: ‘Product 2’,
    path: ‘/shop/product-2’
  },
]
</script>
```
````

3. Display the shop title and navigation data in the `<template>` block via the `v-for` loop on the `shop` page:

````
```html
// pages/shop/index.vue
<template>
  <ul v-if="menu">
    <li v-for="(item, index) in menu">
      <NuxtLink :to="item.path">
        {{ item.title }}
      </NuxtLink>
    </li>
  </ul>
</template>
```
````

4. Create a dummy static data that contains a list of products, in which you can search and display a single user-requested product on the `/pages/shop/[slug].vue` dynamic page:

````
```js
// pages/shop/[slug].vue
<script setup>
const products = [
  {
    slug: 'product-1',
````
````

```
    title: 'Product 1',
    contents: '<p>Contents 1</p>'
  },
  {
    slug: 'product-2',
    title: 'Product 2',
    contents: '<p>Contents 2</p>'
  },
        {
    slug: 'product-3',
    title: 'Product 3',
    contents: '<p>Contents 3</p>'
  }
]
</script>
```

5. Find the user-requested product from the `**posts**` dummy data list with `**useRoute**`, `**reactive**`, `**toRefs**`, and `**find**` methods as follows on the `**/pages/shop/[slug].vue**` dynamic page:

```js
// pages/shop/[slug].vue
<script setup>
const route = useRoute()
const product = reactive({
  title: null,
  contents: null,
  layout: null
})
let { title, contents, layout } = toRefs(product)

const products = [...]

const found = products.find(post => post.slug === route.
params.slug)
title = found.title
contents = found.contents
</script>
```

As you can see that we need to import a few things from Vue and Vue Router to do our dynamic page. The `**reactive**` and `**toRefs**` are used to make our JavaScript object reactive. While the `**useRoute**` is used to trace the route `**params**` from the router. And then the JavaScript built-in `**find**` method is used to find the specific product from the product list. Once a product is found, we update the product's title to the Vue reactive **`title`** object.

Notes:

- The **`reactive`** method is used to create a reactive copy of an object. It is equivalent to the **`data`** option in Options API. For more information about this method, please visit https://vuejs.org/api/reactivity-core.html#reactive.
- The **`toRefs`** method is used to convert a reactive object to a plain object to make each property in the converted object a reference pointing to the property in the original object. Destructuring the **`product`** reactive object will cause the loss of Vue reactivity on the **`title`** property. Hence, we need to covert the **`product`** reactive object using this method. For more information about this method, please visit https://vuejs.org/api/reactivity-utilities.html#torefs.
- The **`useRoute`** method is used to return the information of the current route location. It is equivalent to using **`$route`** in Options API. For more information about this method, please visit https://next.router.vuejs.org/api/#useroute.
- The **`find`** method is a JavaScript built-in method that can be used to search an item in an array. For more information about this method, please visit https://developer.mozilla.org/en-US/docs/Web/JavaScript/Reference/Global_Objects/Array/find.

6. Create a **`<template>`** block to display the current product that is found from the product list on the **`/pages/shop/[slug].vue`** dynamic page:

````
```html
// pages/shop/[slug].vue
<template>
  <h2>
    {{ title }}
  </h2>
  <div v-html="contents" />
</template>
```
````

7. Run the app on the **`dev`** environment:

````
```
$ npm run dev
```
````

You should see the `shop` page at `localhost:3000/shop` with the shop menu. So, if you navigate to `localhost:3000/shop/product-1`, you should see that **`Product 1`** is displayed on the `/shop/[slug].vue` dynamic page, and navigating to `localhost:3000/shop/product-2` will load the `Product 2` on the same dynamic page.

Dynamic routes are useful and unavoidable in a more complex app. They are good for pages that share the same layout. For example, if you have the `/about` and `/contact` routes using the same layout (which is quite unlikely), then creating a `/[slug]/` directory in the preceding dynamic route example code is a good choice. So, just as with the sub-pages under the `/shop` route that share the same layout, the `/[slug].vue` file approach is a good choice for this scenario.

Besides using this (simple) dynamic route to create sub-routes for sub-pages under the `/shop` route, we can also use more complex dynamic routes for them – nested routes. This is a case when you don't want the parent layout to be replaced completely by the child layout when rendering the sub-pages; in other words, when you want to render the sub-page inside the parent layout. Let's find out how you can achieve this in the next section.

Creating Nested Routes and Pages

In some cases, you may want to compose components (child components) that are nested inside other components (parent components), and you will want to render these child components inside particular views of the parent components, instead of having the parent components replaced by the child components.

To do that in a Nuxt app, you will need to insert a `<NuxtPage>` component inside the parent component for the child component. For example, say you have a `blog` parent component and you want the contents of the individual post to be loaded inside this parent when a specific post is called. Then, you can create a nested route for them with the following steps:

1. Create a `blog.vue` page and a `blog` sub-folder with a `[slug].vue` page in the `/pages/` directory as follows:

```
pages
├── blog.vue
└── blog
    └── [slug].vue
```

2. Create a dummy data that contains the blog navigation items on the **`blog`** page in **`/pages/blog.vue`**:

    ```js
    // pages/blog.vue
    <script setup>
    const menu = [
      {
        title: 'Post 1',
        path: '/blog/post-1'
      },
      {
        title: 'Post 2',
        path: '/blog/post-2'
      },
    ]
    </script>
    ```

3. Display the blog navigation data in the **`<template>`** block via the **`v-for`** loop and display it on the **`blog`** page:

    ```html
    // pages/blog.vue
    <template>
      <ul v-if="menu">
        <li v-for="(item, index) in menu">
          <NuxtLink :to="item.path">
            {{ item.title }}
          </NuxtLink>
        </li>
      </ul>
      <NuxtPage :page-key="route.path" />
    </template>

    <script setup>
    const route = useRoute()
    ...
    </script>
    ```

Notice that you need to bind a key, the **`pageKey`** prop, to the **`<NuxtPage>`** component inside this parent component so that Vue won't reuse this component for loading the child component when the route has changed. So, the **`path`** string from the `$route` object is used as the key, which is unique whenever the route has changed. As you can't use `$route` in Composition API, the `useRoute` method must be imported from Vue Router as a `route` constant so that it can be used in the template just like `$route` in Options API.

If you put the preceding code in a diagram, it can be visually explained, as follows:

```
+--------------------+
| Blog               |
| +----------------+ |
| | Post 1, Post 2 | |
| +----------------+ |
| +----------------+ |
| |   <NuxtPage>   | |
| +----------------+ |
+--------------------+
```

Then, the preceding code will produce the following visual when a child link is clicked for example, child `Post 1` and `/blog/post-1` will be dynamically generated as the route:

```
/blog/post-1
+--------------------+
| Blog               |
| +----------------+ |
| | Post 1, Post 2 | |
| +----------------+ |
| +----------------+ |
| |     Post 1     | |
| +----------------+ |
+--------------------+
```

But we are not finished yet because we still need to deal with the empty view in `/blog` when no post has been called yet. So, to fix that, you will create an index child component in `/pages/blog/`, as follows:

```
// pages/blog/index.vue
<template>
  <h2>
```

~~~
    Blog Index
  </h2>
</template>
```
~~~

And that when you navigate to `` `/blog` `` on your browser, you will get the following result:

~~~
```
/blog
+--------------------+
| Blog               |
| +----------------+ |
| | Post 1, Post 2 | |
| +----------------+ |
| +----------------+ |
| |   Blog Index   | |
| +----------------+ |
+--------------------+
```
~~~

So now, you should have the new file structure in your app as follows:

~~~
```
pages
├── blog.vue
└── blog
    ├── index.vue
    └── [slug].vue
```
~~~

4. Create a dummy static data that contains a list of posts, in which you can search and display a single user-requested post on the `` `/pages/blog/[slug].vue` `` dynamic page:

~~~
```js
// pages/blog/[slug].vue
<script setup>
const posts = [
  {
    slug: 'post-1',
~~~

~~~
      title: 'Post 1',
      contents: '<p>Contents 1</p>'
    },
    {
      slug: 'post-2',
      title: 'Post 2',
      contents: '<p>Contents 2</p>'
    },
    {
      slug: 'post-3',
      title: 'Post 3',
      contents: '<p>Contents 3</p>'
    }
  ]
  </script>
  ```
~~~

5. Find the user-requested post from the **`posts`** dummy data list with **`useRoute`**, **`ref`**, and **find** methods as follows on the **`/pages/blog/[slug].vue`** dynamic page:

~~~
```js
// pages/blog/[slug].vue
<script setup>
const route = useRoute()

const title = ref(null)
const contents = ref(null)

const posts = [...]
const found = posts.find(post => post.slug === route.params.slug)

title.value = found.title
contents.value = found.contents
</script>
```
~~~

Notice that instead of using the **`reactive`** method as in the **`/pages/shop/[slug].vue`** dynamic page, you can make a single standalone reactive object directly by using the **`ref`** method. Once a post is found, then you can update its title to the **`title`** standalone reactive object through its inner **`value`** property. This is because the **`title`** reactive object is a reference pointing to its inner **`value`** property. Notes:

- The `ref` method is used to create a single mutable reactive object that you can obtain its inner value without using `.value`, which is the only property it accepts. For more information about this method, please visit https://vuejs.org/api/reactivity-core.html#ref.

6. Create a `<template>` block to display the found post from the `posts` list on the `/pages/blog/[slug].vue` dynamic page:

```html
// pages/blog/[slug].vue
   <template>
       <h2>
         {{ title }}
       </h2>
       <div v-html="contents" />
   </template>
```

7. Run the app on the `dev` environment:

```
$ npm run dev
```

You should see the `blog` page at `localhost:3000/blog` with the blog menu and the `/blog/index.vue` index page (child component). If you navigate to `localhost:3000/blog/post-1`, you should see the `Post 1` is displayed on the `/blog/[slug].vue` dynamic page (child component) is loaded inside the `/blog.vue` parent page (parent component), and navigating to `localhost:3000/blog/post-2` will load the `Post 2` on the same dynamic page inside the `/blog.vue` parent page too.

A nested route is a `children` option of another array of route configuration objects inside the route configuration object of a parent route object. Therefore, you can keep nesting views as much as you need. However, we should avoid deep nesting to keep our application simple as much as possible for better maintenance.

Creating dynamic routes and pages always requires the parameters in the route (in other words, the route `params`) so that we can pass them (whether they are IDs or slugs) to the dynamic pages to be processed. But before processing and responding to the parameters, it is a good idea to validate them. So, let's take a look at how we can validate the route `params` in the next section.

Validating Route Params

As you already know, the `setup` API is a component option that is executed before the component is created. It serves as the entry point for composition APIs. So we can validate the route `params` of a dynamic route inside the `setup` block before the component is created. If the validation rejects the route `params`, then you can immediately throw an error page before any further data is processed or fetched asynchronously. This error page can be a 500, 400, or 404 page. So, let's find out how you can validate the route `params` and throw errors in Nuxt in the following steps:

1. Validate the `slug` parameter and use the `createError` API from Nuxt to throw a 400 error on the `/blog/[slug].vue` page as follows:

```js
// pages/blog/[slug].vue
<script setup>
const route = useRoute()
...

const test = /^[a-zA-Z0-9\-]*$/.test(route.params.slug)
if (test === false) {
  throw createError({
    statusCode: 400,
    statusMessage: 'Invalid request'
  })
}
</script>
```

In the preceding validation rule, the `[a-zA-Z0-9\-]` regex is used to accept alphabets (uppercase or lowercase), numbers, and hyphens only. Anything else will be rejected and an error object will be thrown with `Invalid request` as the message and `400` as the status code. Note that you can apply this validation code to the `/shop/[slug].vue` post page as well. For more information about the `createError` API, please visit https://nuxt.com/docs/api/utils/create-error#createerror.

2. Use the `showError` API from Nuxt on the `/blog/[slug].vue` page to show the 404 error on the Nuxt default error page:

```js
// pages/blog/[slug].vue
<script setup>
```

```
...
const found = posts.find(post => post.slug === route.params.
slug)
if (found === undefined) {
  showError({
    statusCode: 404,
    statusMessage: 'Page Not Found'
  })
}
</script>
```

In the preceding code, the request will be rejected and an error object will be thrown with `Page Not Found` as the message and `404` as the status code. Note that you can apply this validation code to the `/shop/[slug].vue` post page as well. For more information about the `showError` API, please visit https://nuxt.com/docs/api/utils/show-error#showerror.

3. Catch thrown error by the `createError` API on the top-level `app.vue` parent component by using the `onErrorCaptured` (`errorCaptured`) hook and show the error on the Nuxt error page by using the `showError` API as follows:

```js
// app.vue
<script setup>
onErrorCaptured(err => {
  showError({
    statusCode: err.statusCode || 500,
    statusMessage: `${err.name} - ${err.message}`,
    stack: err.stack
  })
  return false
})
</script>
```

Notice that you must return `false` in the `onErrorCaptured` block to prevent the error from propagating further. And note that if you are not catching the thrown errors, you will get the following warning and error on your browser console when your app is in the SPA mode during the runtime:

````
```bash
[Vue warn]: Unhandled error during execution of setup function
...
Uncaught (in promise) Error: Invalid request
...
```
````

Also, note that even if you are using the `showError` API only on the `/blog/[slug].vue` page to handle errors (400, 404, and so on), you must stop your code from being executed further, and the error from propagating further by using the `onErrorCaptured` hook and the `false` return on the `app.vue` component. In other words, the `onErrorCaptured` hook and the `false` return are required for both `createError` and `showError` APIs to call the Nuxt default error page for displaying the errors during the SPA mode. For more information about the `onErrorCaptured` hook, please visit https://vuejs.org/api/composition-api-lifecycle.html#onerrorcaptured.

4. Run the app on the `dev` environment and test with the following routes on your browsers:

````
```
/blog/$
/blog/Ø
/blog/post-*
/blog/post-^
```
````

You should see the Nuxt default error page is called and displaying the 400 error for the invalid input from the user and the 404 error for the posts that are not found:

````
```
/blog/post-4
/blog/post-5
```
````

Note that you also can throw a 404 page when validating the route `params.` But sometimes it is good to distinguish between the invalid routes from unknown routes which are better served with a 404 page. So, when the route `params` has passed the validation, the next thing you need to check is if we can find the article (a post or a product) that matches the route `params`. If no match is found, then we will throw the 404 page. Let's find out how to handle unknown routes in the next section.

Catching All Unknown Routes

Before handling the unknown routes for dynamic routes and pages, we should also handle the unknown routes on the top-level simple routes. You can catch all these unknown routes (also known as 404 not found routes) in the following steps:

1. Create a `[...all].vue` page in the `/pages/` directory as follows:

   ```
   pages
   └─ [...all].vue
   ```

2. Add the template and script in the `/pages/[...all].vue` page:

   ```js
   // pages/[...all].vue
   <script setup>
   showError({
     statusCode: 404,
     statusMessage: 'Page Not Found'
   })
   </script>
   ```

3. Run the app on the `dev` environment and test with the following routes on your browsers:

   ```
   /xyz
   /abc
   ```

You should see the `/pages/[...all].vue` page is executed to call the Nuxt default error page and display the 404 error on your screen.

As you can see catching all the unknown routes in simple routes and pages is very straightforward, while catching them in dynamic routes and pages need some extra work as you have to manually throw the error when no result is found from the existing data. But the extra work is still an easy task that is just a few lines of code.

Routes and pages are inextricably related and inseparable for creating multiple pages in the Nuxt app. Vue Router has provided us with an incredibly straightforward way of making the routes for our app, from simple routes to dynamic routes, and nested routes. And Nuxt has even made it more straightforward by auto-generating and mapping these routes for us. Validating routes and handling unknown ones are very easy with Vue Router and Nuxt. However, you probably have noticed that we use the Nuxt default error page to show the errors which is not ideal for a real project. It would be ideal to customize this default error page or create our own error page. You will discover how to override this default error page and create your own error page in the upcoming chapter when fetching data from APIs. Right now, there is more you can do with Vue Router, such as adding navigation guards (middleware), adding route meta fields, fetching data, and more. So in the next topic, you will discover how to create static and dynamic layouts in Nuxt while leveraging the navigation guards (middleware) from Vue Router. So let's find out!

You can find the example app for this topic in `` `/1.nuxt/1.essentials/2.pages-layouts/` `` in the GitHub repository of this book.

Creating Static and Dynamic Layouts

Like pages, a layout is just a Vue component in nature. It is a parent component that can consist of smaller components of a page. But for the sake of separation of concerns, let's call this type of parent component *layouts* and store them in a new directory called `` `layouts` ``. There is no strict rule that you must do this in Vue apps. But in Nuxt, it is a directory in the Nuxt directory structure that you must follow to make your Nuxt app more manageable. So, in your Nuxt app, you might have the following layouts in the `` `/layouts/` `` directory:

````
```
layouts
├── default.vue
├── light.vue
└── dark.vue
```
````

You might want some pages to use specific layouts. For example, you would like the `` `home` `` page to use the default layout, the `` `about` `` page to use the `` `dark` `` layout, and some single posts to use the `` `light` `` layout but some use the `` `dark` `` or `` `default` `` layout, the `` `product-1` `` page to use the `` `dark` `` layout, and so on. All these are feasible with `` `definePageMeta` ``, `` `setPageLayout` ``, middleware, and the **`<NuxtLayout>`** and **`<slot>`** components. You will discover how to use them in the coming sections. So let's start creating your app layouts with **`definePageMeta`**, the **`<NuxtLayout>`** component, and the **`<slot>`** component.

Creating Static Layouts with definePageMeta

Setting layouts statically in Nuxt is incredibly easy and straightforward. It does all the heavy lifting that you have to do in Vue apps. You just have to create your layouts and use the **`definePageMeta`** API to set the layout statically on the pages you want to apply the layouts from the **`/layouts/`** directory. Let's discover how you can create layouts using this feature with slots and apply them in your Nuxt app in the following steps:

1. Add a very simple structure in each layout to contain a **`<slot>`** component in the **`/layouts/`** directory as follows:

   The **`default`** layout:

   ```
   // layouts/default.vue
   <template>
     <div>
       <p>
         default
       </p>
       <slot />
     </div>
   </template>
   ```

   The **`light`** layout:

   ```
   // layouts/light.vue
   <template>
     <div class="grey">
       <p>
         light
       </p>
       <slot />
     </div>
   ```

```
</template>

<style scoped>
.grey {
  background-color: #ccc;
}
</style>
```

The **`dark`** layout:

```
// layouts/dark.vue
<template>
  <div class="dark">
    <p>
      dark
    </p>
    <slot />
  </div>
</template>

<style>
.dark {
  background-color: #666;
}

.dark {
  color: white;
}

.dark a {
  color: white;
}
</style>
```

A slot can be thought of as a content placeholder. So you can dump your contents from a parent component into the child component that contains a **`<slot>`** component in it. In other words, these preceding layouts are child components. The **`<slot>`** component inside them will be replaced by the contents (or components) you place in the top-level component. For example:

```html
// app.vue (as parent)
```

```html
<template>
  <div>
    <dark>
      <ul>
        <li>Home</li>
        ...
        <li>Contact</li>
      </ul>
      <router-view/>
    </dark>
  </div>
</template>
```

Anything between the opening and closing tags of the `<dark>` element will be distributed down to this `<dark>` component and replaces the `<slot>` component in it as follows:

```html
// layout/dark.vue
<template>
  <div class="dark">
    <ul>
      <li>Home</li>
      ...
      <li>Contact</li>
    </ul>
    <slot />      </div>
</template>
```

For more information about the `<slot>` component, please visit https://vuejs.org/guide/components/slots.html.

2. Wrap the app template with the `<NuxtLayout>` component in the `<template>` block in `app.vue`:

```html
// app.vue
<template>
  <NuxtLayout>
    <h1>
      Layouts and Pages
```

```
      </h1>
      <ul v-if="menu">
        ...
      </ul>
      <NuxtPage />
    </NuxtLayout>
  </template>
```

The `<NuxtLayout>` component in the preceding code is used to activate the `default` layout on `app.vue.` For more information about the `<NuxtLayout>` component, please visit https://nuxt.com/docs/api/components/nuxt-layout#nuxtlayout.

3. Use the `definePageMeta` API to set the layout in the `layout` property on a page that you would like to override the `default` layout, for example:

```js
// pages/about.vue
<script setup>
definePageMeta({
  layout: 'light',
})
</script>
```

4. Run the app on the `dev` environment:

```
$ npm run dev
```

You should see the `home` page is loaded at `localhost:3000` with the `default` layout you just created. If you navigate to `localhost:3000/about`, you should see the `light` layout has been applied to this page and overridden the `default` layout on the `app.vue` component. Notice that the layout will switch back to the `default` layout when no specific component is determined. If you put this process in a diagram, it can be visually explained as follows when the app is loaded at `localhost:3000` and when navigating to those pages have no specific layout set:

```
+---------------------+
| default             |
| +-----------------+ |
| |  Home           | |
| +-----------------+ |
+---------------------+
```

On the other hand, the `default` layout will be overridden when navigating to those pages that have specific layouts set, for example:

```
+---------------------+
| light               |
| +-----------------+ |
| | About           | |
| +-----------------+ |
+---------------------+
```

You may have realized that the `definePageMeta` API actually works the same as using the `meta` property (or the route `meta` field) directly from Vue Router to attach a piece of arbitrary information to a route to set specific layouts for certain pages. The `<NuxtLayout>` component also works the same as creating dynamic components by binding the `is` attribute with a reactive variable, for example:

```html
<component :is="layout">
  //...
</component>
```

The `layout` variable is a reactive object, its value can be computed and changed dynamically. When the value of the `layout` variable is changed, the preceding component is changed too. However, whether you are using the `definePageMeta` API or route `meta` field directly with Vue Router has its limitations as you only can set the data manually in the JavaScript object. If you have your data stored remotely in a database and you have the layout information of each page stored in the database, then you can't use the `definePageMeta` API or the `meta` field to set the arbitrary information for switching layouts around. You will need to fetch the layout data either at the route's end or at the page's end and then pass the fetched data to the `<NuxtLayout>` component or the dynamic component. So, we will first look at how you can fetch the data at the route's end with navigation guards (also known as middleware) in the next sections with the `setPageLayout` API from Nuxt.

Creating Dynamic Layouts with `setPageLayout` and Middleware

Setting layouts dynamically in Nuxt is also very easy and straightforward. Again, it does the heavy lifting that you have to do in Vue apps. You just have to create your layouts and use the `setPageLayout` API and middleware to set the layout dynamically on the pages you want to apply the layouts from the `/layouts/` directory. Let's discover how you can create layouts using this approach in your Nuxt app in the following steps:

1. Create a new directory called `middleware` in the project root with a `layout.ts` file:

   ```bash
   middleware
   └── layout.ts
   ```

2. Create a dummy static data that contains a list of posts, in which you can search the post that contains the layout name of that post:

   ```js
   // middleware/layout.ts
   const posts = [
     {
       slug: 'post-1',
       layout: 'light'
     },
     {
       slug: 'post-2',
       layout: 'dark'
     },
     {
       slug: 'post-3',
     }
   ]
   ```

3. Use the `` `defineNuxtRouteMiddleware` `` API to create a middleware and use the `` `setPageLayout` `` API set the layout that you would like to override the `` `default` `` layout as follows:

```
```js
// middleware/layout.ts
const posts = [ ... ]
export default defineNuxtRouteMiddleware((to, from) => {
  let found = posts.find(post => post.slug === to.params.slug)
  if (!found) {
    return
  }
  setPageLayout(found.layout)
})
```
```

As you can see that we use the JavaScript built-in `` `find` `` method to find the specific post from the `` `posts` `` list and get the layout name from the post. If no post is found from the list, we stop the middleware from executing further. In a real project, you would fetch the data dynamically from an API and set the layout instead of getting the data from static data.

4. Use the `` `definePageMeta` `` API to set the `` `layout` `` middleware in the `` `middleware` `` property on a page that you would like to override the `` `default` `` layout, for example:

```
```js
// pages/blog/[slug].vue
<script setup>
definePageMeta({
  middleware: ['layout']
})
</script>
```
```

Notice that we use the `` `definePageMeta` `` API in the preceding code just like we did in the previous section. The only difference is we use the `` `middleware` `` property in this example, while in the other, we used the `` `layout` `` property.

5. Run the app on the `dev` environment:

```
$ npm run dev
```

You should see the `home` page is loaded at `localhost:3000` with the `default` layout. If you navigate to `localhost:3000/blog/post-1`, you should see the `light` layout has been applied and overridden the `default` layout. The same goes with `/blog/post-2`, you should see the `dark` layout has been applied and overridden the `default` layout. If you put this process in a diagram, it can be visually explained as follows when the app is loaded at `localhost:3000` and when navigating to those pages that have no specific layout set:

```
+--------------------+
| default            |
| +----------------+ |
| | Post 3         | |
| +----------------+ |
+--------------------+
```

On the other hand, the `default` layout will be overridden when navigating to those pages that have specific layouts set, for example:

```
+--------------------+
| light              |
| +----------------+ |
| | Post 1         | |
| +----------------+ |
+--------------------+
```

You may have realized that the `defineNuxtRouteMiddleware` API actually works the same as using the navigation guards directly from Vue Router. For example, in a Vue app, you can use the global guard to fetch the API data and set the layout with the `meta` property whenever a route is changed, as follows:

```js
const router = createRouter({ ... })
```

~~~
router.beforeEach(async (to, from, next) => {
  const slug = to.params.slug ?? undefined
  if (slug === undefined) {
    return next()
  }
  const response = await fetch(`https://my-api.xyz/posts/${slug}`)
  const data = await response.tson()
  to.meta.layout = data.layout

  next()
})
```
~~~

In Nuxt, we can also can create a global middleware and achieve the same result with the `defineNuxtRouteMiddleware` API. You will discover how to create global middleware and more details on middleware in Nuxt in the next topic. But for now, let's find out how you can create dynamic layouts on a per-page basis with a named `NuxtLayout` component in the next section.

Creating Dynamic Per-page Layouts with Named `NuxtLayout`

Setting layouts dynamically with `setPageLayout` and middleware helps us to apply the custom layout to pages (children) and override the layout on the `app.vue` parent component. But depending on how you design your layouts overall if you just want to apply the custom layout on children pages only, for example, the product pages, you can use the following steps in your Nuxt app to achieve that:

1. Create a dummy static data that contains a list of products, in which you can search the product that contains the layout name of that product, for example:

~~~
```js
// pages/shop/[slug].vue
<script setup>
const products = [
  {
    slug: ‘product-1’,
    title: ‘Product 1’,
    contents: ‘<p>Contents 1</p>’,
    layout: ‘light’
  },
  {
~~~

```
    slug: ‘product-2’,
    title: ‘Product 2’,
    contents: ‘<p>Contents 2</p>’,
    layout: ‘dark’
  },
  {
    slug: ‘product-3’,
    title: ‘Product 3’,
    contents: ‘<p>Contents 3</p>’
  }
]
</script>
```

2. Use `reactive` to make a reactive `product` constant with the following properties and deconstruct them, just as you have learned in the *Creating Static and Dynamic Routes* topic, as follows:

```js
// pages/shop/[slug].vue
<script setup>
const product = reactive({
  title: null,
  contents: null,
  layout: null
})
let { title, contents, layout } = toRefs(product)

const products = [ ... ]
</script>
```

3. Use the JavaScript built-in `find` method to find the user-requested product from the `products` list and set the layout value as follows:

```js
// pages/shop/[slug].vue
<script setup>
...
const posts = [ ... ]
const found = products.find(post => post.slug === route.
params.slug)

title = found.title
contents = found.contents
```

```
layout = found.layout
</script>
```

The most important thing in the preceding code is the `layout` reactive object that we will need in the next step. The value of the `layout` reactive object will change with the data from the post we found from the `posts` list. Once again, in a real project, you would fetch the data dynamically from an API and set the layout instead of getting the data from static data.

4. Use the `<NuxtLayout>` component with a `name` attribute to wrap your template as follows:

```html
// pages/shop/[slug].vue
<template>
  <NuxtLayout :name="layout">
    <h2>
      {{ title }}
    </h2>
    <div v-html="contents" />
  </NuxtLayout>
</template>
```

Notice that we set the `layout` reactive object as the value of the `name` attribute on the `<NuxtLayout>` component. So, the value of the `name` attribute will change with the data according to the post we found from the `posts` list.

5. Run the app on the `dev` environment:

```
$ npm run dev
```

You should see the `home` page is loaded at `localhost:3000` with the `default` layout - just as in the previous sections that you have just learned. If you navigate to `localhost:3000/shop/product-1`, you should see the `light` layout has been applied on this product page **within** the `default` layout. The same goes with `/shop/product-2`, you should see the `dark` layout has been applied accordingly. If you put this process in a diagram, it can be visually explained as follows when the app is navigated to those products that have no specific layout set:

```
+--------------------+
| default            |
| +----------------+ |
| | default        | |
| | +------------+ | |
| | | Product 3  | | |
| | +------------+ | |
| +----------------+ |
+--------------------+
```

On the other hand, for those products that have specific layouts set, the diagram can be visually explained as follows:

```
+--------------------+
| default            |
| +----------------+ |
| | light          | |
| | +------------+ | |
| | | Product 1  | | |
| | +------------+ | |
| +----------------+ |
+--------------------+
```

However, this seems odd and does not make sense with this approach as we probably don't want our customized **`default`** layout to be re-applied without itself. So remove the **`default.vue`** file from the **`/layouts/`** directory and refresh your app or restart it on the **`dev`** environment:

```
$ npm run dev
```

You should see the customized **`default`** layout is gone on the **`home`** page when it is loaded at **`localhost:3000`**. If you navigate to **`localhost:3000/shop/product-1`**, you should see the customized **`light`** layout has been applied on this product page only. The same goes with **`/shop/product-2`**, only the customized **`dark`** layout has been applied accordingly. If you put this process in a diagram, it can be visually explained as follows when the app is navigated to those products that have no specific layout set:

```
+--------------------+
| +---------------+ |
| | +-----------+ | |
| | | Product 3 | | |
| | +-----------+ | |
| +---------------+ |
+--------------------+
```

On the other hand, for those products that have specific layouts set, the diagram can be visually explained as follows:

```
+--------------------+
| +---------------+ |
| | light         | |
| | +-----------+ | |
| | | Product 1 | | |
| | +-----------+ | |
| +---------------+ |
+--------------------+
```

As you can see that the `` `default` `` layout now is an empty slot and this makes more sense with this approach to change our layout dynamically.

Again, you may have realized that this can be done in the Vue app also by using the dynamic component with the `` `is` `` attribute. But in Nuxt, you just have to use the `` `<NuxtLayout>` `` component with the `` `name` `` attribute. This approach is ideal if you just want to change the layout on this page only and leave the elements (for example, header and footer elements/components) outside this page as they are. But if you would like to change the outside (top-level) elements through this page, then the first and second approaches that you have just learned in the previous sections are more suitable and ideal.

Having multiple layouts is probably inescapable if you are building a large app that requires different looks and feels on different contents. Unlike traditional server-side scripting apps, rendering different layouts on different pages is quite a challenge in Vue and Nuxt apps. In Nuxt, depending on how complex the look and feel of your Nuxt app is, and how complex the app itself is, you can apply different layouts from using the `<NuxtLayout>` component, slots, middleware, the `definePageMeta` API, and the `setPageLayout` API that you have learned in this topic. In the next topic of this chapter, you will learn to learn more about middleware. Also, you will find how to use the `/plugins/` directory to create reusable functions in Nuxt. So let's get to it.

You can find the example app for this topic in `/1.nuxt/1.essentials/2.pages-layouts/` in the GitHub repository of this book.

Creating Plugins and Middleware

In this topic, we are going to look into the `/plugins/` and `/middleware/` directories in Nuxt. You have learned to use some middleware briefly in the previous topic, but there is more about middleware in Nuxt. For example, apart from using the `/middleware/` directory for creating middleware, you also can use the `/plugins/` directory for doing the same. But before going into more about middleware, you must first learn to `/plugins/` directory in your Nuxt app. So, let's get started!

Creating Plugins with `defineNuxtPlugin` and `provide`

Plugins are just global JavaScript functions by nature, encapsulated in `.js` files that can be installed in your Vue app by using `use` global method. For example, Vue Router is a plugin that has been pre-installed for us in Nuxt. In a Vue app, all plugins are meant for the client-side, whereas in Nuxt, you will need to take care of the both client and server sides. You might want some plugins to run on the client or server-side only, or both. So in this section, we are going to create our own plugins in Nuxt, whether they are for client or server only, or for both, and see how they are installed automatically for us by Nuxt. You are also going to create plugins that are not scanned and installed by Nuxt and we will be installing them manually through the `nuxt.config.ts`. But before that, let's see how you can create plugins that are scanned automatically by Nuxt in the following steps:

1. Create the `/plugins/` directory in your project root with the following files:

```
plugins
├── foo.ts
├── foo.server.ts
└── foo.client.ts
```

2. Use `defineNuxtPlugin` and `provide` to create a `greet` function in `/plugins/foo.ts` as follows:

```js
// plugins/foo.ts
export default defineNuxtPlugin(nuxtApp => {
  return {
    provide: {
      greet: (name: string) => `Greeting, ${name}! I'm a
"foo", client-server, auto-registered!`
    }
  }
})
```

Notice that you can access your Nuxt app information in `defineNuxtPlugin` through its first parameter, `nuxtApp`. So, it is useful if you need to access the app information, such as the runtime configuration, which you can access via `nuxtApp.ssrContext.runtimeConfig` or just using `useRuntimeConfig`, for example:

```js
const runtimeConfig = useRuntimeConfig()
const apiBaseUrl = runtimeConfig.public['apiBaseUrl']
```

Also notice that you can access the `provide` helper through `nuxtApp`. So instead of returning an object with the `provide` key in it, you can create your plugin as follows:

```js
nuxtApp.provide('apiBaseUrl', apiBaseUrl)
```

However, returning an object with the `provide` key is more recommended as you don't need to set the plugin name manually, such as `apiBaseUrl` as in the preceding code, which looks repetitive.

3. Use `defineNuxtPlugin` and `provide` to create a `hello` function in `/plugins/foo.server.ts` as follows:

```js
// plugins/foo.server.ts
export default defineNuxtPlugin(nuxtApp => {
  return {
    provide: {
      hello: (name: string) => `Hello, ${name}! I'm a "foo", server-only, auto-registered!`
    }
  }
})
```

4. Use `defineNuxtPlugin` and `provide` to create a `hi` function in `/plugins/foo.client.ts` as follows:

```js
// plugins/foo.client.ts
export default defineNuxtPlugin(nuxtApp => {
  return {
    provide: {
      hi: (name: string) => `Hi, ${name}! I'm a "foo", client-only, auto-registered!`
    }
  }
})
```

5. Use the preceding `greet` and `hi` functions anywhere you like in the `<template>` block, for example:

```html
// pages/plugins.vue
<template>
  <p>
    $greet (client-server): {{ $greet('Marlene') }}
  </p>
  <ClientOnly>
```

~~~~
      <p>
        $hi (client only): {{ $hi('Molly') }}
      </p>
    </ClientOnly>
  </template>
  ```
~~~~

Note that all functions are prefixed with a `$` automatically when they are created in Nuxt. Also, you must use the `<ClientOnly>` component for the functions created in the files that are suffixed with `.client`, because they are available on the client side only.

6. Use the preceding `greet` and `hello` functions anywhere you like in the `<script>` block, for example:

~~~~
```js
// pages/plugins.vue
<script setup>
const { $hello, $greet } = useNuxtApp()
console.log($greet('Matt'))

if (process.server) {
  console.log('server only:', $hello('John'))
}
</script>
```
~~~~

Notice that you must import the functions from `useNuxtApp` for using the functions in the `<script>` block. Also, you must use the `process.server` if-condition block for the functions created in the files that are suffixed with `.server`, because they are available on the server-side only.

7. Run the app on the `dev` environment:

~~~~
```

$ npm run dev
```
~~~~

Navigate to the page where you use the `greet` and `hi` functions, you should see the following output on your browser screen:

~~~~
```

    $greet (client-server): Greeting, Marlene! I'm a "foo",
client-server, auto-registered!
~~~~

```
    $hi (client only): Hi, Molly! I’m a “foo”, client-only,
auto-registered!
```

If you check your terminal, you should see the following output on your terminal for the `greet` and `hello` functions that you just used:

```
    Greetings, Matt! I’m a “foo”, client-server, auto-registered!
    Server only: Hello, John! I’m a “foo”, server-only,
auto-registered!
```

On the other hand, if you check your browser console, because the `greet` function is created for both client and server sides, and you use it in the `<script>` block for both sides, you should also see the following output on the browser console:

```
    Greetings, Matt! I’m a “foo”, client-server, auto-registered!
```

Notice that the output for the `greet` function on both the client and server sides is identical.

As you can see, custom plugins are very handy when we want to use them in the `<template>` block as they are available automatically. However, if you need to use them in the `<script>` block, you will need to deconstruct them from your Nuxt app through `useNuxtApp`. These plugins that you just created are scanned and installed automatically for you by Nuxt. But there are plugins that Nuxt will skip scanning. So let’s find out.

Creating Plugins with `defineNuxtPlugin`, `provide`, and `nuxt.config.ts`

Keeping our plugins in the `/plugins/` directory root and letting Nuxt scan automatically for us is very convenient. But you would want to organize your plugins into sub-directories in the `/plugins/` directory at some point when your plugins are piling up. When this happens, Nuxt won’t be scanning these plugins that are kept in the sub-directories. Then, you will have to manually register these un-scanned plugins in the `nuxt.config.ts` file. Let’s find out how you can do that in the following steps:

1. Create a `fooz` sub-directory in `/plugins/` with a `fooz-1.ts` file:

    ```
    plugins
    └── fooz
        └── fooz-1.ts
    ```

2. Use `defineNuxtPlugin` and `console.log` to print an output in `/plugins/fooz/fooz-1.ts` as follows:

    ```js
    // plugins/fooz/fooz-1.ts
    export default defineNuxtPlugin(nuxtApp => {
      console.log('"fooz-1", registered via nuxt.config.ts!')
    })
    ```

Note that you also can use the `provide` helper to create a function if you prefer just as in the previous section.

3. Manually register `/plugins/fooz/fooz-1.`ts in `nuxt.config.ts` in the `plugins` key as follows:

    ```js
    // nuxt.config.ts
    export default defineNuxtConfig({
      plugins: [
        '~/plugins/fooz/fooz-1.ts'
      ]
    })
    ```

Note that you also can register the un-scanned plugins as follows:

```js
// nuxt.config.ts
export default defineNuxtConfig({
  plugins: [
    { src: '~/plugins/fooz/fooz-1.ts' }
  ]
```

```
})
```

4. Run the app on the `dev` environment:

```
$ npm run dev
```

Navigate to the page where you use the plugin, and you should see the following output on your browser console and your terminal:

```
"fooz-1", registered via nuxt.config.ts!
```

There you go! You have successfully applied the code on both the client and server sides. However, if you just want to apply the code on the client-side only, you can add a `client` mode to the file you want to register, as follows:

```js
// nuxt.config.ts
export default defineNuxtConfig({
  plugins: [
    { src: '~/plugins/fooz/fooz-1.ts', mode: 'client' }
  ]
})
```

On the other hand, if you just want to apply the code on the server-side only, you can add a `server` mode to the file you want to register, as follows:

```js
// nuxt.config.ts
export default defineNuxtConfig({
  plugins: [
    { src: '~/plugins/fooz/fooz-1.ts', mode: 'server' }
  ]
})
```

There you go! As you can see that it is not difficult at all to register your un-scanned plugins manually. Note that you also can use `nuxt.config.ts` to manually register the scanned plugins in the `/plugins/` directory root if you want to control the order of your plugins. You also can prefix alphabetical numbers to the plugin filenames to control their orders, for example:

```
plugins
├── 01.foo.ts
└── 02.baz.ts
```

Note that filenames are sorted as strings, not as numeric values. So if you have more than 9 plugins to sort alphabetically, prefix the number with an `0` or `00` (if you have more than 99 plugins!).

There is more we can do with plugins in the `/plugins/` directory, such as using composables in plugins and using plugins to create middleware. We will cover using composables in plugins in the next topic, and we will cover using plugins to create middleware in the coming section. Right now, let's first discover more about middleware that you have learned briefly in the previous section.

Creating Middleware with `defineNuxtRouteMiddleware`

Creating middleware in Nuxt is extremely easy, as you have discovered in the previous topic for layout manipulations. Such middleware is named middleware which is executed when they are applied manually and directly to a page. But sometimes you may want to run the middleware on every route change, and such middleware is a global middleware. In this section, you will create the named and global middleware side by side so that you can understand their differences. So let's find out in the following steps:

1. Create the `/middleware/` directory in the project root with a `foo.ts` and a `foo.global.ts` files:

   ```bash
   middleware
   ```

```
├── foo.ts
└── foo.global.ts
```

2. Use **`defineNuxtPlugin`** and **`console.log`** to set a message in **`/middleware/foo.ts`** as follows:

```js
// middleware/foo.ts
export default defineNuxtRouteMiddleware((to, from) => {
  console.log('named middleware from `/middleware/` that runs only when it has been manually applied')
})
```

Note that middleware created under the **`/middleware/`** directory will be named after their filenames, for example, the preceding middleware will be called the `foo` middleware.

3. Use **`defineNuxtPlugin`** and **`console.log`** set a message in **`/middleware/foo.global.ts`** as follows:

```js
// middleware/foo.global.ts
export default defineNuxtRouteMiddleware((to, from) => {
  console.log('global middleware from `/middleware/` that runs on every route change')
})
```

Note that we will call the preceding middleware the **`foo`** global middleware.

4. Use **`definePageMeta`** and its **`middleware`** key to register the **`foo`** middleware on any page you like, for example:

```js
// pages/middleware.vue
<script setup>
definePageMeta({
  middleware: ['foo']
})
</script>
```

````
```
````

Note that you can register multiple middlewares with an array (square brackets). If you just have one middleware to register, you can register it as follows:

````
```js
// pages/middleware.vue
<script setup>
definePageMeta({
  middleware: 'foo'
})
</script>
```
````

5. Run the app on the `dev` environment:

````
```
$ npm run dev
```
````

You should see the `home` page is loaded at `localhost:3000` with the message you set in the `foo` global middleware. If you navigate to any other pages, you should also see the same message on your browser console:

````
```
  global middleware from `/middleware/` that runs on every
route change
```
````

If you navigate to the `middleware` page where you register the `foo` middleware, you should also see the message you set in this middleware on your browser console, as well as the message from the `foo` global middleware:

````
```
  global middleware from `/middleware/` that runs on every
route change
  named middleware from `/middleware/` that runs only when it
has been manually applied
```
````

As you can see, the differences between named and global middleware are how you name them (just suffix the global ones with `.global`) and how you use
````

them. Global middleware is always called before the named ones. Nuxt has made middleware creation extremely easy otherwise you will have to use navigation guards to do so just as in a Vue app. What's more in Nuxt, apart from using the `/middleware/` directory to create our middleware, you also can use plugins to create middleware. So let's find out in the next section.

# Creating Middleware with `defineNuxtPlugin` and `addRouteMiddleware`

It is also very easy to create middleware through plugins if you want to use the `/plugins/` directory to do that. You can use `defineNuxtPlugin` and `addRouteMiddleware` to create middleware in the `/plugins/` directory. Just as those middlewares in the `/middleware/` directory, you can create named and global middleware through plugins in the following steps:

1. Create the `/middleware/` directory in the project root with a `foo-middleware.ts` file:

```bash
middleware
└── foo-middleware.ts
```

2. Use `defineNuxtPlugin`, `addRouteMiddleware`, and `console.log` to create two middleware with messages in `/plugins/foo-middleware.ts` as follows:

```js
// plugins/foo-middleware.ts
export default defineNuxtPlugin(nuxtApp => {
  addRouteMiddleware('global-foo', (to, from) => {
      console.log('global middleware from `/plugin/` that runs on every route change')
    },
    { global: true }
  )

  addRouteMiddleware('named-foo', () => {
    console.log('named middleware from `/plugin/` that runs only when it has been used')
  })
})
```

````
```
````

Note that in the preceding code, the name **`global-foo`** is used for the global route middleware, whereas the name **`named-foo`** is used for the named middleware. The difference between these two middlewares is the **`global`** key set to **`true`** for the **`global-foo`** global route middleware.

3. Use **`definePageMeta`** and its **`middleware`** key to register the **`named-foo`** middleware on any page you like, for example:

````
```js
// pages/middleware.vue
<script setup>
definePageMeta({
  middleware: ['named-foo']
})
</script>
```
````

Note that if you just have one middleware to register, you can register it as follows:

````
```js
// pages/middleware.vue
<script setup>
definePageMeta({
  middleware: 'named-foo'
})
</script>
```
````

4. Run the app on the **`dev`** environment:

````
```
$ npm run dev
```
````

You should see the **`home`** page is loaded at **`localhost:3000`** with the message you set in the **`global-foo`** global middleware. If you navigate to any other pages, you should also see the same message on your browser console:

````
```
global middleware from `/plugin/` that runs on every route
````

```
change
    ```
```

If you navigate to the `middleware` page where you register the `foo` middleware, you should also see the message you set in this middleware on your browser console, as well as the message from the `foo` global middleware:

```
    ```
    global middleware from `/plugin/` that runs on every route
change
    named middleware from `/plugin/` that runs only when it has
been used
    ```
```

Using plugins for middleware creation is just as simple as using the `/middleware/` directory. But note that middleware from the `/middleware/` directory is always called before the ones from the `/plugins/` directory. So unless you need to use plugins as middleware for some reason, it is better off using the /middleware/ directory as this also help you to unclutter your `/plugins/` directory.

Well done! You have managed to create plugins and middleware using the `/plugins/` and `/middleware/` directory. You have learned to create scanned and un-scanned plugins, server or client-side-only plugins, as well as plugins for both sides. You have learned the differences between the named and global middleware. And lastly, you have learned to use plugins to create middleware. However, there is more you can do with plugins that is using composables in them. So let's find out in the next topic.

You can find the example app for this topic in `/1.nuxt/1.essentials/3.plugins-middelware-composables-utils/` in the GitHub repository of this book.

Creating Composables and Utilities

In this topic, we are going to look into the `/composables/` and `/utils/` directories in Nuxt. Just like plugins and middleware, composables, and utilities are extracted JavaScript logic that we organize into meaningful directories. The difference between them is plugins and middleware are always called before composables and utilities. We use composables and utilities differently in practice even though they are just extracted JavaScript logic in nature. We use composables for reusable stateful logic, while utilities for reusable stateless logic. We will be looking into how to create them in this topic using the `/composables/` and `/utils/` directories. So, let's get started!
```

# Creating Composables with `export` and `export default`

Composables are useful when we want to reuse logic that involves reactive states for common tasks such as fetching data from an API and manipulating them. There are many default composables that come with Nuxt such as **`useFetch`** which we will be using often in the coming chapters and topics. But in this section, we will be looking at how to create our own composables using the **`/composables/`** directory and the naming convention when creating them. So let's find out in the following steps:

1. Create the **`/composables/`** directory in your project root with a **`/nested/`** sub-directory and the following files:

   ```
   composables
   ├── use-foo.ts
   └── nested
       └── use-baz.ts
   ```

2. Use **`export`** to export the following functions in **`/composables/use-foo.ts`** as follows:

   ```js
   // composables/use-foo.ts
   export function useA () {
     return 'a'
   }

   function useB () {
     return 'b'
   }

   function useC () {
     return 'c'
   }

   export const useD = () => {
     return 'd'
   }
   ```

````
export { useB, useC }
```
````

In the preceding functions, we return static values only. But in a real function, you would want to use reactive objects and return computed values. You also might want to use export executable functions such as increment and decrement functions for making a counter on a page. We will be using composables a lot and often in the coming chapters and topics in more complicated Nuxt apps. But for now, we will keep it as simple as possible. Note that you also can use `export default` to export a default function in a composable, for example:

````
```js
// composables/use-foo.ts
export default function () {
  ...
  const runtimeConfig = useRuntimeConfig()
  return runtimeConfig.public['apiBaseUrl']
}
```
````

In the preceding `export default` function, you can see that we also can access the runtime configuration, just like plugins and utils. So, to fulfil what the preceding function is looking for from the runtime configuration, let's create a `.env` file in the project root with the following line:

````
```bash
// .env
APP_BASE_URL=http://localhost:3000
```
````

Then, create an `apiBaseUrl` key in the `public` key in the `runtimeConfig` object in `nuxt.config.ts` and use `process.env` to get the value of `API_BASE_URL` as follows:

````
```js
// nuxt.config.ts
export default defineNuxtConfig({
  runtimeConfig: {
    public: {
      apiBaseUrl: process.env.APP_BASE_URL
    }
  }
}
````

````
```
````

3. Use **`export default`** to create and export a function in **`/composables/nested/use-baz.ts`** as follows:

```js
// composables/nested/use-baz.ts
export default () => {
  return ‘baz’
}
```

4. Use the preceding functions anywhere you like in the script block, for example:

```js
// pages/composables.vue
<script setup>
import useBaz from ‘~/composables/nested/use-baz’
const a = useA()
const b = useB()
const c = useC()
const d = useD()
const foo = useFoo()
console.log(useBaz())
</script>
```

Note that there is no need to de-structure the exported functions from composables.

5. Use the preceding functions anywhere you like in the **`&lt;template&gt;`** block, for example:

```html
// pages/composables.vue
<template>
  <p>
    Named export `useA`: {{ a }}
  </p>
  <p>
    Named export `useB`: {{ b }}
  </p>
  <p>
    Named export `useC`: {{ c }}
```
```

```
    </p>
     <p>
       Named export `useD`: {{ d }}
    </p>
     <p>
       Default export `useFoo`: {{ foo }}
    </p>
     <p>
       Nested default export `useBaz`: {{ useBaz() }}
    </p>
  </template>
```

Note that you can use composables directly in the `**<template>**` block such as `**useBaz()**` if you don't want to assign them as constants in the `**<script>**` block.

7. Run the app on the `**dev**` environment:

```
$ npm run dev
```

Navigate to the page where you use the composable functions, and you should see the following output on your browser screen:

```
Named export `useA`: a
Named export `useB`: b
Named export `useC`: c
Named export `useD`: d
Default export `useFoo`: http://localhost:4000
Nested default export `useBaz`: baz
```

As you can see that it is a naming convention to prefix the composable file with a `**use-**` in the `**/composables/**` directory. It is also a convention to initial composables using **use** (e.g. `**useA()**`) in the `**<script>**` block. We can use such conventions in the `**template**` block or reassign them to constants before using them. Notice that composables are imported automatically by Nuxt so you don't need to use the `**import**` statement to import them manually from the `**/composables/**` directory.

For more information about composition functions, please visit https://vuejs.org/guide/extras/composition-api-faq.html.

Using Composables in Plugins

We also can use composable functions in plugins that you have learned in the previous topic. We can use our composable functions directly in a plugin without having to import them, just as how you use them in the previous section. So let's find out how you can do that in the following steps:

1. Create a **`baz.ts`** file in **`/plugins/`**:

   ```
   plugins
   └── baz.ts
   ```

2. Use **`defineNuxtPlugin`** and import the **`useFoo`** composable in **`/plugins/baz.ts`** as follows:

   ```js
   // plugins/baz.ts
   export default defineNuxtPlugin(nuxtApp => {
     const foo = useFoo()
     return {
       provide: {
         foo
       }
     }
   })
   ```

Note that you also can use the **`provide`** helper to create a function if you prefer just as in the previous section.

3. Prefix **`foo`** with a **`$`** and use it anywhere you like in the **`<template>`** block, for example:

   ```html
   // pages/plugins.vue
   <template>
     <p>
       $foo (client-server, a composable used in the plugin): {{
   $foo }}
     </p>
   </template>
   ```

4. Run the app on the `dev` environment:

   ```
   $ npm run dev
   ```

Navigate to the page where you use the plugin composable function, you should see the following output on your browser screen:

```
    $foo (client-server, a composable used in the plugin):
http://localhost:4000
```

There you go! As you can see that it is extremely easy to create and use composables in Nuxt. You just have to follow some conventions and Nuxt will do the rest of the job for you. What about utilities? How do we create and use them in a Nuxt app? Let's find out in the next section!

Creating Utilities with `export default`

Utilities or utility functions are common reusable logic that does not involve reactive states, such as a function that takes some input and immediately returns the expected output. It is best to regard utilities as those Utility functions from **lodash,** https://lodash.com/ , which is a JavaScript utility library that you may have heard of already. We will create some meaningful utilities in the coming chapters and topics, but in this section, we will be looking at how to create them using the `/composables/` directory.

1. Create the `/utils/` directory in the project root with a `do-something.ts` file:

   ```bash
   utils
   └── do-something.ts
   ```

2. Use **`export`** **`default`** to create and export a function in **`/utils/do-something.ts`** as follows:

```js
// utils/do-something.ts
export default () => {
  const runtimeConfig = useRuntimeConfig()
  return runtimeConfig.public['apiBaseUrl']
}
```

You can see from the preceding code, you can access the runtime configuration in utility functions, just like composables.

3. Use the **`doSomething`** util anywhere you like in the **`<template>`** block, for example:

```html
// pages/utils.vue
<template>
  <p>
    doSomething: {{ doSomething() }}
 </p>
</template>
```

4. Run the app on the **`dev`** environment:

```
$ npm run dev
```

Navigate to the page where you use the utility function, and you should see the following output on your browser screen:

```
doSomething: http://localhost:4000
```

You probably have noticed that there is no naming convention for the utility file. Neither any convention for initiating and using them in the **`<script>`** and **`<template>`** block or anywhere. So it is up to you to give your utility files meaningful names. You can even create utilities and use them in composables, plugins, and middleware - anywhere. But you should always give them meaningful names so that you or other collaborators know what they are for.

Conclusion

In this short topic, you have managed to create composables and utilities using the **`/composables/`** and **`/utils/`** directory. You have learned the difference between them and know that they are scanned and imported automatically by Nuxt. You will use them more in the coming chapters and topics, especially composables. In the next chapter, you will discover how to serve public and static assets, such as images, in Nuxt projects. You will create some meaningful and useful utilities to help you to serve them, as well as use Windi CSS to make them responsive on your layouts. Apart from making responsive layouts and images, you will also be using Less CSS preprocessor to speed up your frontend development. So let's find out!

You can find the example app for this topic in **`/1.nuxt/1.essentials/3.plugins-middelware-composables-utils/`** in the GitHub repository of this book.

Chapter 3
Managing Assets and Adding UI Frameworks

Introduction

Welcome to *Chapter* 3. In this chapter, you will use Windi CSS as a UI framework for your Nuxt apps and create responsive layouts with Windi CSS; write local and global CSS styles by using Less as the CSS preprocessor; discover how to serve public and static assets such as images and fonts; serve dynamic assets from using composables in the `` `<template>` `` block; learn the difference of serving assets between the `` `/public/` `` and `` `/assets/` `` directories.

Structure

The topics that will be covered in this chapter are as follows:

- Adding UI Frameworks: Windi CSS
- Adding CSS Preprocessors: Less
- Serving Static Assets
- Serving Dynamic Assets

Adding UI Frameworks: Windi CSS

There are many UI frameworks out there you can choose for your Nuxt apps, such as Bootstrap (https://getbootstrap.com/), Bulma(https://bulma.io/), Uikit (https://getuikit.com/), Tailwind CSS (https://tailwindcss.com/), Windi CSS (https://windicss.org/), and so on. These frameworks help you to bootstrap your app UI so that you don't have to do it yourself from scratch with your own CSS. And that can increase your productivity significantly.

Tailwind CSS and Windi CSS are utility-first frameworks. If you are familiar with Tailwind already, you will pick up Windi easily. Most of the class names in Tailwind and Windi are identical. So if you are stuck in Windi and the documentation (https://windicss.org/utilities/) doesn't help, you can always use the Tailwind documentation (https://tailwindcss.com/docs) to help you to get going.

There are more benefits to using Windi CSS than Tailwind CSS, such as the installation of Windi is more straightforward than Tailwind CSS which is more complicated. Therefore, we will use Windi CSS in this topic and throughout the course. So, let's find out how you can add Windi CSS into Nuxt apps and leverage this framework in the following sections.

Adding Windi CSS as Your UI Framework

Using Windi CSS as the UI Framework is fun and joyful whether in Nuxt or Vue projects. It is fast and easy to get the styles sorted by adding classes to HTML elements directly. If you need the styles again for another new project, you just have to copy the HTML elements over – no need for any CSS files anymore! This makes your HTML elements more readable and semantic. And it is also easier for future maintenance. So, let's find out how you can install Windi CSS for your Nuxt apps in the following steps:

1. Install Windi CSS as a **`dev`** dependency via **`npm`** on your terminal:

```
$ npm i -D nuxt-windicss
```

Note that the installation of Node.js packages may change over time, you should always confirm the installation command lines with their official documentation. For this package, please check it out at https://windicss.org/integrations/nuxt.html.

2. Register **`nuxt-windicss`** in **`nuxt.config.ts`** as follows:

```js
// nuxt.config.ts
export default defineNuxtConfig({
  modules: [
```

```
      'nuxt-windicss',
    ]
  })
```

3. Start using classes on any page throughout the site, for example:

```html
// pages/index.vue
<template>
  <p class="text-blue-500">
    Hello World!
  </p>

  <button
    class="bg-gray-900
    hover:bg-violet-600
    text-white
    font-bold
    py-2
    px-4
    rounded
    focus:outline-none"
  >
    I am a button
  </button>
</template>
```

4. Run the app on the **`dev`** environment:

```
$ npm run dev
```

You should see the **`Hello World!`** paragraph and the **`I am a button`** button are loaded at **`localhost:3000`** and they are converted into CSS behind the scene for you.

For more options and variants of the preset text color from Windi CSS, please visit https://windicss.org/utilities/general/colors.html.

Using utility-first CSS frameworks such as Windi CSS, you write less native CSS code and get the styles done faster. If you ever need to change the style on an

HTML element, you just have to do it directly on that element, without having to look through messy CSS style sheets, which can be impossible to maintain over time. Besides styling HTML elements, utility-first CSS frameworks also can help us to create responsive layouts easily. So, let's find out in the next section how you can use Windi CSS to achieve that!

Creating Responsive Layouts with Windi CSS

The most common approach in making a responsive layout is using Flexbox (https://developer.mozilla.org/en-US/docs/Learn/CSS/CSS_layout/Flexbox). Assuming that you want to create a 3-column layout for large screens (desktop) that will collapse into a 2-column layout for medium screens (tablet) and will collapse into a 1-column layout for small screens (mobile). We can achieve this easily with the utilities (https://windicss.org/utilities/) from Windi CSS in the following steps:

1. Create a **desktop-first** responsive layout by using a **`<div>`** parent block to contain 3 **`<div>`** child blocks and then wrap them in a **`<div>`** container block (optional) on any page, for example:

```html
// pages/responsive.vue
<div class="container mx-auto">
    <div class="flex flex-wrap justify-center items-center
    px-1.5">
    <div class="w-4/12 <lg:w-1/2 <md:w-full px-2.5">
      <img alt="R0001844" src="/static/R0001844.jpg" />
    </div>
    <div class="w-4/12 <lg:w-1/2 <md:w-full px-2.5">
      <img alt="R0001844" src="/static/R0001844.jpg" />
    </div>
    <div class="w-4/12 <lg:w-1/2 <md:w-full px-2.5">
      <img alt="R0001844" src="/static/R0001844.jpg" />
    </div>
  </div>
</div>
```

In the preceding code:

- The **`flex-wrap`** class is essential for collapsing the columns for different screens. For more information about this utility class, please visit https://windicss.org/utilities/flexbox.html#flex-wrap.
- The **`justify-center`** class is used to make the child items vertically

centered. For more information about this utility class, please visit https://windicss.org/utilities/positioning.html#justify-content.

- The **`items-center`** class is used to make the child items horizontally centered. For more information about this utility class, please visit https://windicss.org/utilities/positioning.html#align-items.
- The **`w-4/12`** class is used to make 3 columns, the **`w-1/2`** class is used to make 2 columns, and the **`w-full`** class is used to make 1 column. For more information about the width classes, please visit https://windicss.org/utilities/sizing.html#width.
- The **`container`** and **`mx-auto`** classes are used to fix the width of the element to the current breakpoint. For more information about them, please visit https://windicss.org/utilities/container.html.
- The **`<lg`** and **`<md`** prefixes are desktop-first variants. The **`<lg`** variant is applied to screen sizes that are **smaller than** the large screen, and that means they are tablet screens. While the **`<md`** variant is applied to screen sizes that are **smaller than** the medium screen, which means they are mobile screens. For more information about the variants, please visit https://windicss.org/utilities/variants.html.
- The **`px-1.5`** and **`px-2.5`** classes are used to set X paddings. For more information about padding classes, please visit https://windicss.org/utilities/spacing.html.

2. Create a **mobile-first** responsive layout using the same preceding elements and utility classes on the same **`pages/responsive.vue`** file as follows:

```html
// pages/responsive.vue
<div class="container mx-auto">
  <div class="flex flex-wrap justify-center items-center
  px-1.5">
    <div class="w-full md:w-1/2 lg:w-4/12 px-2.5">
      <img alt="R0001844" src="/static/R0001844.jpg" />
    </div>
    <div class="w-full md:w-1/2 lg:w-4/12 px-2.5">
      <img alt="R0001844" src="/static/R0001844.jpg" />
    </div>
    <div class="w-full md:w-1/2 lg:w-4/12 px-2.5">
      <img alt="R0001844" src="/static/R0001844.jpg" />
    </div>
  </div>
</div>
```

The difference in mobile-first is using these utility classes: `w-full`, `md:w-1/2`, `lg:w-4/12`. Notice that the `w-full` class for 1 column is set as default. Then the `md` variant resets the layout to 2 columns with `w-1/2` for medium screens and above. Lastly, the `lg` variant resets the layout to 3 columns with `w-4/12` for large screens and above.

3. Run the app on the `dev` environment:

```
$ npm run dev
```

You can see that the `flexbox` items are stacked to each other and on top of each other perfectly when the screen size changes between desktop, tablet, and mobile. Also, obviously, there is no difference between desktop-first and mobile-first layouts. They both work and look the same. It is all down to which approach you are more comfortable with.

There are many great features and built-in utility classes from Windi CSS out of the box such as the **Desktop First** variants that you have just discovered in this section. Such useful variants are not available in Tailwind CSS by default. Both Tailwind CSS and Windi CSS have the **Mobile First** variants that you also have learned in this section. On top of that, with Windi CSS, you also can use **Only Screen** variants to suit your need for making responsive columns. For more information about these variants, please visit https://windicss.org/utilities/general/variants.html.

Utility-first UI frameworks like Tailwind CSS and Windi CSS can appear intimidating and overwhelming at first for new beginners. As you have noticed in the preceding example of responsive layouts, you are expected to use and read tons of classes on HTML elements. This is what a utility-first UI framework is meant to be – you can tell what an element actually does by reading the classes that are applied to it, without having to read the CSS code in a style sheet. So, you write less CSS code in the style sheet but just write more class names in the HTML elements.

However, occasionally you may need to extract a list of classes that are applied to an element and store it in a global style sheet so that you can reuse it elsewhere. Or, you may need to write some custom CSS styles that you cannot find in the utility classes, you may need to mix your custom styles with the utility classes. Then, you will need to do this on a global style sheet. So, let's explore in the next lesson how you can achieve this with a CSS preprocessor – Less.

Note that Windi CSS is **sunsetting**. That means that there won't be any new features added to Windi CSS in the future. This is because the core team of Windi is pursuing the successor of Windi CSS - UnoCSS. So, no worries you could make the transition easily to UnoCSS if you are already familiar with features from Windi CSS, as they are incorporated into UnoCSS already. However, it is still an early stage for using UnoCSS in the Nuxt project. So be cautious and ready to see bugs in your Nuxt apps for using UnoCSS right now. If you would like to find out more information about UnoCSS and experiment with it with your Nuxt or Vue projects, please visit https://unocss.dev/.

You can find the example app for this topic in **`/1.nuxt/1.essentials/4.windicss-less-assets/`** in the GitHub repository of this book.

Adding CSS Preprocessors: Less

There are a number of CSS preprocessors available these days, such as Less (https://lesscss.org/), Stylus (https://stylus-lang.com/), and Sass (https://sass-lang.com/). Sass is more well-known. But Less is easier to get started with. We will use Less in this lesson and throughout the course where it is necessary.

The installation of Less for Nuxt project is very easy. So, let's find out how you can add it to Nuxt apps and use it with Windi CSS in the following sections.

Adding Less as a CSS Preprocessor

Just like utility-first CSS frameworks, CSS preprocessors like Less help you write less CSS code and make your code more manageable. The learning curve with Less is lower and flatter than with Sass. You can start writing styles right away with Less as soon as it is installed. So, let's find out how you can install it and start using it in the following steps:

1. Install Less as a **`dev`** dependency via **`npm`** on your terminal:

   ```

   $ npm i -D less
   ```

2. Create a simple custom class in the **`<style>`** block in **`/pages/index.vue`** (or any page) and apply this class on the element in the **`<template>`** block as follows:

   ```css
   // pages/index.vue
   <style lang="less">
   ```

~~~
@text-color: red;

.text-red {
  color: @text-color;
}
</style>

<template>
  <p class="text-red">
    I am red
  </p>
</template>
```
~~~

Notice that you need to set a **`less`** value to the **`lang`** attribute in the **`<style>`** block. In the preceding code, **`@text-color`** is a variable that holds **`red`** as its value. This variable is then applied to the **color** property in the **`text-red`** class. For more information about variables in Less, please visit https://lesscss.org/features/#variables-feature.

3. Mix the preceding Less code with Windi CSS in **`/pages/index.vue`** as follows:

~~~
```css
<style lang="less">
...
.text-red {
  ...
  &:hover {
    @apply
      text-blue-500;
  }
}
</style>
```
~~~

Note that the **`@apply`** directive is required to mix the Windi utility classes with your custom styles.

4. Run the app on the **`dev`** environment:

~~~
```
$ npm run dev
```
~~~

You should see the `I am red` paragraph is loaded at `localhost:3000` and is applied with the CSS you set in the `<style>` block. The text should turn to blue (`text-blue-500` from Windi CSS) when you hover it.

Notice that there is no need to configure the `nuxt.config.ts` file for using Less. You literally can start writing your CSS code with Less right after the installation and have set `lang="less"` in the `<style>` block. Besides writing styles locally on specific pages, you also can use Less to use global styles and mix them with utility classes from Windi CSS. So, let's find out in the next section.

Writing Global Styles with Less

Global styles can help us reduce repetitive code and you will need them to speed up your productivity. They are particularly useful when you need to abstract styles and reuse them on multiple pages. Using Less for writing global styles is no different from using native CSS for global styles. You can also mix Less code with utility classes from Windi CSS by using an `@apply` directive. So, let's find out in the following steps:

1. Create a `styles` directory with `css` and `less` sub-directories in the `/assets/` directory with a `main.css` file in the `/css/` sub-directory and a `main.less` file in the `/less/` sub-directory as follows:

   ```
   assets
   └── styles
       ├── css
       │   └── main.css
       └── less
           └── main.less
   ```

2. Create a `text-blue` class with the following styles in `/assets/styles/css/main.css` as follows:

   ```css
   // assets/styles/css/main.css
   .text-blue {
     color: blue;
   }
   ```

3. Create a `has-links` class and mix some Less code with Windi CSS in `/assets/styles/less/main.less` as follows:

    ```
    // assets/styles/less/main.less
    .has-links {
      a {
        @apply
          text-red-500;

        &:hover {
          @apply
            text-blue-500;
        }
      }
    }
    ```

4. Extract the Windi classes from the button that you did in the previous *Adding UI Frameworks: Windi CSS* topic and keep them in `/assets/styles/less/main.less` as follows:

    ```
    // assets/styles/less/main.less
    .button {
      @apply
        bg-gray-900
        hover:bg-violet-600
        text-white
        font-bold
        py-2
        px-4
        rounded
        focus:outline-none;
    }
    ```

5. Register the preceding `main.css` and `main.less` files in `nuxt.config.ts` as follows:

    ```
    // nuxt.config.ts
    export default defineNuxtConfig({
      css: [
    ```

````
      '@/assets/styles/css/main.css',
      '@/assets/styles/less/main.less',
    ]
  })
  ```
````

6. Apply the preceding global custom **`text-blue`** class from **`/assets/styles/css/main.css`** on any page, for example:

````
```html
// pages/index.vue
<p class="text-blue">
  I am blue
</p>
```
````

7. Apply the preceding global custom **`button`** and **`has-links`** classes from **`/assets/styles/less/main.less`** on any page, for example:

````
```html
// pages/index.vue
<button class="button">
  I am a button
</button>

<div class="container mx-auto space-y-3 has-links border-1">
  <p>
    I am a paragraph with a <a href="#">link</a>.
  </p>
  <p>
    I am another paragraph with a <a href="#">link</a>.
  </p>
  <p>
    I am another paragraph with a <a href="#">link</a>.
  </p>
</div>
```
````

The **`space-y-3`** class is used to adjust the vertical space between the child elements. For more information about the **Space Between Y** utility classes, please visit https://windicss.org/utilities/spacing.html#space-between-y.
````

8. Run the app on the `dev` environment:

    ```
    $ npm run dev
    ```

You should see `I am blue`, `I am a button`, and `I am a paragraph with a link`. are loaded at `localhost:3000` and they are applied with the global styles you set in `/assets/styles/css/main.css` and in `/assets/styles/less/main.less`.

Global styles are indeed useful and can be tempting, but overusing them can lead to code that is impossible to maintain over time just like using the native CSS for writing global styles. So use global styles cautiously and sparsely for better future maintenance. Unless it is necessary and you are certain, global styles should be kept to a minimum.

There you go, you have installed and applied the custom global styles successfully in your Nuxt app. Now, how you make use of the rest of the Windi utility classes with your custom Less code will be up to your creativity. There are benefits of using a CSS preprocessor in your apps rather than writing native CSS styles. One of the benefits is the improvement in your productivity and code readability. It also makes your style succinct and neat. You can check out the official site of Less and explore how you can make use of it at https://lesscss.org/usage/.

Besides what you have learned so far in these topics, Windi CSS also helps us make our images responsive out of the box and you probably have noticed in the previous topic in creating responsive layouts. This is definitely a huge benefit for using a CSS framework like Windi CSS. In the coming sections, you will see this benefit of asset serving. So, let's explore more on serving assets in Nuxt products from the `/public/` and `/assets/` directories in the next topic.

You can find the example app for this topic in `/1.nuxt/1.essentials/4.windicss-less-assets/` in the GitHub repository of this book.

Serving Static Assets

A complex app that is good-looking is required to serve images and fonts on the browser. So, knowing how to serve these assets correctly is very important in web development. Vite uses the `/src/` directory as the root directory for serving assets and all other files like `.js` and `.vue` files. So, you can request your assets by using `/assets/` as follows:

```html
<img alt="logo" src="./assets/logo.png" />
```

All the asset files in this directory will be processed and hashed. On the other hand, you can request files that you don't want to be processed and hashed in the `/public/` directory by using `/` as follows:

```html
<img alt="logo" src="/logo.png" />
```

However, it is useful to extract `./` and replace it with an `@`, alias for example, that uses `./src` instead. You then can use this alias in deep-level components easily, instead of using multiple one-level-up file paths like `../../../../`. This `@` alias will always assure that you are requesting and importing files from `./src` no matter where you are. So, let's take a look at how you can use aliases from Nuxt in the following section to serve your images.

Serving `asset` and `public` Images

In Nuxt, the `/src/` directory is omitted and we use an `~` alias to point our project root in the `<template>` block. So, if you want to point your assets to the **/assets/**directory, you can use the `~` alias followed by `/assets/` such as `~/assets/R0001844.jpg`. However, if you want to get your images from the `/public/` directory, you don't need to use the `~` alias. You can just require your assets from this directory directly with**/**. Just like Vite projects, if you want your assets in Nuxt projects to be processed and hashed, then store them in the `/assets/` directory, otherwise use the `/public/` directory. So, let's find out in the following steps:

1. Create a `static` sub-directory in the `/public/` directory and an `images` sub-directory in the `/assets/` directory with your images as follows:

    ```
    ├── public
    │   └── static
    │       └── R0001844.jpg
    └── assets
        └── images
    ```

```
        └── R0003515.jpg
```

2. Use the `~` alias to request the image from the `/assets/` directory in the `<template>` block on any page, for example:

```html
// pages/assets.vue
<template>
  <img alt="R0003515" src="~/assets/images/R0003515.jpg" />
</template>
```

3. Request the image from the `/public/` directory directly without any alias in the `<template>` block on any page, for example:

```html
// pages/assets.vue
<template>
  // ...
  <img alt="R0001844" src="/static/R0001844.jpg" />
</template>
```

4. Run the app on the `dev` environment:

```
$ npm run dev
```

Now you should see two images on your browser immediately. The first image is coming from the `/assets/` directory, while the other is from the `/public/` directory.

5. Build the app with the following command:

```
$ npm run build
```

You should see a similar output as follows on your terminal:

```
    ```
    i Building client
    i vite v4.3.9 building for production...
    i ✓ 124 modules transformed.
    i .nuxt/dist/client/manifest.json
2.91 kB | gzip: 0.53 kB
    i .nuxt/dist/client/_nuxt/R0003515.d2634427.jpg
1,418.10 kB
    ...
    ...
    ```
```

You can see that only the image in the `` `/assets/` `` directory is processed and hashed into the `` `/.output/public/_nuxt/` `` directory. On the other hand, the images from the `` `/public/` `` directory are not processed but are just simply copied into the `` `/.output/public/` `` directory as they are with the `` `/static/` `` directory. This `` `/static/` `` directory that you created is placed in the `` `/public/` `` root directory. If you inspect the `` `/.output/` `` directory, you should able to find your images in it as follows:

```
```
public
├── favicon.ico
├── static
│   └── R0001844.jpg
└── _nuxt
    ├── ...
    └── R0003515.d2634427.jpg
```
```

You may find that having the `` `~` `` alias is unnecessary in a simple and small app. But you will find that aliases like this one are extremely beneficial as it saves you some space and from getting confused with the file paths when your app is getting large and complex.

What about fonts? Let's find out in the next section. But before that, it is also worth mentioning that you may have noticed that the oversized images that cause a visible Y scrollbar at the bottom of your page if you have a smaller screen. The image doesn't scale itself to fit the screen and is not responsive when resizing the browser.

But using a UI framework like Windi CSS can solve this issue on the fly for us. Windi CSS fixes the image oversized issue immediately and makes the image responsive on the fly without having you write any code. That's a prominent benefit of using a UI/CSS framework.

Serving Custom Fonts from the `assets` Directory

You will probably need custom fonts to display your app content beautifully on browsers, for example, Open Sans (https://fonts.google.com/specimen/Open+Sans?query=open+sans). So, assuming that you have generated the `.woff` format of your chosen fonts and you have installed a fresh copy of your `Nuxt` app. You can install custom fonts in Nuxtapps in the following steps:

1. Create a new directory called `fonts` in the `/assets/` directory to store the custom font as follows:

```
assets
└── fonts
    └── open-sans
        ├── OpenSans-Regular.woff
        └── OpenSans-Regular.woff
```

2. Create a new directory called `styles` in the `/assets/` directory with the following sub-directories which contain `.css` files as follows:

```
assets
└── styles
    └── css
        ├── main.css
        └── font-face.css
```

3. Create the style of the custom font in `/styles/css/font-face.css` as follows:

```css
// assets/styles/css/font-face.css
@font-face {
  font-family: 'Open Sans';
  src: url('~/assets/fonts/open-sans/OpenSans-Regular.woff2')
```

````
    format('woff2'),
         url('~/assets/fonts/open-sans/OpenSans-Regular.woff')
         format('woff');
    font-weight: normal;
    font-style: normal;
    font-display: swap;
  }
  ```
````

4. Apply the preceding `Open Sans` font face globally in `/assets/styles/less/main.less` as follows:

````
```css
// assets/styles/less/main.less
html,
body {
  font-family: 'Open Sans', sans-serif;
}
```
````

Note that you also can apply the preceding code in `/assets/styles/css/main.css` instead if you prefer.

5. Register the `font-face.css` file before other global styles in `nuxt.config.ts` as follows:

````
```js
export default defineNuxtConfig({
  css: [
    '@/assets/styles/css/font-face.css',
    '@/assets/styles/css/main.css',
    '@/assets/styles/less/main.less',
  ]
})
```
````

6. Run the app on the `dev` environment:

````
```
$ npm run dev
```
````

Now you should see the custom font has been reflected on your browser. Note that if you apply the custom font locally in a Vue component, it will reflect on
````

that single component only. But if you apply the custom font throughout the app, then you should apply it globally in a style sheet.

7. Finally, you should see the custom fonts are processed and hashed when you build the app for production, for example:

```
    i Building client...
    i vite v4.3.9 building for production...
    i ✓ 128 modules transformed.
    i .nuxt/dist/client/manifest.json
4.41 kB │ gzip:  0.74 kB
    i .nuxt/dist/client/_nuxt/OpenSans-Regular.586bd95c.woff2
50.05 kB
    i .nuxt/dist/client/_nuxt/OpenSans-Light.9706f674.woff2
51.50 kB
    i .nuxt/dist/client/_nuxt/OpenSans-SemiBold.98584192.woff2
52.04 kB
    i .nuxt/dist/client/_nuxt/OpenSans-Regular.5da100e7.woff
67.49 kB
    i .nuxt/dist/client/_nuxt/OpenSans-Light.2bbe2d12.woff
69.34 kB
    i .nuxt/dist/client/_nuxt/OpenSans-SemiBold.1ec2b2d6.woff
69.84 kB
    ...
    ...
```

There you go, you have installed and applied the custom font successfully in your Nuxt app. You also can apply multiple variants (bold, semi-bold, light, etc.) of your custom font if you like and that will be up to your creativity. Note that you also can store your fonts in the `/public/` directory if you don't want to process them. If you do so, then you just need to remove the `~` alias from the `@font-face` styles as follows:

```css
// assets/styles/css/font-face.css
@font-face {
  font-family: 'Open Sans';
  src: url('/fonts/open-sans/OpenSans-Regular.woff2') format('woff2'),
       url('/fonts/open-sans/OpenSans-Regular.woff') format('woff');
```

```
    font-weight: normal;
    font-style: normal;
    font-display: swap;
  }
  ```
```

For more information about working with fonts from the `/public/` directory, you can visit https://nuxt.com/docs/getting-started/styling#working-with-fonts.

There are benefits to serving assets from the `/assets/` directory. One of the benefits of it is that assets from this directory are optimized for production, whether they are images, fonts, or preprocessed styles such as Less, Sass, or Stylus. Styles written in Less, Sass, and Stylus are transformed into generic CSS during development on the fly and during production out of the box, while the `/public/` directory is just a place where you can put all of your static assets that will never be touched but simply copied into the `/dist/` directory. Optimized assets are also hashed for better caching.

You can find the example app for this topic in `/1.nuxt/1.essentials/4.windicss-less-assets/` in the GitHub repository of this book.

## Serving Dynamic Assets

In a complex Nuxt app, you will probably need to serve the app images dynamically. In other words, you wouldn't insert the image path manually and directly into the `<img>` tag just as in the previous topic. You would store your image data in a database with detailed information such as `src`, `alt`, and `caption`. Then you can request that information and bind them to the `<img>` tag using the `v-bind` attribute in your template as follows:

```html
<img :alt="image.alt" :src="`./assets/` + image.src" />
```

However, the preceding code won't work. You will get a 404 error, telling you that the image is not found in your browser's console, for example:

```
GET http://localhost:3000/assets/R0001844.jpg 404 (Not Found)
```
```

That is because dynamic images must be imported as modules so that they can be processed for production and their paths can be resolved correctly in development and production. In Webpack, you can require dynamic images by using the `require` method in your template as follows:

```html
<img :alt="image.alt" :src="require(`./assets/` + image.src)" />
```

In Vite, you can import your image with the **`import`** statement inside the **`<script>`** block:

```js
import imgUrl from './assets/img.png'
```

But this is not good as you need to manually import and set the image. Imagine you have ten images to import. So, let's move on to the following sections to see how you can resolve this issue and discover ways of simplifying your code. For more information about handling assets in Vite, please visit https://vitejs.dev/guide/assets.html.

Requiring `public` Images Dynamically

Requiring images from the **`/public/`** directory is easier because they don't need to be processed and hashed during the build process. You just have to make sure to store them in this directory and then require them dynamically. Let's find out how you can do that in the following steps:

1. Make sure you have images stored in the **`/public/`** directory, for example:

    ```
    public
    └── static
        └── R0001844.jpg
    ```

2. Create an **`use-static.ts`** file in the **`/composables/`** directory:

    ```
    composables
    ```

```
└── use-static.ts
```

3. Add the following logic in `/composables/use-static.ts` to require images from the `/public/` directory:

   ```js
   // composables/use-static.ts
   export default (file) => {
     if (!file) {
       return
     }
     return ‘/static/’ + file
   }
   ```

4. Create the dummy data that returns the information of the images from the `/public/` directories:

   ```js
   // pages/assets.vue
   <script setup>
     const images = {
       public: [
         {
           src: ‘R0001844.jpg’,
           alt: ‘R0001844’
         }
       ]
     }
   </script>
   ```

5. Use the `v-for` attribute in the `<template>` block to loop the image data and require the images with the `useStatic` composable function:

   ```html
   // pages/assets.vue
   <template>
     <ul>
       <li v-for="image in images.public">
         <img
           :alt="image.alt"
           :src="useStatic(image.src)"
   ```

```
        />
      </li>
    </ul>
</template>
```

6. Run the app on the `dev` environment:

```
$ npm run dev
```

You should see the `public` images loaded on your browser dynamically from the `/public/` directory.

When you build your app, you won't see images from the `/public/` directory being processed and printed on your terminal. But if you inspect the `/.output/` directory, you should be able to find them in the root of the `/.output/` directory just as you have learned in the previous topic when serving your app images.

Requiring assets Images Dynamically

On the other hand, requiring images from the `/assets/` directory is more complicated because they need to be processed and hashed during the build process. You need to make sure to store them in this directory and then require them dynamically. Let's find out how you can do that in the following steps:

1. Make sure you have images stored in the `/assets/` directory, for example:

```
assets
└── images
    └── R0003515.jpg
```

2. Create a `use-asset.ts` file in the `/composables/` directory:

```
composables
└── use-asset.ts
```

3. Add the following logic in `` `/composables/use-asset.ts` `` to import images from the `` `/assets/` `` directory:

    ````
    ```js
    // composables/use-asset.ts
    export default (src) => {
      if (!src) {
        return
      }

      const array = src.split('/')
      const filename = [...array].pop()
      const images = import.meta.glob('/assets/images/*.
      {jpg,jpeg,png,svg}', { eager: true })
      const image = images[`/assets/images/${filename}`]
      if (image !== undefined) {
        return image.default
      }
      console.log(`${filename} doesn't exist locally!`)

      if (src.startsWith('http://') || src.
      startsWith('https://')) {
        return src
      }
      return
    }
    ```
    ````

Let's see what the preceding code does:

- The `` `images` `` constant will give you the list of images that are kept in `` `/assets/images/` ``. These images are imported as modules by using the `` `import.meta.glob` `` function through the absolute path (`` `/assets/` ``). Then you just have to return the specific image if the required image's filename is provided in the `` `file` `` variable. The path of the imported image is stored in the `` `default` `` key of the image module. For more information about the bulk import in Vite, please visit [https://vitejs.dev/guide/features.html#glob-import].
- Finally, the imported image, for example, `` `/assets/images/img.jpg` ``, during development will become `` `/assets/img.2d8efhg.jpg` ``, for example, in the production build.

Note that you can include more image extensions in the `` `globEager` `` function if they are needed, for example, `` `gif` ``, `` `jpeg` ``, `` `pjpeg` ``, and `` `webp` ``.

4. Create the dummy data that returns the information of the images from the `/assets/` directories:

```js
// pages/assets.vue
<script setup>
  const images = {
    assets: [
      {
        src: ‘R0003515.jpg’,
        alt: ‘R0003515’
      }
    ]
  }
</script>
```

5. Use the `v-for` attribute in the `<template>` block to loop the image data and require the images with the `useAsset` composable function:

```html
// pages/assets.vue
<template>
  <ul>
    <li v-for="image in images.assets">
      <img
        :alt="image.alt"
        :src="useAsset(image.src)"
      />
    </li>
  </ul>
</template>
```

6. Run the app on the `dev` environment:

```
$ npm run dev
```

You should see the `assets` images loaded on your browser dynamically from the `/assets/` directory.

When you build your app, you should see images from the `/assets/` directory being processed and printed on your terminal. And if you inspect the `/.output/` directory, you should be able to find them in the root of the `/.output/` directory and are hashed just as you have learned in the previous topic when serving your app images.

There you go, you have learned how to require dynamic images in a Nuxt project with two composable functions that you just learned in this topic. You can use the `/utils/` directory and create them as utility functions if you prefer. These two composables may seem unnecessary at this point, but you will realize how useful they are in the coming chapters when fetching data remotely from APIs. So stay tuned!

You can find the example app for this topic in `/1.nuxt/1.essentials/4.windicss-less-assets/` in the GitHub repository of this book.

Conclusion

In this chapter, you have managed to use Windi CSS as a UI framework for your Nuxt apps and create desktop-first and mobile-first responsive layouts with Windi CSS. You have written local and global CSS styles by using Less as the CSS preprocessor in your Nuxt project. You have discovered how to serve public and static assets such as images and fonts; learned the difference in serving assets between the `/public/` and `/assets/` directories. Lastly, you have discovered how to serve dynamic images from the `/public/` and `/assets/` directories using composable functions and the `import.meta.globEager` function.

In the next chapter, you will discover how to fetch data from remote APIs using the `useFetch` Nuxt API and handling HTTP errors from fetching data, such as 404 and 500 errors. You will find out how to display errors using the `showError` Nuxt API and the `error.vue` file. Besides handling HTTP errors from data fetching, you will also learn to handle unknown routes, internal server errors, and JavaScript default errors during development and runtime. So let's get to it!

CHAPTER 4
Fetching Data and Handling Errors

Introduction

Welcome to *Chapter 4*. In this chapter, you will fetch data from remote APIs using the `useFetch` API; handle HTTP errors, such as 404 and 500 errors, with the `showError` API and the Nuxt default error page for unknown routes, internal server errors, and JavaScript default errors during development and runtime; customize the Nuxt default error page with the `error.vue` file; and lastly, abstracted the error-handling logic.

Structure

The topics that will be covered in this chapter are as follows:

- Fetching Data with `useFetch`
- Creating and Handling HTTP Errors
- Customizing the Error Page for HTTP Errors

Fetching Data with `useFetch`

Nuxt is shipped with `useFetch` and `useAsyncData` composables, and a `$fetch` helper for fetching data asynchronously in the browser and on the server side. The `$fetch` helper is built on top of `ofetch` (https://github.com/unjs/ofetch), which is a fetch API, equivalent to the Node.js native `fetch` API.

During SSR rendering, the `$fetch` helper fetches data once on the server, and then again on the client side during hydration. In other words, it fetches data twice. So using `useAsyncData` with `$fetch` will ensure to fetch data once only on the server and then transfer the fetched data to the client.

The `useFetch` composable is a shorthand of fetching data using `useAsyncData` with `$fetch`. You are encouraged to use `useFetch` or `useAsyncData` with `$fetch` to prevent double data fetching when fetching the component data. We will use **useFetch** throughout the book, so let's get started.

Fetching Remote Data with the `useFetch` API

To make a quick jump-start, we will use **DummyJSON** (https://dummyjson.com/) as our REST API for fetching data remotely on this topic. DummyJSON is a free dummy or fake JSON data that we can use as placeholder data in project development or prototype testing. It is very useful when you want to test your code without building the REST API from scratch on your own. We can use the `useFetch` composable to make HTTP requests to DummyJSON for data fetching in the following steps:

1. Create a `.env` text file in the project root with a `API_BASE_URL` set to `https://dummyjson.com` as follows:

```bash
// .env
API_BASE_URL=https://dummyjson.com
```

Note that you also can use the free fake REST API from JSONPlaceholder (https://jsonplaceholder.typicode.com/) for fetching dummy data to test your code. To see the available API endpoints, please check out their guide for more details at https://jsonplaceholder.typicode.com/guide/.

2. Access the `API_BASE_URL` environment variable through `nuxt.config.ts` and assign it to a `apiBaseUrl` key in the `runtimeConfig` property as follows:

```js
// nuxt.config.ts
export default defineNuxtConfig({
  runtimeConfig: {
    public: {
      apiBaseUrl: process.env.API_BASE_URL,
    }
  },
})
```

Notice that you must define your custom keys in the **`public`** property in the **`runtimeConfig`** object.

3. Use the **`useRuntimeConfig`** function to access the **`apiBaseUrl`** key in the **`<script setup>`** block on any page that you want to call the API endpoint with the composable **`useFetch`** API, for example:

    ```js
    // pages/about.vue
    <script setup>
    const runtimeConfig = useRuntimeConfig()
    const { data, error } = await useFetch('/posts/100', {
      baseURL: runtimeConfig.public['apiBaseUrl']
    })
    </script>
    ```

Note that the result of the asynchronous function is passed on to a **`data`** constant, while a **`false`** Boolean will be passed on to an **`error`** constant in the **`useFetch`** composition function. So, you need to destructure them for the data you need in the template.

4. Display data on the template as follows:

    ```html
    // pages/about.vue
    <template>
      <div v-if="!error">
        <h1>{{ data.title }}</h1>
        <div v-html="data.contents"></div>
      </div>
    </template>
    ```

Note that you need to access data items through the object properties in the **`data`** *ref* reactive object. But if you prefer to display the data items without using the object properties, you can unwrap them using the **`unref`** API in the next step.

5. Define **`title`** and **`contents`** constants, fetch the remote with the **`useFetch`** API, and then use the **`unref`** API to unwrap the **`data`** reactive object, then populate the **`data`** properties as follows:

```js
// pages/about.vue
<script setup>
const title = ref(null)
const contents = ref(null)

const runtimeConfig = useRuntimeConfig()
const { data, error } = await useFetch('/posts/100', {
  baseURL: runtimeConfig.public['apiBaseUrl']
})

const post = unref(data)
title.value = post.title
contents.value = post.body
</script>
```

6. Display the data of `title` and `contents` on the template:

```html
// pages/index.vue
<template>
  <div v-if="!error">
    <h2>
      {{ title }}
    </h2>
    <div v-html="contents" />
  </div>
</template>
```

Notice that we can use the `v-if` condition to make sure no error occurs from the `error` reactive object before displaying the data.

7. Use the `useRoute` API with `useRuntimeConfig` and `useFetch` APIs to fetch remote data on dynamic pages, for example:

```js
// pages/blog/[id].vue
<script setup>
```

````
    const route = useRoute()
    const runtimeConfig = useRuntimeConfig()

    const { data: post, error } = await
useFetch(`/posts/${route.params.id}`, {
      baseURL: runtimeConfig.public['apiBaseUrl']
    })
    </script>
    ```
````

8. Display the fetched data on the template:

````
```html
// pages/blog/[id].vue
<template>
  <div v-if="!error">
    <h2>
      {{ post.title }}
    </h2>
    <div v-html="post.body" />
  </div>
</template>
```
````

9. Run the app on the `dev` environment:

````
```

$ npm run dev
```
````

You should see the dummy data from DummyJSON are loaded as expected on the `about` page and the `blog` pages at `localhost:3000`.

You can use the preceding steps to fetch the data for the rest of the pages in your Nuxt app. For more information about the `useFetch` composable, please visit https://nuxt.com/docs/api/composables/use-fetch and https://nuxt.com/docs/getting-started/data-fetching.

As mentioned before, `useFetch` is a sugar **syntax** of writing `useAsyncData` with `$fetch` for making HTTP requests and fetching data. If you need more control with the `$fetch` helper, then you may need to use `useAsyncData` instead. But whether you are using `useFetch` or `useAsyncData`, you can use the same options (`method`, `baseURL`, `query`, `params`, `body`, `headers`, `key`, `lazy`, `watch`, and so on) and get the same return values (`data`, `error`,
````

`pending`, `status`, and `refresh/execute`) from both of them. You even can use `useLazyFetch` and `useLazyAsyncData` instead of writing the `lazy` option in the options. They are just wrappers around `useFetch` and `useAsyncData`. We will use some of the options and return values in the upcoming chapters. You will learn to create your own fetch composable wrapping around `useFetch` to provide shortcut options and modify the error value. For now, we will keep it here short and simple. Before diving deeper, you must know how to handle HTTP request errors when fetching data, as well as handling JavaScript errors during development. So, let's find out in the next topic!

You can find the example app for this topic in `/1.nuxt/1.essentials/5.fetch-data-handle-errors/` in the GitHub repository of this book.

Creating and Handling HTTP Errors

Errors in Nuxt apps can happen during development and runtime. These errors can be HTTP errors such as 404 and 500. They can be internal server errors due to typo mistakes from developers. They can be the mistakes we make in the Vue and Nuxt lifecycles. Luckily, Nuxt comes with a handy default error page that handles these errors for us during development and runtime. Even though Nuxt handles some of these errors for us automatically, we must know how to send errors to Nuxt so it can display the error message and status code that we want to display on the error page. And we must know how to handle errors that Nuxt can't handle for us automatically such as the HTTP error when fetching data. You may also want to handle the error in the `<script>` block before Nuxt catches them in the `<template>` block and throws them to the error page. So, let's find out in the following sections.

Handling HTTP Errors with the Nuxt Default Error Page

Nuxt comes with a `showError` utility API that lets us handle errors in the quickest and simplest way. You can use this utility API on any page, components, and even in plugins to catch and throw errors to the Nuxt default page. The `showError` API is SSR-friendly, meaning the error you encounter is shared across the server and client sides. It also means that you won't get a hydration error during hydration on the client side. You can easily use `showError` with the Nuxt default error page by following these steps:

1. Use the `**showError**` API to throw error from any page, for example:

```js
// pages/blog/[id].vue
<script setup>
...
const { data: post, error } = await
useFetch(`/posts/${route.params.id}`, {
  baseURL: runtimeConfig.public['apiBaseUrl']
})

const failure = unref(error)
if (failure !== null) {
  showError({
    statusCode: failure.statusCode || 500,
    statusMessage: failure.message
  })
}
</script>
```

In the preceding code, we process the `**error**` return value from the `**useFetch**` API by unwrapping and storing it to the `**failure**` constant. If an error occurs, the error data is unpacked and passed to the `**showError**` API. For more information about the `**showError**` API, please visit https://nuxt.com/docs/api/utils/show-error.

2. Make sure you have the following template with the `**v-if**` condition in the `**<template>**` block to display the fetched data:

```html
// pages/blog/[id].vue
<template>
  <div v-if="!error">
    <h2>
      {{ post.title }}
    </h2>
    <div v-html="post.body" />
  </div>
</template>
```

3. Run the app on the `dev` environment:

```
$ npm run dev
```

When you navigate to `/blog/200`, you will get the Nuxt default error page with a 404 error status code and some information on your browser screen:

```
404
(404 (https://dummyjson.com/posts/200))
```

4. Navigate to a route that does not exist at all, for example, `/localhost:3000/xyz`, you will get the Nuxt default error page with a 404 error status code and some information on your browser screen:

```
404
Page not found: /xyz
```

Without handling the HTTP error in the `<script>` block with the `showError` API manually, Nuxt simply won't know there is an error to display. And you will just get an empty result on the page that has occurred. If you remove the `v-if` block in the `<template>` block, Nuxt will catch the errors in the template only and throw them to the default error page as follows:

```
500
TypeError - Cannot read properties of null (reading 'title')
...
...
```

Such errors are not helpful during development and they are a sign of bad UX during runtime for users. So to avoid this kind of bad development experience and UX, you must always handle the error in the `<script>` block. Even though we can use the `v-if` condition in the `<template>` block to suppress our error from Nuxt, it is a bad UX to give the users a blank empty page. A good UX and user-friendly app must be able to handle such HTTP errors properly and tell users what to do when they happen.

Handling JavaScript Errors with the Nuxt Default Error Page

Errors can occur in the code logic during our development process. This can be caused by the typo or syntax errors done by developers, such as `TypeError` and `RangeError` in JavaScript. When such errors happen, browsers will catch them and throw them to the browser console. But without looking into the browser console, this normally leaves us not knowing what happens but just a blank page on the browser screen. So, it is very useful to be able to throw the error on the browser screen during development so that we can trace the error origin and debug it quickly. Nuxt helps us to catch such errors and display them on its default error page. This benefits our development experience and helps to fix our bugs quickly. So, let's find out with some experiments in the following steps:

1. Create a `contact.vue` page and a `login.vue` page in the `/pages/` directory:

   ```bash
   └── pages
       └── contact.vue
       └── login.vue
   ```

2. Add the following code to the `<script>` block in `/pages/contact.vue` to trigger JavaScript `TypeError` as follows:

   ```js
   // pages/contact.vue
   <script setup>
   const num = 123
   num.toUpperCase()
   </script>
   ```

3. Add the following code to the `<script>` block in `/pages/login.vue` to trigger JavaScript `RangeError` as follows:

   ```js
   // pages/login.vue
   <script setup>
   ```

~~~
const l = console.log
const arr = [90,88]
arr.length=90**99
</script>
```
~~~

4. Run the app on the `dev` environment:

~~~
```

$ npm run dev
```
~~~

When you navigate to `/contact`, you will get the Nuxt default error page with a 500 error status code and the error stack on your browser screen:

~~~
```

500
TypeError - num.toUpperCase is not a function
...
...
```
~~~

When you navigate to `/login`, you will get the Nuxt default error page with a 500 error status code and the error stack on your browser screen:

~~~
```

500
RangeError - Invalid array length
...
...
```
~~~

As you can see in this experiment, Nuxt handles JavaScript errors in our code automatically without us lifting an afford. If you are developing a Vue app or a Vue SSR app, you will have to catch and display such errors manually and programmatically. Otherwise, you will only get the error reported on the browser console. So, this is indeed one of the great features of Nuxt that makes your development experience more joyful. You can focus on tracing and fixing the bug more easily and quickly.

The Nuxt default error is great; however, what if you want to apply the theme and styles of your Nuxt app into this error page? Nuxt default error is a generic error page with a default layout and styles from Nuxt. But, in a real app, you would want to personalize this page so that it does not look the same as other Nuxt apps from others. You may want to change how the error status code is being displayed, or add more info on this error page, and add a button to tell the user what to do or where to go when errors happen. You may also want to have the app menu on this error page so that the user can navigate away from this page more easily. So how can we modify and customize that? Let's find out in the next topic.

You can find the example app for this topic in `/1.nuxt/1.essentials/5.fetch-data-handle-errors/` in the GitHub repository of this book.

Customizing the Error Page for HTTP Errors

You wouldn't want the look and feel of your Nuxt app to look identical to other Nuxt apps. If you care about that, then you should always take care of the error page for handling errors. You should always customize and make it unique so that it is not identical to the error page in other Nuxt apps. Therefore, in this topic, we will look into that and also look into how to abstract the logic of handling errors in the `<script>` block. Abstracting the logic of handling errors in the `<script>` block can improve your development experience too and speed up productivity. However, let's look into customizing the Nuxt default error page first.

Handling HTTP and JavaScript Errors with `error.vue`

Nuxt has made it super easy to customize its default error page by just using an `error.vue` file. From this custom `error.vue` file, we can add the app menu, styles, and so on. We will look into that and also customize the error status code, error message, and error stack. So, let's get started with the following steps:

1. Create an `error.vue` file in your Nuxt project root directory as follows:

```bash
└── error.vue
└── pages
    └── ...
```

2. Add the following code to the `<script>` block in `error.vue` as follows:

    ```js
    // error.vue
    <script setup>
    defineProps({
      error: Object
    })
    </script>
    ```

This will enable the `error.vue` page to receive the error data that is passed down through the `defineProps` API. The error data will be stored in the `error` property.

3. Add the following template to the `<template>` block in `error.vue` as follows:

    ```html
    // error.vue
    <template>
      <site-header/>
      <nav-main/>
      <h2>
        {{ error.statusCode }} Error
      </h2>
      <p>
        {{ error.message }}
      </p>
      <div
        v-if=”error.stack”
        v-html=”error.stack”
      />
      <NuxtLink to=”/” class=”button”>
        Navigate home
      </NuxtLink>
    </template>
    ```

The error data will be displayed on the template from the `error` property when the error occurs throughout the pages.

4. Use the `showError` API to throw and show an error on any page, for example:

```js
// pages/blog/[id].vue
<script setup>
...
const { data: post, error } = await
useFetch(`/posts/${route.params.id}`, {
  baseURL: runtimeConfig.public['apiBaseUrl']
})

const failure = unref(error)
if (failure !== null) {
  showError({
    statusCode: failure.statusCode || 500,
    statusMessage: failure.message
  })
}
</script>
```

In the preceding code, just as you have learned in the previous topic, *Creating and Handling HTTP Errors*, we process the `error` return value from the `useFetch` API by unwrapping and storing to the `failure` constant. If error occurs, the error data is unpacked and passed to the `showError` API.

5. Run the app on the `dev` environment:

```
$ npm run dev
```

If you navigate to `/blog/200`, you will see the custom `error.vue` page with a 404 error status code and the error stack on your browser screen when the app is running on the client side:

```
404 Error
(404 (https://dummyjson.com/posts/200))

Error: (404 (https://dummyjson.com/posts/200)) at...
```

However, if you refresh your browser on `/blog/200`, you will see the custom `error.vue` page with a 404 error status code **without** the error stack on your browser screen when the app is running on the server side:

````
```
404 Error
(404 Not Found (https://dummyjson.com/posts/200))
```
````

On the other hand, if you navigate to `/contact`, you will see the custom `error.vue` page with a 500 error status code and the error stack on your browser screen when the app is running on the client side:

````
```
500 Error
TypeError - num.toUpperCase is not a function

TypeError: num.toUpperCase is not a function at setup
(http://localhost:3000/_nuxt/pages/contact.vue:25:5) at...
```
````

And lastly, it is the same if you navigate to `/login`, you will see the custom `error.vue` page with a 500 error status code and the error stack on your browser screen when the app is running on the client side:

````
```
500 Error
RangeError - Invalid array length

RangeError: Invalid array length at setup
(http://localhost:3000/_nuxt/pages/login.vue:10:11) at...
```
````

Well done! You have managed to customize the Nuxt default error page in just a few preceding steps. How you want to style and customize it further to match the look and feel of your Nuxt app is totally up to your imagination, and achieving it is not a far stretch now that you know where to start and how to tweak it in any way you want.

Abstracting Error Logic with `<slot>` and `if-else` Blocks

It is important to handle the `<script>` block manually using the `showError` API before Nuxt automatically handles the error in the `<template>` block for us. But writing the error-handling logic in each `<script>` block across the app is tedious, repetitive, and counter-productive. So, to avoid that, we can abstract the error-handling logic into a new component and then we just have to apply this component wherever we need to handle errors. There are two ways of doing that so let's find out in the following steps:

1. Create an `error-boundary.vue` component and an `error-handler.vue` component in the `/components/` directory as follows:

```bash
└── components
    └── error-boundary.vue
    └── error-handler.vue
```

2. Add the following code to the `<script>` block in `/components/error-boundary.vue` as follows:

```js
// components/error-boundary.vue
<script setup>
const props = defineProps({
  error: {
    type: [ Object, Boolean ],
    default: false
  }
})

if (props.error) {
  showError({
    statusCode: props.error.statusCode || 500,
    statusMessage: `${props.error.name} - ${props.error.message}`,
    stack: props.error.stack
  })
}
</script>
```

In the preceding code, we define props to receive error data from the parent component and the error data can be an object or just a `false` Boolean. When an error occurs, the received error data is passed to the `showError` API just as you did in the previous topic, *Creating and Handling* HTTP *Errors*.

3. Add a `<slot>` component to the `<template>` block in `/components/error-boundary.vue` as follows:

    ```html
    // components/error-boundary.vue
    <template>
      <slot />
    </template>
    ```

4. Add the following code to the `<script>` block `/components/error-handler.vue` as follows:

    ```js
    // components/error-handler.vue
    <script setup>
    const props = defineProps({
      error: {
        type: [ Object, Boolean ],
        default: false
      }
    })

    if (props.error) {
      showError({
        statusCode: props.error.statusCode || 500,
        statusMessage: `${props.error.name} - ${props.error.
        message}`,
        stack: props.error.stack
      })
    }
    </script>
    ```

Notice that the `<script>` block in `/components/error-handler.vue` is exactly the same as in `/components/error-boundary.vue`.

5. Add a `**<div>**` HTML element to the `**<template>**` block in `**/components/error-handler.vue**` as follows:

```html
// components/error-handler.vue
<template>
  <div />
</template>
```

6. Apply the `**<error-boundary>**` component in the `**<template>**` block on any page, for example:

```html
// pages/profile.vue
<template>
  <error-boundary v-bind:error=”error”>
    <h2>
      {{ title }}
    </h2>
    <div v-html=”contents” />
  </error-boundary>
</template>
```

7. Fetch the data through the `**<script>**` block in `**/pages/profile.vue**` as follows:

```js
// pages/profile.vue
<script setup>
const title = ref(null)
const contents = ref(null)

const runtimeConfig = useRuntimeConfig()
const { data, error } = await useFetch(‘/posts/1000000’, {
  baseURL: runtimeConfig.public[‘apiBaseUrl’]
})
const failure = unref(error)
if (failure === null) {
  const post = unref(data)
  title.value = post.title
  contents.value = post.body
}
```

```
</script>
```

Notice that we fetch the data from the `/posts/1000000` REST API endpoint, which does not exist in DummyJSON (https://dummyjson.com/). So, this will trigger a 404 not found error. Otherwise, we will populate the data.

8. Use the `<error-handler>` component with the `if-else` condition in the `<template>` block on any page, for example:

```html
// pages/cart.vue
<template>
  <div v-if="!error">
    <h2>
      {{ title }}
    </h2>
    <div v-html="contents" />
  </div>
  <error-handler
    v-else
    v-bind:error="error"
  />
</template>
```

9. Fetch the data through the `<script>` block in `/pages/cart.vue` as follows:

```js
// pages/cart.vue
<script setup>
const title = ref(null)
const contents = ref(null)

const runtimeConfig = useRuntimeConfig()
const { data, error } = await useFetch('/posts/2000000', {
  baseURL: runtimeConfig.public['apiBaseUrl']
})
const failure = unref(error)
if (failure === null) {
  const post = unref(data)
  title.value = post.title
  contents.value = post.body
}
```

```
</script>
```

Notice that we fetch the data from the `/posts/2000000` REST API endpoint, which does not exist in DummyJSON. So, this will trigger a 404 not found error. Otherwise, we will populate the data.

10. Run the app on the `dev` environment:

```
$ npm run dev
```

When you navigate to `/profile`, you will see the custom `error.vue` page with a 404 error status code and the error stack on your browser screen:

```
404 Error
Error - (404 (https://dummyjson.com/posts/1000000))

    FetchError: (404 (https://dummyjson.com/posts/1000000)) at
async setup (http://localhost:3000/_nuxt/pages/profile.vue:25:12)
```

On the other hand, when you navigate to `/cart`, you will see the custom `error.vue` page with a 404 error status code and the error stack on your browser screen:

```
404 Error
Error - (404 (https://dummyjson.com/posts/2000000))

    FetchError: (404 (https://dummyjson.com/posts/2000000))
at async setup (http://localhost:3000/_nuxt/pages/cart.
vue?t=1689179321888:25:12)
```

There you go. Now you have two different components that handle the error in the same way. Whichever component you prefer, or which one you find easier and neater, it is all up to you. We have tucked away the error-handling logic with the `showError` API, we don't need to look and think about it every time. You just have to fiddle with this abstracted logic and components when you need to change the `statusCode`, `statusMessage`, and `stack` options that you need to pass to the `showError` API.

In this another short and simple topic, you have managed to customize the Nuxt default error page and abstracted the error-handling logic into reusable components. It may not seem much and important, but it is an essential part to make your Nuxt app great and standout. The few preceding steps have shown you where to start and tweak, the rest are known to you.

You can find the example app for this topic in `/1.nuxt/1.essentials/5.fetch-data-handle-errors/` in the GitHub repository of this book.

Conclusion

In this short chapter, you have managed to fetch data from remote APIs using the `useFetch` API. You have learned that `useFetch` is a sugar **syntax** or shortcut of using `useAsyncData` with `$fetch`, which is built on `ofetch`, for making HTTP requests and fetching data. You have handled HTTP errors, such as 404 and 500 errors, with the `showError` API and the Nuxt default error page for unknown routes, internal server errors, and JavaScript default errors during development and runtime. You have customized the Nuxt default error page using the `error.vue` file and have customized the error status code, error message, and error stack. Lastly, you have abstracted the error-handling logic into reusable components to improve the development experience, productivity, and future maintenance.

In the next chapter, you will discover how to create global states with the Nuxt `useState` API to be shared between the server and client across components and pages; manipulate global states from specific pages; build a counter and a shopping cart system with Pinia; create a client-server data-persistent store with the `useCookie` Nuxt API; and more excitingly, create a client-server data-persistent store with `localStorage` and Redis. So, let's get to it!

Chapter 5

Managing States and Stores

Introduction

Welcome to *Chapter* 5. In this chapter, you will create global states to be shared between the server and client across components and pages. You will discover which methods you should avoid and which ones you should use when creating global states in Nuxt apps. In addition, you will build a counter and a shopping cart program with Pinia, and you will also create client-server data-persistent stores with Pinia, cookies, **`localStorage`**, Nuxt's built-in Nitro web server, middleware, and Redis.

Structure

The topics that will be covered in this chapter are as follows:

- Creating Global States with **`useState`**
- Creating Data-Persistent Stores with Pinia and Cookies: A Counter
- Creating Stores with Pinia: A Shopping Cart
- Creating Data-Persistent Stores with Pinia, **`localStorage`**, Cookies, and Redis

Creating Global States with `useState`

Whether you are building a Vue or Nuxt app, you will need to pass some data around across your app. You would use **`defineProps`** and **`defineEmits`** to pass data up and down between two components. However, it is tedious when we need to pass data to more distant components or multi-layer deep components.

So, this can be resolved with global states, which centralize the data we need to share across the app, allowing us to access data from anywhere regardless of how distant and how deep our components are. In this topic, we will explore a few methods to create global states for Nuxt apps. By the end of this topic, you will find out which method to go for and which ones to avoid. So, let's find out in the following sections!

Using Custom Composables

It is possible to use custom composable to create global states in a Vue or Nuxt app. However, it is more of a **hack** than anything officially written in Vue or Nuxt documentation. It has never been the proper global state creation from any of these frameworks. Furthermore, it has insidious consequences. In this section, we will explore this method of creating global states in Nuxt apps and study what is wrong with it through the following steps:

1. Create a **`use-count.ts`** file in the **`/composables/`** directory:

```bash
composables
└─ use-count.ts
```

2. Create a **`count`** reactive constant **outside** the exported function that returns the **`count`** reactive constant only:

```js
const count = ref(0)
export default () => {
  return count
}
```

3. Use the **`useCount`** composable on the **`index`** page as follows:

```js
// pages/index.vue
<script setup>
  const countA = useCount()
</script>
```

4. Display the data on the template as follows:

````
```html
// pages/index.vue
<template>
  <p>
    countA (composable): {{ countA }}
  </p>
</template>
```
````

5. Use the **`useCount`** composable again on another page and change its default value, for example:

````
```js
// pages/about.vue
<script setup>
  const countA = useCount()
  countA.value = 1
</script>
```
````

6. Display the data on the template as follows:

````
```html
// pages/about.vue
<template>
  <p>
    countA (composable): {{ countA }}
  </p>

  <button type="button" @click="countA++">
    count is {{ countA }}
  </button>
</template>
```
````

7. Use the **`useCount`** composable again on another page, for example:

````
```js
// pages/contact.vue
````
````

~~~
<script setup>
  const countA = useCount()
</script>
```
~~~

8. Display the data on the template as follows:

~~~
```html
// pages/contact.vue
<template>
  <p>
    countA (composable): {{ countA }}
  </p>
</template>
```
~~~

9. Run the app on the `dev` environment:

~~~
```
$ npm run dev
```
~~~

You should see the following result on your browser screen at `localhost:3000`:

~~~
```
countA (composable): 0
```
~~~

You should see the following result on your browser screen when navigating to `/about`:

~~~
```
countA (composable): 1
```
~~~

If you navigate back to `/` or `/contact`, you should see the same result on your screen as on `/about`:

~~~
```
countA (composable): 1
```
~~~

This shows that the global `count` state is shared across the app successfully. If you click the button on `/about` to increase the `count` value, you will see the same result on other pages.

However, creating global states by placing reactive constants outside the exported function in composable has insidious consequences. If you refresh your browser on `/about` and then navigate to `/` or `/contact` and refresh your browser again, you will get a warning of hydration text content mismatch in your browser console. If you inspect the rendered HTML on `/` at `view-source:http://localhost:3000/`, you will see the following rendered element:

```html
<p> countA (composable): 1</p>
```

The preceding is rendered on the server side. However, the browser on the client side rendered the element as follows:

```html
<p> countA (composable): 0</p>
```

This phenomenon happens because the following script runs on the server side first when your browser is being refreshed on `/about`:

```js
const countA = useCount()
countA.value = 1
```

However, this has set the `count` constant on the `useCount` composable permanently to `1` on the server side – unless you make sure that the preceding script runs on the client side only. However, if we want it to run on both the client and server sides, then creating global states in this way must be avoided at any cost. It is insidious and incorrect. It is because such global states are shared with all users visiting your website from different browsers and geographies across the globe, which can overwhelm the server memory.

Creating global states just by placing the reactive constant outside the function scope in composable looks neat and simple. It looks like a holy grail for global states, providing a magically fast and easy way to create them. However, it is too good to be true. It entails issues hidden in plain sight from the start. The correct global states should be available only across the components and pages, not across all components, pages, and users. There are several proper ways for creating global reactive states in Vue; one of them is using the **`provide`** and **`inject`** APIs from Vue itself. You will find out about this in the next section and compare it with the global states presented in this section. So, let's find out!

# Using provide and inject APIs

The **`provide`** and **`inject`** APIs from Vue itself are the official and proper methods for creating global states in Vue apps. They can be used in Nuxt apps without any trouble. In this section, we will explore this method of creating global states in Nuxt apps and see if they work well on both the server and client sides or not through the following steps:

1. Use **`provide`** to create a reactive **`count`** global state in **`app.vue`** as follows:

    ```js
    // app.vue
    <script setup>
      const countB = ref(0)
      provide(‘count’, countB)
    </script>
    ```

2. Use **`inject`** to receive data from the provider on any page, for example:

    ```js
    // pages/index.vue
    <script setup>
      const countB = inject(‘count’)
    </script>
    ```

3. Display the data on the template as follows:

    ```html
    // pages/index.vue
    <template>
      <p>
        countB (provide/inject): {{ countB }}
      </p>
    </template>
    ```

4. Use **`inject`** to receive data again from the provider on another page and change its default value, for example:

```js
// pages/about.vue
<script setup>
  const countB = inject('count')
  countB.value = 100
</script>
```

5. Display the data on the template as follows:

```html
// pages/about.vue
<template>
  <p>
    countB (provide/inject): {{ countB }}
  </p>

  <button type="button" @click="countB++">
    countB (provide/inject) is {{ countB }}
  </button>
</template>
```

6. Use **`inject`** to receive data again from the provider on another page, for example:

```js
// pages/contact.vue
<script setup>
  const countB = inject('count')
</script>
```

7. Display the data on the template as follows:

```html
// pages/contact.vue
<template>
  <p>
```

```
    countB (provide/inject): {{ countB }}
  </p>
</template>
```

8. Run the app on the `dev` environment:

```
$ npm run dev
```

You should see the following result on your browser screen at `localhost:3000`:

```
countB (composable): 0
```

You should see the following result on your browser screen when navigating to `/about`:

```
countB (composable): 100
```

If you navigate back to `/` or `/contact`, you should see the same result on your screen as on `/about`:

```
countB (composable): 100
```

This shows that the global `count` state is shared across the app successfully. If you click the button on `/about` to increase the `count` value, you will see the same result on other pages.

If you refresh your browser on `/about` and then navigate to / or `/contact` and refresh your browser again, you won't get the warning of hydration text content mismatch on your browser console, as seen with `countA`. If you inspect the rendered HTML on `/` at `view-source:http://localhost:3000/`, you will see the following rendered element:

```html
<p> countB (composable): 100</p>
```

The preceding element is rendered on the server side as expected, and the browser on the client side also renders the element as expected, as follows:

```html
<p> countB (composable): 100</p>
```

There you go. It takes two APIs, **`provide`** and **`inject`**, to create proper global reactive states in Vue or Nuxt apps. It is SSR-friendly and does not have the hydration mismatch issue observed in the previous section, which places the reactive constant outside the function scope in composable. For more information about **`provide`** and **`inject`** APIs, please visit https://vuejs.org/api/composition-api-dependency-injection.html and https://vuejs.org/guide/components/provide-inject.html.

We definitely can use **`provide`** and **`inject`** to create global reactive states in Nuxt apps. However, Nuxt has a **`useState`** API that does the same thing for us. It is simpler and easier to implement and use just one API instead of two like **`provide`** and **`inject`**. It is definitely worth a shot for many, especially for those who are fond of using composable. So, let's find out in the next section.

# Using The `useState` API

The **`useState`** API from Nuxt is the official and proper method for creating global states in Nuxt apps. In this section, we will explore this method in creating global states in Nuxt apps and see if it works well on both the server and client sides or not through the following steps:

1. Use **`useState`** to create a reactive **`count`** global state in **`app.vue`** as follows:

```js
// app.vue
<script setup>
  const countC = useState('count', () => 0)
</script>
```

Note that `useState` is a `ref` replacement and is SSR-friendly. Hence, any global shared state that is created using `useState` is reactive by nature.

2. Use `useState` to receive data by providing `count` as the key on any page, for example:

   ````
   ```js
   // pages/index.vue
   <script setup>
     const countC = useState('count')
   </script>
   ```
   ````

3. Display the data on the template as follows:

   ````
   ```html
   // pages/index.vue
   <template>
     <p>
       countC (useState): {{ countC }}
     </p>
   </template>
   ```
   ````

4. Use `useState` again with the `count` key to retrieve the data and change it on another page, for example:

   ````
   ```js
   // pages/about.vue
   <script setup>
     const countC = useState('count')
     countC.value = 200
   </script>
   ```
   ````

5. Display the data on the template as follows:

   ````
   ```html
   // pages/about.vue
   <template>
     <p>
       countC (useState): {{ countC }}
     </p>
   ````
   ````

```
  <button type="button" @click="countC++">
    countC (useState) is {{ countC }}
  </button>
</template>
```

6. Use **`useState`** again with the **`count`** key to retrieve the data on another page, for example:

```js
// pages/contact.vue
<script setup>
  const countC = useState('count')
</script>
```

7. Display the data on the template as follows:

```html
// pages/contact.vue
<template>
  <p>
    countC (useState): {{ countC }}
  </p>
</template>
```

8. Run the app on the **`dev`** environment:

```
$ npm run dev
```

You should see the following result on your browser screen at **`localhost:3000`**:

```
countC (composable): 0
```

You should see the following result on your browser screen when navigating to **`/about`**:

```
countC (composable): 200
```

If you navigate back to **`/`** or **`/contact`**, you should see the same result on your screen as on **`/about`**:

```
countC (composable): 200
```

This shows that the global **`count`** state is shared across the app successfully. If you click the button on **`/about`** to increase the **`count`** value, you will see the same result on other pages.

If you refresh your browser on **`/about`** and then navigate to **`/`** or **`/contact`** and refresh your browser again, you won't get the warning of hydration text content mismatch on your browser console, as seen with **`countA`**. If you inspect the rendered HTML on **`/`** at **`view-source:http://localhost:3000/`**, you will see the following rendered element:

```html
<p> countC (composable): 200</p>
```

The preceding element is rendered on the server side as expected, and the browser on the client side also renders the element as expected, as follows:

```html
<p> countC (composable): 200</p>
```

As you can see, **`useState`** is SSR-friendly. This means that any global state you create has its value re-populated on both the client and server sides when the browser is refreshed. And that you won't get the hydration mismatch error. It is a great alternative to the **`provide`** and **`inject`** APIs in Nuxt apps. For more information about this API, please visit https://nuxt.com/docs/api/composables/use-state and https://nuxt.com/docs/getting-started/state-management.

Finally, you should have realized and known already which methods should be used for your Nuxt apps without causing any unexpected outcome. Once again, you should avoid creating global states by placing reactive constants out of the functions in composable. Internally available options such as `provide`, `inject`, and `useState` should be used for creating proper global states when required. Besides these internal APIs, you can also use external libraries to help you to create global states. These libraries are also called store management libraries, such as Pinia, which you will use in the upcoming sections. So, let's find out!

The example app for this topic can be found in `/1.nuxt/1.essentials/6.state-management/` in the GitHub repository of this book.

Creating Data-Persistent Stores with Pinia and Cookies: A Counter

Global states can be useful and necessary in your Nuxt app, and there are multiple ways of creating them, as shown in the previous section with the `useState` composable, the `provide` and `inject` APIs, and local component functions. However, if you want to organize your global states into separate files, with the functions that are used to manipulate the states, you can use a store management library, such as Pinia (https://pinia.vuejs.org/). With stores, you can organize your global states into manageable and extendable modules. So, let's find out how you can leverage Pinia to manage stores for you in the upcoming sections!

Creating Global States with Pinia

Creating global states with Pinia is surprisingly easy and the learning curve is really flat. In this section, we will create a counter program in which it has a global state and a global function to increase its state value. However, before that, you will need to install Pinia and its Nuxt module in your Nuxt app. So, let's get started and create our counter program through the following steps:

1. Create a `/stores/` directory with a `counter.ts` file in the project root and a `counter.vue` file in the `/pages/` directory as follows:

````
```bash
├── pages
│   └── counter.vue
└── stores
    └── counter.ts
```
````

2. Install `pinia` and `@pinia/nuxt` in your Nuxt project:

```
$ npm i pinia @pinia/nuxt
```

Note that the installation of Node.js packages may change over time, you should always confirm the installation command lines with their official documentation if you start your project afresh. For installing the `@pinia/nuxt` Nuxt module with `pinia`, please visit https://pinia.vuejs.org/ssr/nuxt.html.

3. Register `@pinia/nuxt` to the `modules` key in `nuxt.config.ts` as follows:

```js
// nuxt.config.ts
export default defineNuxtConfig({
  modules: [
    '@pinia/nuxt'
  ]
})
```

4. Create a `counter` store using `defineStore` in `/stores/counter.ts` as follows:

```js
// stores/counter.ts
import { defineStore } from 'pinia'
export const useCounterStore = defineStore('counter', () => {
  const count = 0
  return {
    count
  }
})
```

Notice that in this `counter` store, we also created a `count` constant and return it to the store object.

5. Create an `increment` function to increase the `count` value incrementally and then return it:

```js
```

```
// stores/counter.ts
import { defineStore } from 'pinia'
export const useCounterStore = defineStore('counter', () => {
  ...
  function increment () {
    count.value++
  }
  return {
    decrement
  }
})
```

6. Import the **`counter`** store as **`useCounterStore`** and assign it to a **`store`** constant in **`/pages/counter.vue`**:

```js
// pages/counter.vue
<script setup>
import { useCounterStore } from '@/stores/counter'
const store = useCounterStore()
</script>
```

7. Display the **`count`** value and attach the **`increment`** store function to a button on the template as follows:

```html
// pages/counter.vue
<template>
  <p>
    store.count: {{ store.count }}
  </p>
  <button @click="store.increment()">
    +
  </button>
</template>
```

8. Import the **`counter`** store again on another page and display the **`count`** value, for example:

```
// pages/index.vue
```

```
<script setup>
import { useCounterStore } from '@/stores/counter'
const store = useCounterStore()
</script>

<template>
  <p>
    store.count: {{ store.count }}
  </p>
</template>
```

9. Run the app on the `dev` environment:

```
$ npm run dev
```

You should see the `count` value starts at `0` on / and `/counter`. If you click the increment button on `/counter`, you should see the `count` value has been increased the same on `/` and `/counter`. If you refresh your browser on any of these two pages, you should see the `count` value reset back to `0`.

Note that the `count` value is reset back to `0` is an expected behavior, as global states are not persistent unless the increment value is re-populated on both the client and server sides when refreshing the browser. This means that the increment value has to be stored in a place that both the client and server can access and then re-populate the `count` value. And that place is cookies, which you might have considered already. So, let's find out how you can use cookies to make the `count` value persistent in the upcoming section.

Creating Data-Persistent Stores with Cookies

Nuxt is shipped with an `useCookie` composable to help us to create cookies out of the box without the need for installing any extra module in your Nuxt app or creating your own cookie functions. In this section, we will further the counter program you just created in the previous section by implementing `useCookie`. We will also create additional global functions to decrease and reset the global counter's state. So, let's find out through the following steps:

1. Use `useCookie` to create the `count` constant instead and assign the `count` value from cookies as follows:

```js
// stores/counter.ts
import { defineStore } from ‘pinia’
export const useCounterStore = defineStore(‘counter’, () => {
  const day = 1
  const count = useCookie(‘count’, {
    maxAge: day * 24 * 60 * 60
  })
  count.value = count.value || 0
  return {
    count
  }
})
```

Notice that the `count` cookie is set to expire in one day. If no `count` cookie can be retrieved, then use the `0` as the `count` value.

2. Create a `decrement` function and a `reset` function and then return them:

```js
// stores/counter.ts
import { defineStore } from ‘pinia’
export const useCounterStore = defineStore(‘counter’, () => {
  ...
  function decrement () {
    count.value--
  }
  function reset () {
    count.value = 0
  }
  return {
    decrement,
    reset
  }
})
```

The `decrement` function will decrease the `count` value detrimentally, while the reset function will reset the `count` value to `0`.

3. Create a **`doubleCount`** computed function to double the **`count`** value and then return it:

```js
// stores/counter.ts
import { defineStore } from ‘pinia’
export const useCounterStore = defineStore(‘counter’, () => {
  ...
  const doubleCount = computed(() => count.value * 2)
  return {
    doubleCount
  }
})
```

4. Import the **`counter`** store (as before) in **`/pages/counter.vue`** and create a **`doubleValue`** computed function to get the value from the **`doubleCount`** function:

```js
// pages/counter.vue
<script setup>
import { useCounterStore } from ‘@/stores/counter’

const store = useCounterStore()
const doubleValue = computed(() => store.doubleCount)
</script>
```

5. Display the **`count`** value (as before) and the **`doubleValue`** values, and then attach the **`decrement`** and **`reset`** store functions to the buttons on the template as follows:

```html
// pages/counter.vue
<template>
  <p>
    store.count: {{ store.count }}
  </p>
  ...
  ...
  <p>
    doubleValue: {{ doubleValue }}
```

```
    </p>
    <button @click="store.increment()">
      +
    </button>
    <button @click="store.decrement()">
      -
    </button>
    <button @click="store.reset()">
      Reset
    </button>
  </template>
  ```
```

6. Run the app on the `dev` environment:

```
  ```
  $ npm run dev
  ```
```

You should see that the `count` value starts at `0` on `/` and `/counter`. If you click the increment or decrement button on `/counter`, you should see the `count` value has either increased or decreased the same on / and `/counter`. Upon refreshing your browser on any of these two pages, you should see the `count` value is re-populated with the last value that you set to it. If you click the reset button, the value will be reset to `0` and it will be re-populated as `0` when you refresh your browser.

There you go. You have just managed to make a data-persistent counter by following these steps using `useCookie`. All you need is to attach `useCookie` to the counter's global state and set the expiration time. `useCookie` is SSR-friendly, which means that it re-populates the value on both the client and server sides when the browser is being refreshed, avoiding hydration mismatch error. That's sweet as we don't even have to think about it and Nuxt has done the heavy lifting for us out of the box! For more information about the `useCookie` composable, please visit https://nuxt.com/docs/api/composables/use-cookie#usecookie.

Well done! In this topic, you have managed to use Pinia and cookies to create a simple data-persistent counter store. You should have noticed that writing variables and functions in the store is exactly similar to writing them in components using Composition API. You may not even realize that writing stores with Pinia because of this. However, if you prefer, you still use Option API. Besides Pinia, you can also use Vuex (https://vuex.vuejs.org/) or Harlem (https://harlemjs.com/) to create stores. For more store examples and
```

information about Pinia, please visit https://pinia.vuejs.org/core-concepts/. In the next topic, we will use Pinia to create a more advanced store – a shopping cart program. You will discover how to store large data on the server and client sides for your stores. So, let's find out!

The example app for this topic can be found in **`/1.nuxt/1.essentials/6.state-management/`** in the GitHub repository of this book.

Creating Stores with Pinia: A Shopping Cart

The ultimate aim of the counter program in the previous section was to make its data persistent for both the client and server sides, which was only possible with cookies. However, we can only use cookies to store small data. If you need to store larger data, such as the data of a shopping cart, then we must look for other options. Therefore, in this section, we will use the storage technology on the client and server sides that allow us to achieve that. However, before making the data persistent for larger data, we must first build a program to collect the data. So, let's build a shopping cart program!

Creating the Shopping Cart

In the shopping cart program that we are going to create, we aim to enable user to add items to their cart, update them, and remove them from their shopping cart. We also allow users to set the item quantity. Additionally, we want to calculate the total cost of the cart, the total cost of each item, as well as the total and unique items in the cart. So, let's get started and create our store cart through the following steps:

1. Create a **`/stores/`** directory with a **`cart.ts`** file, a **`shop.vue`** file in the **`/pages/`** directory, and a **`product-item.vue`** file in the **`/components/`** directory as follows:

```
├── stores
│   └── cart.ts
├── pages
│   └── shop.vue
└── components
    └── product-item.vue
```

2. Create a `.env` file in the project root with the following variables and values:

    ```bash
    // .env
    APP_BASE_URL=http://localhost:3000
    APP_CART_ID=example.com:cart
    API_BASE_URL=https://dummyjson.com
    ```

3. Pass the preceding env variables to the runtime configuration's `public` key in `nuxt.config.ts`:

    ```js
    // nuxt.config.ts
    export default defineNuxtConfig({
      runtimeConfig: {
        public: {
          apiBaseUrl: process.env.API_BASE_URL,
          appBaseUrl: process.env.APP_BASE_URL,
          appCartId: process.env.APP_CART_ID
        }
      },
      modules: [
        ‘@pinia/nuxt’
      ]
    })
    ```

4. Create a `cart` store using `defineStore` in `/stores/cart.ts` as follows:

    ```js
    // stores/cart.ts
    import { defineStore } from ‘pinia’

    export const useCartStore = defineStore(‘cart’, () => {
      const runtimeConfig = useRuntimeConfig()
      const cartId = runtimeConfig.public[‘appCartId’]
      const cart = ref([])
      return {
        cart
      }
    })
    ```

Notice that in this `cart` store, we use `useRuntimeConfig` to get the `appCartId` value, then create a `cart` reactive constant with an empty array by default and return it in the store object.

5. Create `uniqueLength`, `sumQuantity`, and `sumCost` computed functions to compute the cart's total items, total cost, and total unique items:

````
```js
// stores/cart.ts
import { defineStore } from ‘pinia’
export const useCartStore = defineStore(‘cart’, () => {
  ...
  const uniqueLength = computed(() => cart.value.length)
  const sumQuantity = computed(() => {
    return cart.value.reduce((accumulator, object) =>
      Number(object.quantity) + accumulator, 0
    )
  })
  const sumCost = computed(() => {
    const costs = cart.value.reduce((accumulator, object) =>
      Number(object.cost) + accumulator, 0
    )
    return costs.toFixed(2)
  })
  return {
    uniqueLength,
    sumQuantity,
    sumCost
  }
})
```
````

Note that we must return the preceding computed functions/constants so that they can be accessed publicly anywhere throughout the app. The `sumQuantity` computed constant is used to sum the total items in the cart through the `quantity` key from each item in the cart. Similarly, the `sumCost` computed constant is used to sum the total cost of the cart through the `cost` key from each item in the cart. Both use the `reduce` method from JavaScript built-in methods. For more information about this method, please visit https://developer.mozilla.org/en-US/docs/Web/JavaScript/Reference/Global_Objects/Array/reduce.

6. Create an `addItem` async function to add items to the `cart` array and return it:

```js
// stores/cart.ts
import { defineStore } from ‘pinia’
export const useCartStore = defineStore(‘cart’, () => {
  ...
  async function addItem (item) {
    const exist = cart.value.some(product => product.id ===
    item.id)
    if (exist === true) {
      await updateItem(item)
      return
    }

    cart.value.push(item)
  }
  return {
    ...
    addItem
  }
})
```

In this `addItem` function, we would want to make sure any new item that the user wants to add to the cart must not exist already in their shopping cart. If the new item has not existed, then add it to the cart; otherwise, update the item's quantity through a `updateItem` function. We use the `some` method from JavaScript built-in methods to look for a match in the `cart` array. For more information about this method, please visit https://developer.mozilla.org/en-US/docs/Web/JavaScript/Reference/Global_Objects/Array/some.

7. Create a `updateItem` async function to update items in the `cart` array and return it:

```js
// stores/cart.ts
import { defineStore } from ‘pinia’
export const useCartStore = defineStore(‘cart’, () => {
  ...
  async function updateItem (item) {
    const index = cart.value.findIndex((element, index) => {
      if (element.id === item.id) {
```

```
          return true
        }
      })
      cart.value[index].quantity = item.quantity
      cart.value[index].cost = item.cost
    }
    return {
      ...
      updateItem
    }
  })
```

In this `updateItem` function, we would want to make sure any existing item that the user wants to update in the cart already exists in their shopping cart. If the updated item does not exist, it should be ignored; otherwise, the existing item's quantity and cost should be updated based on what is provided by the user. We use the `findIndex` from JavaScript built-in methods to find the index of the incoming item in the `cart` array, and then get this item using the index to update its quantity and cost. For more information about this method, please visit https://developer.mozilla.org/en-US/docs/Web/JavaScript/Reference/Global_Objects/Array/findIndex.

8. Create a `deleteItem` async function to delete items from the `cart` array and return it:

```js
// stores/cart.ts
import { defineStore } from 'pinia'
export const useCartStore = defineStore('cart', () => {
  ...
  function deleteItem (item) {
    const index = cart.value.findIndex((element, index) => {
      if (element.id === item.id) {
        return true
      }
    })
    cart.value.splice(index, 1)
  }
  return {
    ...
    deleteItem
  }
})
```

9. Create an `empty` function to remove all items from the `cart` array completely and return it:

```js
// stores/cart.ts
import { defineStore } from 'pinia'
export const useCartStore = defineStore('cart', () => {
  ...
  function empty () {
    cart.value = []
  }
  return {
    ...
    empty
  }
})
```

10. Import the `cart` store as `useCartStore` and assign it to a `store` constant in `/pages/shop.vue`:

```js
// pages/shop.vue
<script setup>
import { useCartStore } from '@/stores/cart'
const store = useCartStore()

const runtimeConfig = useRuntimeConfig()
const { data, error } = await useFetch(`/products/?limit=10`,
{
  baseURL: runtimeConfig.public['apiBaseUrl']
})
</script>
```

11. Display the `cart` value and attach the `empty` store function to a button on the template as follows:

```html
// pages/shop.vue
<template>
  <h2>
    Shop
  </h2>
```

```
    {{ store.cart }}
    <ul v-if=”!error”>
      <button @click=”store.empty”>
        Empty Cart
      </button>
      <li
        v-for=”product in data.products”
        :key=”product.id”
      >
        <product-item
          v-bind:product=product
        />
      </li>
    </ul>
  </template>
```

12. Import the `` `cart` `` store in `` `/components/product-item.vue` ``, get the `` `product` `` data from `` `/pages/shop.vue` ``, and create an `` `add` `` local component function as follows:

```js
// components/product-item.vue
<script setup>
import { useCartStore } from ‘@/stores/cart’

const store = useCartStore()
const props = defineProps({
  product: {
    type: Object
  }
})
const quantity = ref(1)

function add () {
  const cost = quantity.value * props.product.price
  const order = {
    quantity: quantity.value,
    cost: cost.toFixed(2),
    timestamp: Date.now()
  }

  // Merge object properties with the spread operator.
  store.addItem({ ...props.product, ...order })
}
</script>
```

````
```
````

In the `add` function on this component, we use the `toFixed` from JavaScript built-in methods to make sure only 2 decimals are used in the item cost. For more information about this method, please visit https://developer.mozilla.org/en-US/docs/Web/JavaScript/Reference/Global_Objects/Number/toFixed.

13. Display the `product` data and attach the `add` component function to a button on the template as follows:

````
```html
// components/product-item.vue
<template>
  <h3>
    {{ product.title }}
  </h3>
  <p>
    <img
      :alt=”product.title”
      :src=”product.thumbnail”
    />
  </p>
  <p>
    {{ product.description }}
  </p>
  <p>
    $ {{ product.price }}
  </p>
  <p>
    Stock: {{ product.stock }}
  </p>
  <input
    v-model=”quantity”
    type=”number”
    min=”1”
    v-bind:max=”product.stock”
  />
  <button @click=”add”>
    Add to Cart
  </button>
</template>
```
````
````

14. Run the app on the `dev` environment:

```
$ npm run dev
```

You should see a list of products fetched from `dummyjson.com` displayed on `/shop` successfully with an empty array, `[]`. If you click the `Add to Cart` button to add a product to the store cart, you should see the empty array is populated with the product data, for example:

```
    [ { "id": 1, "title": "iPhone 9", "description": "An apple mobile
which is nothing like apple", "price": 549, "discount
Percentage": 12.96, "rating": 4.69,
"stock": 94, "brand": "Apple", "category": "smartphones", "thumbnail":
"https://i.dummyjson.com/data/products/1/thumbnail.jpg", "images": [
"https://i.dummyjson.com/data/products/1/1.jpg",
"https://i.dummyjson.com/data/products/1/2.jpg",
"https://i.dummyjson.com/data/products/1/3.jpg",
"https://i.dummyjson.com/data/products/1/4.jpg",
"https://i.dummyjson.com/data/products/1/thumbnail.jpg" ],
"quantity": 1, "cost": "549.00", "timestamp": 1691522410731 } ]
```

You should see the cart array growing on the screen as you click add more items. If you click the `Empty Cart` button, the cart array will be reset back to `[]`. However, if you would like to delete some specific items from the cart array, there is currently no button created to attach with the store `deleteItem` async function. So, to have this button and a button for updating the product quantity on the product already added to the cart, we will need to have a `cart` page to list the cart items with these buttons. So, let's create this page in the next section.

Creating the Cart Page

Having a user interface that allows users to add items to the store cart isn't enough. We also need a user interface or a page that allows users to see their cart items and modify or remove them. In this cart page we are going to create, you will be able to apply the rest of the store functions that you just created in the previous section, such as the `sumQuantity`, `uniqueLength`, `deleteItem`, and `updateItem` functions. So, let's find out in the following steps:

1. Create a **`cart.vue`** file in the **`/pages/`** directory and a **`cart-item.vue`** file in the **`/components/`** directory as follows:

```
├── pages
│   └── cart.vue
└── components
    └── cart-item.vue
```

2. Import the **`cart`** store as **`useCartStore`** and assign it to a **`store`** constant in **`/pages/cart.vue`**:

```js
// pages/cart.vue
<script setup>
import { useCartStore } from '@/stores/cart'
const store = useCartStore()
</script>
```

3. Display the **`cart`** contents with the **`sumQuantity`**, **`uniqueLength`**, and **`sumCost`** store functions, as well as attach the **`empty`** store function to a button on the template as follows:

```html
// pages/cart.vue
<template>
  <h2>
    Cart
  </h2>
  <p>
    Total Items: {{ store.sumQuantity }}
  </p>
  <p>
    Total Unique Items: {{ store.uniqueLength }}
  </p>
  <p>
    Total Cost: $ {{ store.sumCost }}
  </p>
   <button @click="store.empty">
    Empty Cart
  </button>
  <ul v-if="store.cart.length > 0">
```

````
    <li
      v-for=”item in store.cart”
      v-bind:key=”item.id”
    >
      <cart-item
        v-bind:product=item
      />
    </li>
  </ul>
</template>
```
````

4. Import the `` `cart` `` store in `` `/components/cart-item.vue` ``, get the `` `product` `` data from `` `/pages/cart.vue` ``, and create an `` `update` `` local component function and a `` `remove` `` local component function as follows:

````
```js
// components/cart-item.vue
<script setup>
import { useCartStore } from ‘@/stores/cart’

const store = useCartStore()
const props = defineProps({
  product: Object
})
const quantity = ref(props.product.quantity)

function remove () {
  store.deleteItem(props.product)
}
function update () {
 // Use toFixed to make sure only 2 decimals in the cost.
  const cost = quantity.value * props.product.price
  const order = {
    quantity: quantity.value,
    cost: cost.toFixed(2),
    timestamp: Date.now()
  }

  // Merge object properties with the spread operator.
  store.updateItem({ ...props.product, ...order })
}
</script>
```
````
````

5. Display the `product` data and attach the `update` and `remove` component functions to the buttons on the template as follows:

```html
// components/cart-item.vue
<h3>
  {{ product.title }}
</h3>
<p>
  <img
    :alt=”product.title”
    :src=”product.thumbnail”
  />
</p>
<p>
  Unit Price: $ {{ product.price }}
</p>
<p>
  Total Cost: $ {{ product.cost }}
</p>
<input
  v-model=”quantity”
  type=”number”
  min=”1”
  v-bind:max=”product.stock”
/>
<button @click=”update”>
  Update
</button>
<button @click=”remove”>
  Remove
</button>
```

6. Run the app on the `dev` environment:

```
$ npm run dev
```

You should see the list of added items in the store cart displayed on `/cart`, along with the buttons for updating and deleting them. The total items, total unique items, and total cost of all items in the cart should be computed and displayed properly on the screen. These values will be updated immediately on the screen without having to refresh your browser whenever you update or delete the items in the cart.

There you go. By following these steps in two sections, you have just created a shopping cart system with Pinia. The exported public variables, constants, and functions are global, and you can access them easily from anywhere across the app. Simply import the cart module from the **`/stores/`** directory, and then you can add, update, and delete items in the cart array. However, there are still some minor improvements we can make to improve the user experience on our shopping cart system, such as showing some notes or messages to the user when a new item is added to the cart or when an item in the cart is updated. So, let's find out how you can implement that to your cart's UX in the next section!

Handling Shopping Cart Statuses

It is not a good UX for not having a notification when an item is added to the cart. Users wouldn't realize that they have added an item. Therefore, it is necessary to notify users whenever their selected items are added to the cart successfully. In this section, we will refactor our store and the existing store functions for having simple notifications when items are added and updated. You will find out how easy and simple it is to do the notification through the following steps:

1. Add a **`response`** reactive constant with **`message`** and **`data`** properties in it and then return it:

```js
// stores/cart.ts
import { defineStore } from ‘pinia’
export const useCartStore = defineStore(‘cart’, () => {
  ...
  const response = reactive({
    message: ‘’,
    data: ‘’
  })
  return {
    response
  }
})
```

2. Create a `delay` local async function for making Promise timeouts as follows:

```js
// stores/cart.ts
import { defineStore } from ‘pinia’
export const useCartStore = defineStore(‘cart’, () => {
  ...
  async function delay (ms) {
    return new Promise(res => {
      setTimeout(res, ms)
    })
  }
})
```

We don’t need to return this `delay` function like the other functions because it is only used locally in the `cart` module.

3. Add a response and a timeout to reset the response in the `addItem` async function for when items are added to the cart:

```js
// stores/cart.ts
import { defineStore } from ‘pinia’
export const useCartStore = defineStore(‘cart’, () => {
  ...
  async function addItem (item) {
    ...
    response.message = ‘Added ok’
    response.data = item
    await delay(3000)
    response.message = ‘’
    response.data = ‘’
  }
})
```

4. Add a response and a timeout to reset the response in the `updateItem` async function for when items are updated in the cart:

```js
// stores/cart.ts
import { defineStore } from ‘pinia’
```

~~~~
export const useCartStore = defineStore(‘cart’, () => {
  ...
  async function updateItem (item) {
    ...
    response.message = ‘Updated ok’
    response.data = item
    await delay(3000)
    response.message = ‘’
    response.data = ‘’
  }
})
```
~~~~

5. Add the store response in **`/components/product-item.vue`** for the event when items are added to the cart:

~~~~
```html
// components/product-item.vue
<template>
  ...
  <button @click=”add”>
    Add to Cart
  </button>
  <span v-if=”
    store.response.message &&
    store.response.data &&
    store.response.data.id === product.id
  “>
      {{ store.response.message }}
  </span>
</template>
```
~~~~

6. Add the store response in **`/components/cart-item.vue`** for the event when items are updated in the cart:

~~~~
```html
// components/cart-item.vue
<template>
  ...
  <button @click=”update”>
    Update
  </button>
  <button @click=”remove”>
    Remove
~~~~

```
    </button>
    <span v-if="
      store.response.message &&
      store.response.data &&
      store.response.data.id === product.id
    ">
        {{ store.response.message }}
    </span>
  </template>
```

7. Run the app on the `dev` environment:

```
$ npm run dev
```

You should see the status `Added ok` appear for 3 seconds when adding items to the cart at `/shop`. Similarly, you should see the status `Updated ok` appear for 3 seconds when updating items in the cart at `/cart`.

There you go. You have just improved the UX of our shopping cart in a few steps by adding some lines in the `addItem` and `updateItem` functions in the cart module. However, we still need to improve the cart UX when the user tries to add more order quantity than the available stock. So, how do we do that? Let's find out in the next section!

Handling Shopping Cart Statuses

It is also not a good UX not to have a warning when users make mistakes in adding and updating their cart. They wouldn't realize if no warning is given to them on the screen. So, it is also necessary to warn users when they make mistakes, such as exceeding the cart quantity limit or the product quantity limit. In this section, we will refactor the existing component functions in `/components/product-item.vue` and `/components/cart-item.vue` for having simple warnings when such errors occur. You will find out how easy and simple it is to do the error warning through the following steps:

1. Create an `error` constant with a `null` value by default in `/components/product-item.vue` and add an if-condition to inject the error message when the input quantity is exceeding the product stock:

```js
// components/product-item.vue
<script setup>
...
const error = ref(null)

function add () {
  if (quantity.value < 1 || quantity.value > props.product.
  stock) {
    error.value = `Please input between 1 - ${props.product.
    stock} only`
    return
  }
  error.value = null
  ...
}
</script>
```

2. Display the error message on the template when the error occurs:

```html
// components/product-item.vue
<template>
  ...
  <button @click=”add”>
    Add to Cart
  </button>
  <span v-if=”error”>
      {{ error }}
  </span>
  ...
</template>
```

3. Create an `error` constant with a `null` value by default in `/components/cart-item.vue` and add an if-condition to inject the error message when the input quantity is exceeding the product stock:

```js
// components/cart-item.vue
<script setup>
...
const error = ref(null)
```

````
function update () {
  if (quantity.value < 1 || quantity.value > props.product.
  stock) {
    error.value = `Please input between 1 - ${props.product.
    stock} only`
    return
  }
  error.value = null
  ...
}
</script>
```
````

4. Display the error message on the template when the error occurs:

````
```html
// components/cart-item.vue
<template>
  ...
  <button @click="update">
    Update
  </button>
  <button @click="remove">
    Remove
  </button>
  <span v-if="error">
      {{ error }}
  </span>
  ...
</template>
```
````

5. Run the app on the **`dev`** environment:

````
```
$ npm run dev
```
````

You should see the error message appear when trying to add the order quantity more than the product stock on **`/shop`** and when updating the order quantity more than the available stock on **`/cart`**.
````

Finally, you have further improved the UX of your shopping cart in a few steps by adding some lines in `/components/cart-item.vue` and `/components/cart-item.vue` to prevent the order quantity from exceeding the product stock from the user and warn them with messages. Well done!

We have managed to build a program to collect larger data on this topic. However, if you refresh your browser either on `/shop` or `/cart` (especially, on `/cart`), you will see that all the collected data will disappear immediately. All the values will be reset to their original values. This is because we haven't yet made the data persist with any storage technology offered by the client and server. The storage candidates we will be looking into are `localStorage`s from the client side and Redis from the server side. You will find out how they can be used to help us to make the cart data we collected persistent. So, stay tuned.

The example app for this topic can be found in `/1.nuxt/1.essentials/7.store-management/` in the GitHub repository of this book.

Creating Data-Persistent Stores with Pinia, `localStorage`, Cookies, and Redis

Building a shopping cart program isn't as quick and easy as a counter program, similar to those you have seen and built in the previous sections. It requires more logic, lines, and scripts to build the shopping cart program just to collect the data. Making the data persist in a shopping cart program also isn't as quick and straightforward as a counter program. It also requires more logic, lines, and scripts to persist the data for both the client and server in the shopping cart. However, it is neither difficult nor impossible at all. We will start with `localStorage` for the client and then move on to Redis for the server. In the end, they will complement each other to make our data persistent on both ends. So, let's get started!

Creating Data-Persistent Stores with `localStorage`

Using `localStorage`s to create a data-persistent store is very easy and straightforward. We don't have to install anything because `localStorage` comes with all modern browsers. In this section, we will refactor our store and the existing store functions for injecting cart data into `localStorage` whenever a new item is added to the cart or whenever an existing cart item is updated. So, let's find out how you can achieve this through the following steps:

1. Create a `storeCart` async function in `/stores/cart.ts` to set the store cart to the `localStorage` property and unset from it:

```js
// stores/cart.ts
import { defineStore } from 'pinia'
export const useCounterStore = defineStore('cart', () => {
  ...
  async function storeCart (cart) {
    const body = JSON.stringify(unref(cart))
    localStorage.setItem(cartId, body)

    if (unref(cart).length === 0) {
      localStorage.removeItem(cartId)
    }
  }
})
```

Notice that we need to unpack the store cart using `unref` and stringify it before storing it in `localStorage`. If the cart is empty, then we will remove the cart from `localStorage`. The store cart is stored in `localStorage` with the app cart ID, which is `example.com:cart`, and it will be used later to retrieve the cart data from `localStorage`.

2. Call `storeCart` in the `addItem` async function whenever an item is added to the store cart:

```js
// stores/cart.ts
import { defineStore } from 'pinia'
export const useCartStore = defineStore('cart', () => {
  ...
  async function addItem (item) {
    ...
    cart.value.push(item)
    storeCart(cart)
    ...
  }
})
```

3. Call **`storeCart`** in the **`updateItem`** async function whenever an item is updated in the store cart:

~~~
```js
// stores/cart.ts
import { defineStore } from 'pinia'
export const useCartStore = defineStore('cart', () => {
  ...
  async function updateItem (item) {
    ...
    cart.value[index].quantity = item.quantity
    cart.value[index].cost = item.cost
    storeCart(cart)
    ...
  }
})
```
~~~

4. Call **`storeCart`** in the **`deleteItem`** async function whenever an item is deleted from the store cart:

~~~
```js
// stores/cart.ts
import { defineStore } from 'pinia'
export const useCartStore = defineStore('cart', () => {
  ...
  function deleteItem (item) {
    ...
    cart.value.splice(index, 1)
    storeCart(cart)
  }
})
```
~~~

5. Call **`storeCart`** in the **`empty`** function whenever the store cart is being emptied:

~~~
```js
// stores/cart.ts
import { defineStore } from 'pinia'
export const useCartStore = defineStore('cart', () => {
  ...
  function empty () {
    cart.value = []
~~~

```
    storeCart(cart)
  }
})
```

6. Import the `cart` store in `/app.vue`, get the app cart ID from `runtimeConfig` to retrieve the cart data from `localStorage`, and repopulate the store cart on the client side whenever the browser is being refreshed:

```js
// app.vue
<script setup>
import { useCartStore } from '@/stores/cart'

if (!import.meta.env.SSR) {
  const runtimeConfig = useRuntimeConfig()
  const cartId = runtimeConfig.public['appCartId']
  const store = useCartStore()
  const cartFromLocalStorage = localStorage.getItem(cartId)
  store.cart =  JSON.parse(cartFromLocalStorage) ?? []
}
</script>
```

Notice that we must parse the JSON string from `localStorage` to become a JSON object before repopulating the store cart.

7. Run the app on the `dev` environment:

```
$ npm run dev
```

You should see all the products that are added to the cart are re-populated when refreshing on `/cart`.

However, if you inspect `/cart at view-source:http://localhost:3000/cart`, you will see that the cart is not being rendered into HTML at all. You will also get the hydration mismatch warning in your browser console. This is just because `localStorage` is a client property, and we only can use it to re-populate our cart on the client side. So, it is important to store our cart somewhere on the server side, and then retrieve the data and re-populate our cart on the client side. We can use cookies, as discussed in the previous section *Creating*

Data-Persistent Stores with Pinia and Cookies. However, we can't use cookies to store our cart because of the limited data capacity in cookies. Cookies are only suitable to store small data. Our cart can expand when multiple items are added, so it is important to use server-side technology to store the cart data, such as Redis. We will use cookies and Redis to re-populate the store cart on the server side for us. So, let's find out in the upcoming sections!

Creating a Custom Cookie Composable

As you have already realized that Nuxt is shipped with the **`useCookie`** composable to help us to create cookies out of the box. However, creating our own cookie functions can give us more control over cookie creation, deletion, and debugging. In this section, we will refactor our store and the existing store functions and variables for creating, updating, and deleting cookies whenever a new item is added to the cart or whenever an existing cart item is updated. So, let's find out how you can achieve this through the following steps:

1. Create a **`use-cooki3.ts`** file in the **`/composables/`** directory:

    ```bash
    composables
    └── use-cooki3.ts
    ```

2. Create the **`useCooki3`** composable that accepts **`options`** as its first parameter in **`/composables/use-cooki3.ts`**:

    ```js
    // composables/use-cooki3.ts
    export default (options) => {
      //
    }
    ```

3. Create a **`get`** function to retrieve cookies by **`name`** from the **`document`** object or a provided cookie object and then return the function:

    ```js
    // composables/use-cooki3.ts
    export default (options) => {
      function get (name, cookie) {
        const resource = cookie ?? document.cookie
    ```

```
      let string = resource.match(
        `(?:(?:^|.*; *)${name} *= *([^;]*).*$)|^.*$`
      )[1]
      if (string) {
        string = decodeURIComponent(string)
      }
      if (string === 'undefined'
        || string === undefined
        || string === ''
      ) {
        string = null
      }

      return JSON.parse(string)
    }

    return {
      get
    }
  }
```

In the preceding code, the cookie can be retrieved through the `document` object when the `get` function is used on the client side. The cookie can also be retrieved through a provided cookie object when this function is used on the server side. You just have to trace the cookie data from the Node.js HTTP request object. We must parse the stored cookie, ensuring that it is a stringified object that can be parsed as a JSON object before parsing.

4. Create a `set` function to set a new cookie to the `document` object with a name (for example, `example.com:cart`) and its value (for example, `1691413316500`) and then return the function:

```js
// composables/use-cooki3.ts
export default (options) => {
  function set (name, value) {
    let maxAge = 0

    if (options.maxAge) {
      maxAge = options.maxAge
    }
    if (options.days) {
      maxAge = options.days * 60 * 60 * 24
```

```
      }

      document.cookie = `${name}=${encodeURIComponent(value)};
max-age=${maxAge}; path=/`
    }

    return {
      ...
      set
    }
  }
```

In the preceding code, the cookie is stored as `example.com:cart=1691413316500`, as an example. Then, the cookie's name, which is `example.com:cart`, is used to retrieve the cookie value, which is `1691413316500`. So, each user will have their own unique specified cart key in their shopping cart, for example, `1691413316500`.

5. Create a `drop` function to remove cookies by `name` from the `document` object and then return the function:

```js
// composables/use-cooki3.ts
export default (options) => {
  function drop (name) {
    document.cookie = name + '=;expires=Thu, 01 Jan 1970
    00:00:00 GMT; path=/'
  }

  return {
    ...
    drop
  }
}
```

6. Create an `observe` function (optional) to watch the reactive object that is intended to be stored as the cookie value and then return the function:

```js
// composables/use-cooki3.ts
export default (options) => {
  function observe (ref, name) {
    watch(ref, (newVal, prevVal) => {
      set(name, JSON.stringify(ref.value))
```

```
    }, {
      deep: true
    })
  }

  return {
    ...
    observe
  }
}
```

Note that cookies should only be used for storing small data. If you have very large data, such as the reactive store cart, then cookies should not be used to store your cart data.

7. Import `useCooki3` and use the `set`, `get`, and `drop` cookie functions from it as `setCookie`, `getCookie`, and `dropCookie` in `/stores/cart.ts`:

```js
// stores/cart.ts
import { defineStore } from ‘pinia’
export const useCounterStore = defineStore(‘counter’, () => {
  ...
  const options = {
    path: ‘/’,
    maxAge: 5 * 60
  }
  const {
    set: setCookie,
    get: getCookie,
    drop: dropCookie
  } = useCooki3(options)

  const cart = ref([])
  ...
})
```

Notice that we have set the cookie to expire in 5 minutes in development, but it should be set to expire in days for production.

8. Add the following if-condition blocks in the `` `addItem` `` async function to set and update cookies:

    ````
    ```js
    // stores/cart.ts
    import { defineStore } from 'pinia'
    export const useCartStore = defineStore('cart', () => {
      ...
      async function addItem (item) {
        ...
        if (uniqueLength.value === 0) {
          const timestamp = Date.now()
          setCookie(cartId, timestamp)
        }
        if (uniqueLength.value > 0) {
          const value = getCookie(cartId)
          setCookie(cartId, value)
        }
        cart.value.push(item)
        ...
      }
    })
    ```
    ````

In the preceding code, the first if-condition block is used to set a new cookie whenever the store cart is started empty. While the second if-condition block is used to update the saved cookie's expiration whenever the store cart is being updated.

9. Add an if-condition block in the `` `updateItem` `` async function to update the cookie's expiration again whenever the cart is updated:

    ````
    ```js
    // stores/cart.ts
    import { defineStore } from 'pinia'
    export const useCartStore = defineStore('cart', () => {
      ...
      async function updateItem (item) {
        ...
        cart.value[index].quantity = item.quantity
        cart.value[index].cost = item.cost

        if (uniqueLength.value > 0) {
          const value = getCookie(cartId)
          setCookie(cartId, value)
    ````
    ````

```js
      }
      ...
    }
  })
```

10. Add an if-condition block in the `deleteItem` async function to update the cookie's expiration again whenever items are removed from the cart:

```js
// stores/cart.ts
import { defineStore } from ‘pinia’
export const useCartStore = defineStore(‘cart’, () => {
  ...
  function deleteItem (item) {
    ...
    cart.value.splice(index, 1)

    if (uniqueLength.value > 0) {
      const value = getCookie(cartId)
      setCookie(cartId, value)
    }
  }
})
```

11. Use `dropCookie` in the existing if-condition block in the `storeCart` async function to drop the saved cookie whenever the cart is being emptied:

```js
// stores/cart.ts
import { defineStore } from ‘pinia’
export const useCounterStore = defineStore(‘counter’, () => {
  ...
  async function storeCart (cart) {
    const body = JSON.stringify(unref(cart))
    localStorage.setItem(cartId, body)

    if (unref(cart).length === 0) {
      localStorage.removeItem(cartId)
      dropCookie(cartId)
    }
  }
})
```

12. Add an if-condition block in `/app.vue` to remove the stored cart from `localStorage` whenever the saved is gone (expired):

    ```js
    // app.vue
    <script setup>
    import { useCartStore } from '@/stores/cart'

    if (!import.meta.env.SSR) {
      const runtimeConfig = useRuntimeConfig()
      const cartId = runtimeConfig.public['appCartId']
      const cookie = useCookie(cartId)
      const store = useCartStore()

      if (!cookie.value) {
        localStorage.removeItem(cartId)
      }
      const cartFromLocalStorage = localStorage.getItem(cartId)
      store.cart =  JSON.parse(cartFromLocalStorage) ?? []
    }
    </script>
    ```

13. Run the app on the `dev` environment:

    ```
    $ npm run dev
    ```

You should see that all the products, which are previously added to the store cart, will be gone from `/cart` within 5 minutes once the set cookie for the store cart expires. A new cookie will be created when a new item is added to the store cart again. And the expired time for the existing cart cookie will be extended when more items are added on top, or when the existing items are being updated on `/cart`.

However, if you inspect `/cart` at `view-source:http://localhost:3000/cart`, you will still see that the cart is not rendered into HTML at all. You will still get the hydration mismatch warning on your browser console. This occurs because cookies are only used to store an identifier (for example, `1691413316500`) for the user's active cart. This identifier will be expired in 5 minutes. The cart data is yet to be stored anywhere on the server side, as for that, we will use Redis. So, let's find out in the next section!

# Creating Data-Persistent Stores with Cookies, Nitro Web Server, Middleware, and Redis

Redis is an in-memory key–value database and storage on the server side. You can imagine it as a hybrid of cookies and `localStorage` to store and retrieve data, as discussed in the previous sections and topics. The data stored in `localStorage` is permanent until you delete it, whereas the data in cookies have an expiration. The data we will store in Redis also will have an expiration, but Redis can help us to store larger data like `localStorage`.

In this section, we will use the `/server/` directory in our Nuxt project to create HTTP server APIs to store and retrieve our cart data. Then, we will refactor the existing `storeCart` function only to send the cart data to Redis over HTTP requests whenever a new item is added to the cart or whenever an existing cart item is updated. So, let's find out how you can achieve this through the following steps:

1. Create a `/server/` directory with a `[id].ts` file and a `one.post.ts` file in the following sub-directories as follows:

```
└── server
    └── api
        └── carts
            ├── [id].ts
            └── create
                └── one.post.ts
```

2. Install the Redis client in your project root:

```
$ npm i redis
```

Note that the installation of Node.js packages may change over time, so you should always confirm the installation command lines with their official documentation if you start your project afresh. For installing the Redis client package, please visit https://redis.io/docs/clients/nodejs/.

3. Import the Redis client and use it to store the cart data in the Redis database on the server side in `/server/api/carts/create/one.post.ts`:

```js
// server/api/carts/create/one.post.ts
import { createClient } from 'redis'

export default eventHandler(async event => {
  const runtimeConfig = useRuntimeConfig()
  const cartId = runtimeConfig.public['appCartId']
  const value = getCookie(event, cartId) || null
  const key = value ? `${cartId}:${value}` : null

  if (!key) {
    return null
  }

  const body = await readBody(event)

  const client = createClient()
  client.on('error', err => console.log('Redis Client Error',
  err))
  await client.connect()

  const expire = 5 * 60
  return await client.set(key, JSON.stringify(body), { 'EX':
  expire })
})
```

In the preceding code, we get the individual user's cart ID (for example, `1683665729834`) from the cookies and use it to create a namespace key for the Redis database (for example, `example.com:cart:1683665729834`) and assign the cart data (which is stored in the **body** constant) as its value. The cookie is obtained from the HTTP headers using the `getCookie` API, while the cart data is obtained from the HTTP body using the `readBody` API. Both `getCookie` and `readBody` APIs are built-in utility functions from h3 (https://www.jsdocs.io/package/h3 or https://github.com/unjs/h3), a minimal web server that Nitro web server is built on.

If the namespace key is created successfully, then the cart data can be stored in the Redis database using the `set` command, which will be expired in 5 minutes. For more information about the `set` command and the time-to-live (TTL) options, please visit https://redis.io/commands/set/.

Notice that the cart data must be turned into a string before saving it to the Redis database. During development, it is set to expire in 5 minutes; however, in production, it should be set to expire in days. Note that if the client-side cart data is set to expire in 10 minutes, then the server-side cart data must do the same.

4. Import the Redis client and use it to retrieve the stored cart data from the Redis database in **`/server/api/carts/[id].ts`**:

```js
// server/api/carts/[id].ts
import { createClient } from 'redis'

export default eventHandler(async event => {
  const id = event.context.params.id
  if (!id) {
    return null
  }

  const client = createClient()
  client.on('error', err => console.log('Redis Client Error',
  err))
  await client.connect()

  return JSON.parse(await client.get(id))
})
```

Notice that in the preceding code, we must obtain the namespace key from the client side, which is passed down as a parameter ID in the Nuxt server, for retrieving the stored data from the Redis database. Then, finally, we must parse the retrieved cart string into a JSON object before returning it to the client side.

5. Post the cart data in a string to the server via **`/api/carts/create/one`** from the **`storeCart`** async function in **`/stores/cart.ts`**:

```js
// stores/cart.ts
import { defineStore } from 'pinia'
export const useCounterStore = defineStore('counter', () => {
  ...
  async function storeCart (cart) {
    const body = JSON.stringify(unref(cart))
    ...
```

```
      const { data } = await useFetch(`/api/carts/create/one`, {
        method: 'POST',
        body
      })
      ...
    }
  })
  ```
```

6. Create a global **`populate-cart.global.ts`** middleware in the **`/middleware/`** directory to fetch the cart data from the Redis database and repopulate the store cart on the server side whenever the app route is changed:

```
  ```js
  // middleware/populate-cart.global.ts
  import { useCartStore } from '@/stores/cart'

  export default defineNuxtRouteMiddleware(async (to, from) => {
    if (import.meta.env.SSR) {
      const runtimeConfig = useRuntimeConfig()
      const cartId = runtimeConfig.public['appCartId']
      const store = useCartStore()

      store.cart = []
      const cookie = useCookie(cartId) || null
      const key = cookie.value ? `${cartId}:${cookie.value}` :
      null

      if (key) {
        const { data } = await useFetch(`/api/carts/${key}`)
        const cartFromRedis = data.value ?? []
        store.cart = cartFromRedis
      }
    }
  })
  ```
```

In the preceding code, we get the individual user's cart key (for example, **`1691413316500`**) from cookies and use it to create a namespace key (for example, **`example.com:cart:1691413316500`**) for the Redis database to retrieve the cart data for us. Notice that we use **`useCookie`** from Nuxt in the preceding code, but you can use **`useCooki3`** if you prefer. Note that you must use the if-condition to make sure only to execute the preceding code on the server side.
```

7. Run the app on the `dev` environment:

```
$ npm run dev
```

You should see that all the products, which are previously added to the store cart, will be re-populated on both the client and server sides on `/cart`. If you inspect `/cart at view-source:http://localhost:3000/cart`, you should see the cart data are rendered into HTML from the server. You will no longer get the hydration mismatch error on the browser console. And then everything previously stored and active will be gone in 5 minutes on both sides.

There you go. By following these steps, you have just managed to make a data-persistent store using Redis and the Nitro web server. Well done! you just need two server API endpoints: one to store and another to retrieve the cart data. The `/api/carts/create/one` API endpoint is used to store the cart data whenever a product is added to the store cart. It is also used to update the stored data whenever the product in the store cart is being updated. On the other hand, the `/api/carts/[id]` API endpoint is used to retrieve the stored data whenever the browser is being refreshed. And then, finally, you see how seamlessly the technologies from both the server and client sides complement each other to create a data-persistent store on both ends.

As you can see, it takes more effort and logic to create a data-persistent store on the server side. It requires cookies, a web server, and Redis to make it happen. However, if you just want to make the data persistent on the client side, then you need to make sure that the cart data are only re-populated on the server side with an `if` condition when the browser is being refreshed. Also, besides `localStorage`, you can use IndexedDB instead as the client-side storage if you prefer. While `localStorage` calls all its methods synchronously, IndexedDB does it asynchronously without blocking the rest of your script when injecting and accessing the data. For further information about IndexDB and `localStorage`, as well as some code examples, please have a read at https://developer.mozilla.org/en-US/docs/Learn/JavaScript/Client-side_web_APIs/Client-side_storage. Whichever client storage you go for, you are encouraged to make the data persistent on the server, instead of using an `if` condition to re-populate the cart data on the client side only. It takes more effort, but it is definitely worth it in the end!

The example app for this topic can be found in `/1.nuxt/1.essentials/7.store-management/` in the GitHub repository of this book.

# Conclusion

In this chapter, you have learned to create global states for Nuxt apps and learned that you should avoid placing reactive variables outside the function scope in composable. You should use the `useState` API instead for creating global states in Nuxt apps, or use the `provide` and `inject` APIs from Vue. You have also learned that you can use external store management libraries to create global states, such as Pinia and Vuex, ultimately using Pinia to create a counter data-persistent program with the `useCookie` API. Finally, you have managed to build a data-persistent shopping cart program with Pinia, cookies, `localStorage`, Nuxt's built-in Nitro web server, and Redis for storing larger data on both the client and server sides, as cookies only allow small data to be stored.

In the next chapter, you will further discover how to use Nuxt's built-in Nitro web server to create built-in API layers, API routes, and API calls with server middleware, server plugins, and server utilities. You will also learn to store and manage data with Nitro's default in-memory data storage, integrate MongoDB database internally in the Nuxt apps, and use the Nuxt Content module and Markdown documents as your database in the Nuxt apps. So, let's venture further!

CHAPTER 6

# Managing Data with Nitro Server Engine in Nuxt

## Introduction

Welcome to *Chapter* 6. In this chapter, you will use Nuxt's built-in API layer to create APIs with server routes, server middleware, server plugins, and server utilities. You will learn how to store and manage data using Nitro's default in-memory data storage. You will also use MongoDB as on-disk data storage for your Nuxt app, along with the Nuxt Content module and Markdown documents as the data storage in your Nuxt app.

## Structure

The topics that will be covered in this chapter are as follows:

- Creating Server Routes, Server Middleware, Server Plugins, and Server Utilities
- Managing Data with In-Memory Data Storage
- Managing Data with MongoDB Database
- Managing Data with the Nuxt Content Module

# Creating Server Routes, Server Middleware, Server Plugins, and Server Utilities

Internally, Nuxt uses the Nitro framework (https://nitro.unjs.io/), which is built on top of UnJS h3 (https://www.jsdocs.io/package/h3), as the web server for SSR rendering and server-side handling. Since it has a web server behind the scenes, we can use the web server for creating server APIs to serve both sides of our Nuxt app – the client and server sides. To do that, we just need to create a `/server/` directory in the Nuxt directory root. Then, Nuxt will automatically scan the files and sub-directories in the `/server/` directory and create APIs for us with HMR support. In this section, we will explore how to create our API routes, middleware, plugins, and utility functions in the `/server/` directory.

## Creating Server Routes and Middleware

Creating server routes and server middleware in the `/server/` directory in Nuxt is just as easy as creating app routes in the `/pages/` directory and app middleware in the `/middleware/` directory. They are auto-scanned and auto-imported. So, you just need to focus on creating the server routes and their middleware without worrying about registering them, as Nuxt takes care of them automatically for us. Let's find out in the following steps:

1. Create an `api` sub-directory with an `index.ts` file and a `middleware` sub-directory with a `log.ts` file in the `/server/` directory:

````
```
server
├── api
│   └── index.ts
└── middleware
    └── log.ts
```
````

2. Create a **'Hello World!'** API response with `eventHandler` in `/server/api/index.ts`:

````
```js
// server/api/index.ts
export default eventHandler(() => {
````
````

```
  return { message: 'Hello World!' }
})
```

Note that `eventHandler` is an alias of `defineEventHandler`. So, you can use `eventHandler` or `defineEventHandler` to define a new server route. The `defineEventHandler` function is one of the built-in functions from UnJS h3. For more information about this function, please visit https://www.jsdocs.io/package/h3#package-index-functions.

3. Create a `log` middleware using `defineEventHandler` in `/erver/middleware/log.ts` just to log the request URL on the terminal:

```js
// server/middleware/log.ts
export default defineEventHandler(event => {
  console.log('Request URL: ' + event.node.req.url)
})
```

4. Run the app on the `dev` environment:

```
$ npm run dev
```

You should see the following JSON response on `localhost:3000/api` on your browser screen:

```json
{
  "message": "Hello World!"
}
```

Also, you should see the requested URLs logged on your terminal:

```
Request URL: /
Request URL: /api
```

As you can see in the preceding steps and code, Nuxt has taken care of the mandate and trivial task of importing and registering the server routes and their middleware. All server routes created in the server `/api/` sub-directory are automatically prefixed with `/api`. If you want to omit this prefix, then you just have to rename the `/api/` sub-directory to `routes`. Then, you will get the JSON response of `/server/routes/index.ts` on `localhost:3000`. However, be careful when omitting the prefix of `/api`, because the app routes from the `/pages/` directory will be overridden by the server routes if they use the same route names. And the routes from both ends will eventually get mixed up over time, leading to confusion, unless you choose different names for the server routes to avoid conflicts, for example, by renaming `/server/routes/index.ts` to `/server/routes/hello-world.ts`.

# Creating Server Plugins and Utilities

The same goes for server plugins and server utility functions; creating them in the `/server/` directory is as easy as creating app plugins and app utility functions in the top-level `/plugins/` and `/utils/` directories. They are auto-scanned and auto-imported. So, you just need to focus on creating the server plugins and server utility functions without worrying about registering them, as Nuxt takes care of them automatically for us. Let's find out in the following steps:

1. Create a `plugins` sub-directory with a `plugin-1.ts` file and a `utils` sub-directory with a `to-uppercase.ts` file in the `/server/` directory:

```
server
├── plugins
│   └── plugin-1.ts
└── utils
    └── to-uppercase.ts
```

2. Create a `log` plugin using `defineNitroPlugin` in `/server/plugins/plugin-1.ts` just to run this plugin once to log the information of the Nitro app when the server is started:

```js
// server/plugins/plugin-1.ts
export default defineNitroPlugin((nitroApp) => {
  console.log('Nitro plugin runs when server is started: ',
  nitroApp)
```

```
})
```

The **`defineNitroPlugin`** function is a built-in function from the Nitro framework to extend the runtime behavior of your web server that you build with Nitro. For more information about plugins and this function, please visit https://nitro.unjs.io/guide/plugins.

3. Create a **`toUppercase`** utility async function in **`/server/utils/to-uppercase.ts`** to make all letters in a string uppercase:

```js
// server/utils/to-uppercase.ts
export default async (text) => {
  return text.toUpperCase()
}
```

4. Use **`toUppercase`** in **`/server/api/index.ts`** as follows:

```js
// server/api/index.ts
export default eventHandler(async () => {
  const message = await toUppercase('Hello World!')
  return { message }
})
```

Notice that **`toUppercase`** is auto-imported by Nitro. Also, note that you can only use the server utility functions within the **`/server/`** directory. In other words, you cannot use them in **`/pages/`** or any other directories, which are outside the **`/server/`** directory.

5. Run the app on the **`dev`** environment:

```
$ npm run dev
```

You should see the following JSON response on **`/api`** on your browser screen:

```json
{
```

~~~~
    "message": "HELLO WORLD!"
}
```
~~~~

Also, you should see the information of your Nitro web server logged on your terminal:

~~~~
```
Nitro plugin runs when server is started:  {
  hooks: Hookable {
    _hooks: {},
    _before: undefined,
    _after: undefined,
    ...
  },
  h3App: {
    use: [Function: use],
    handler: [AsyncFunction (anonymous)] { __is_handler__:
    true },
    stack: [ [Object], [Object], [Object], [Object] ],
    options: { debug: true, onError: [AsyncFunction:
    errorhandler] }
  },
  router: {
    add: [Function (anonymous)],
    use: [Function (anonymous)],
    connect: [Function (anonymous)],
    ...
  },
  localCall: [Function: callHandle],
  localFetch: [AsyncFunction: ufetch]
}
```
~~~~

Once again, as you can see in the preceding steps and code, Nuxt has taken care of the mandate and trivial task of importing and registering the server plugins and server utility functions. All server utilities are automatically imported as camel-case names. You just use them in camel case. Notice that the use of server plugins is very different from the app plugins created in the top-level **`/plugins/`** directory. The app plugins can be used in **`<template>`** blocks, but since there is no template on the server side, the server plugins can be used only to control or to get insight of the Nitro web server. We most likely need the server plugins the least.

There you go! Creating server APIs within the Nuxt project itself is as easy and simple as you have just learned in the preceding steps and sections. Once again, note that all server routes, middleware, plugins, and utilities created in the **`/server/`** directory are only available and accessible within the **`/server/`** directory. You can't use them on the front side of your Nuxt app. However, you can access the server routes via APIs. There is more we can do with the Nitro web server. The Nitro framework has a built-in storage layer that we can use to hook up with an external database server (for example, Redis, MongoDB) for storing our API data remotely and separately. The storage layer can also be used to store our API data in-memory without the need for any external database server. We will explore and venture into this area in the upcoming sections. So, let's find out!

You can find the example app for this topic in **`/1.nuxt/2.signle-domain/1.in-memory/`** in the GitHub repository of this book.

# Managing Data with In-Memory Data Storage

In-memory storage – You should already be familiar and comfortable with this idea and technology since you have learned to use Redis to store the cart data in the memory on the server side in the previous chapter. Remember, Redis is an in-memory key-value database and storage on the server side. By default, the Nitro framework also has an in-memory data storage layer. This can be very useful if you need to make a data persistent store in your Nuxt app, similar to what you did in the previous chapter. Hence, it raises a question: Do we still need Redis then? If we don't, then does that make what you have learned in the previous chapter obsolete? We will find out and answer this question in this section. So, let's get started!

## Using Nitro's In-Memory Data Storage

Nitro comes with a built-in storage layer that you can use to work with many other database options, such as MongoDB and Redis. The default data storage is an in-memory storage driver. With this default in-memory storage driver, you don't need to install any additional Node.js database package. For example, if you want to use the Nitro storage layer with MongoDB for your Nuxt app, then you will need to install **`mongodb`** in your Nuxt project. However, in this section, we are only interested on in-memory storage. So, let's find out how you can manage data for Nuxt apps without having any additional Node.js package and any separate server for serving data in the following steps:

1. Create a `connect-db.ts` file in the `/utils/` sub-directory and a `users` sub-directories in the `/api/` sub-directory with the following files in `/server/`:

    ```
    server
    ├── api
    │   ├── ...
    │   └── users
    │       ├── index.ts
    │       └── create
    │           └── one.post.ts
    └── utils
        ├── ...
        └── connect-db.ts
    ```

2. Create a `.env` file with a `NITRO_DB_DBNAME` variable and `advanced-nuxtjs-course` as its value in the project root:

    ```
    // .env
    NITRO_DB_DBNAME=advanced-nuxtjs-course
    ```

3. Get the value of the `NITRO_DB_DBNAME` env variable and set it as the base name for `useStorage` in `/server/utils/connect-db.ts`:

    ```js
    // server/utils/connect-db.ts
    export default () => {
      const base = import.meta.env.NITRO_DB_DBNAME
      return useStorage(base)
    }
    ```

The `useStorage` composable is a built-in function from the Nitro framework to create an instance of `createStorage` from Unstorage (https://unstorage.unjs.io/) for creating storage for your Nitro app. The default storage driver of `createStorage` is an in-memory driver. For more information about the default in-memory driver from Unstorage's `createStorage`, please visit https://unstorage.unjs.io/drivers/memory. For more information about `useStorage` from Nitro, please visit https://nitro.unjs.io/guide/storage.

4. Verify the posted data from the HTTP request body for injecting new users in **`/server/api/users/create/one.post.ts`** as follows:

```js
// server/api/users/create/one.post.ts
export default eventHandler(async event => {
  const body = await readBody(event)

  if (body.name === undefined) {
    throw createError({
      statusCode: 500,
      statusText: ‘name is undefined’
    })
  }

  if (body.slug === undefined) {
    throw createError({
      statusCode: 500,
      statusText: ‘slug is undefined’
    })
  }

  if (body.name === ‘’) {
    throw createError({
      statusCode: 400,
      statusText: ‘name is required’
    })
  }

  if (body.slug === ‘’) {
    throw createError({
      statusCode: 400,
      statusText: ‘slug is required’
    })
  }
})
```

In the preceding code, we need to get the data from the request body using **`readBody`** and make sure that the **`name`** and **`slug`** inputs are not defined and empty. If they are, we will throw errors using **`createError`**.

Both **`readBody`** and **`createError`** are built-in functions from UnJS h3. The **`readBody`** async function is used to read the request body, while the **`createError`** function is used to create a new **`Error`** object. For more information about them, please visit https://www.jsdocs.io/package/h3#readBody and https://www.jsdocs.io/package/h3#createError.

5. Use the `connectDb` utility to inject users when the data have passed the verification, as follows:

```js
// server/api/users/create/one.post.ts
export default eventHandler(async event => {
  const body = await readBody(event)
  ...

  const timestamp = Date.now()
  const user = {
    name: body.name,
    slug: body.slug,
    email: body.email,
    createdAt: timestamp
  }

  const db = connectDb()
  const users = await db.getItem(‘users’) || []
  users.push(user)
  await db.setItem(‘users’, users)
  return user
})
```

In the preceding code, we prepare new user data from the verified request body with a timestamp using `Date.now` before injecting the user data into a `users` collection in the database. First, we use `getItem` to get the `users` collections and then use `setItem` to reset it in the database. For more information about `getItem` and `setItem`, please visit https://unstorage.unjs.io/usage#interface.

6. Use the `connectDb` util to retrieve all users in `/server/api/users/index.ts`:

```js
// server/api/users/index.ts
export default eventHandler(async event => {
  const db = connectDb()
  return await db.getItem(‘users’) || []
})
```

7. Run the app on the `dev` environment:

```
$ npm run dev
```

You should see an empty `[]` array on `localhost:3000/api/users`.

8. Add a user from your terminal using `curl` as follows:

```
$ curl -X POST http://localhost:3000/api/users/create/one \
 -H "Content-Type: application/json" \
 -d '{"name": "John", "slug": "john"}'
```

You should see the following JSON output on your terminal when the user is added successfully:

```json
{
  "name": "John",
  "slug": "john",
  "createdAt": 1692464528950
}
```

If you try to add a new user with an empty `slug`:

```
$ curl -X POST http://localhost:3000/api/users/create/one \
 -H "Content-Type: application/json" \
 -d '{"name": "John", "slug": ""}'
```

Then, you should see the following JSON output with a `400` error code, an error message, and an error stack on your terminal:

```json
{"url":"/api/users/create/one","statusCode":400,"status
Message":"slug is required","message":"Error","stack":"<pre><span
class=\"stack internal\">at createError (…)</span></p"e>"}
```

You should see the following JSON response on your browser at `` `/api/users` `` when there are users stored in your database:

```
```json
[
  {
 “  “n”me“: “J”hn”,
 “  “s”ug“: “j”hn”,
 “  “create”At”: 1692464528950
  }
]
```
```

Note that besides using `` `curl` `` for adding new users to your database, you can also use an API test tool like Kong Insomnia (https://insomnia.rest/) to debug and test APIs.

In the preceding steps and code, we have stored data for our Nuxt app using the Nitro in-memory storage, without adding any additional Node.js package to our project. This can keep our Nuxt project neat and thin, making it easy to maintain in the future. We have kept everything within one project and one place. So, you might be wondering, since Nuxt/ Nitro provides in-memory storage by default, can we store the store cart data, as learned in the previous chapter, with this default storage instead? Remember that we used Redis for persisting the store data? The short answer is yes, you can. However, the trouble with the Nitro built-in in-memory storage is the lack of documentation. Unstorage is still new, and its official documentation is way far behind Redis' documentation (https://redis.io/docs/). Moreover, it also lacks examples. For example, it's unclear how to expire the stored data with the in-memory storage from Unstorage. In contrast, the technology of Redis is more developed and well-thought. It has a large community and therefore is easier to get help if you ever get stuck. It suits perfectly what we need to achieve on data expiration in the previous chapter and syncs seamlessly with our client-side stored data with `` `localStorage` `` and cookies. Hence, it definitely gives developers more assurance and reliability compared to Unstorage.

Nonetheless, Unstorage's in-memory storage can be as well documented, developed, and supported as Redis someday. So, it is definitely worth noting that there is another alternative out of the box for Nuxt apps. But what about the Redis driver (https://unstorage.unjs.io/drivers/redis) that is shipped with Unstorage? Remember, we directly import the Redis client and then just use it right away in our server routes? Since Unstorage has the Redis driver, can we make use of it instead? The short answer is yes, you can. However, the trouble remains the same, which is the lack of documentation and examples from Unstorage. Also, it is always safer and more recommended to use the direct software and client provided by the vendor, instead of using another layer of software on top of the original one. So, in the end, what you have learned in the previous chapter is not wasted at all. It is the way we are following throughout this book. We will, and should, pipe in directly to the source instead of using layers of layers to poke around the source. You will discover that we will do the same in the next section for using MongoDB as the data storage for our Nuxt apps. So, let's move on!

You can find the example app for this topic in `` `/1.nuxt/2.signle-domain/1.in-memory/` `` in the GitHub repository of this book.

# Managing Data with MongoDB Database

Sometimes, an in-memory database is not enough or might not be the right choice for us. An on-disk database might be a better solution or a complement to an in-memory database. MongoDB is another modern NoSQL database that stores data on disk by default. Even though in-memory storage is available with MongoDB Enterprise Edition, we will look into the community edition, which helps us to store data on disk for our Nuxt apps, in the following sections on this topic. So, let's get started!

## Using MongoDB as Data Storage: MongoDB Server and MongoDB Shell

There are a few routes to install MongoDB server, depending on the edition (Community Edition or Enterprise) and the platform (Windows, Ubuntu, macOS, or Docker) you choose. Regardless of the edition and platform you choose, always confirm the installation command lines from the official documentation at https://www.mongodb.com/docs/manual/installation/. This is just because the installation command lines may change over time.

For the **MongoDB Community Edition**, please refer to https://www.mongodb.com/docs/manual/administration/install-community/. Then, choose the installation guide for the specific platform that you need, for example, the **Ubuntu** platform: https://www.mongodb.com/docs/manual/tutorial/install-mongodb-on-ubuntu/#std-label-install-mdb-community-ubuntu.

Assuming that you have installed the MongoDB server successfully on your machine, you can start creating and manipulating your database, collections, and documents in the following steps:

1. Connect to MongoDB Shell via `mongosh` or `mongo` on your terminal:

```
$ mongosh
```

Whether using `mongosh` or `mongo` depends on the version of the MongoDB server on your machine. The latest version uses `mongosh`. However, it can change over time. So, you should always refer to the official documentation on MongoDB Shell at https://www.mongodb.com/docs/mongodb-shell/.

2. List all the existing databases in your Mongo server:

```
> show dbs
```

If you install MongoDB from scratch, then you should see the following default databases used by MongoDB:

```
admin                   0.000GB
config                0.000GB
local                   0.000GB
```

3. Create an `advanced-nuxtjs-course` database if it doesn't exist:

```
> use advanced-nuxtjs-course
```

If you ever want to drop a database, for example, the `advanced-nuxtjs-course` database:

```
> db.dropDatabase()
```

You should get the following output on your terminal if the database is dropped successfully:

```
> { "dropped" : "advanced-nuxtjs-course", "ok" : 1 }
```

4. Select the `advanced-nuxtjs-course` database:

```
> use advanced-nuxtjs-course
```

5. Create a `users` collection if it doesn't exist:

```
> db.createCollection("users", {})
```

You should get the following output on your terminal if the collection is created successfully:

```
{ "ok" : 1 }
```

When you want to drop a collection, for example, the `users` collection:

```
> db.users.drop()
```

For more information about `createCollection`, please visit https://www.mongodb.com/docs/v7.0/reference/method/db.createCollection/.

6. Insert multiple user documents with a timestamp type in the `users` collection:

```
db.users.insertMany( [
```

```
    { name: "John", slug: "john", email: "john@example.com",
createdAt: new Timestamp() },
    { name: "Jane", slug: "jane", email: "jane@example.com",
createdAt: new Timestamp() },
    { name: "Molly", slug: "molly", email: "molly@example.
com", createdAt: new Timestamp() },
  ] );
```

You should get the following output on your terminal if the user documents are created successfully:

```
{
    "acknowledged" : true,
    "insertedIds" : [
        ObjectId("64e0fafde3939a03c2dac6eb"),
        ObjectId("64e0fafde3939a03c2dac6ec"),
        ObjectId("64e0fafde3939a03c2dac6ed")
    ]
}
```

If you just want to insert a single-user document:

```
db.inventory.insertOne(
    { name: "John", slug: "john", email: "john@example.com",
createdAt: new Timestamp() }
)
```

You should get the following output on your terminal if it is created successfully:

```
{
    "acknowledged" : true,
    "insertedId" : ObjectId("64e0fcc8e3939a03c2dac6f1")
}
```

Notice that IDs such as **`64e0fafde3939a03c2dac6eb`** are a BSON **`ObjectId`** type generated by MongoDB when a new document is created. For more information about the BSON `ObjectId` type, please visit https://www.mongodb.com/docs/v7.0/reference/bson-types/#objectid. For more information about inserting documents, please visit https://docs.mongodb.com/manual/tutorial/insert-documents/. For more information about inserting the timestamp type, please visit https://www.mongodb.com/docs/manual/reference/bson-types/#timestamps.

7. Find all user documents in the `users` collection:

```
> db.users.find()
```

If you want to delete all documents from the `users` collection:

```
> db.users.deleteMany({})
```

You should get the following output on your terminal if all the documents are deleted successfully:

```
{ “acknowledged” : true, “deletedCount” : 3 }
```

For more information about deleting documents, please visit https://docs.mongodb.com/manual/tutorial/remove-documents/.

8. Exit the MongoDB Shell:

```
> exit
```

MongoDB offers tons of CRUD operations and methods for us to work with data. We have only used a few of them in the preceding steps and code. Once again, these methods and operations may change over time. So, you should always refer to their official documentation to update and upgrade your MongoDB knowledge, which can be found at https://www.mongodb.com/docs/manual/crud/ and https://www.mongodb.com/docs/v7.0/reference/method/. The current latest version of MongoDB is 7.0, and as a result, the current existing methods may change in future versions.

# Fetching Data from MongoDB: MongoDB Drivers and MongoDB GUI

Depending on the language you use to code (C, Java, Node.js, PHP, Python, etc.), there are many official MongoDB drivers you can use to connect your apps to your MongoDB server. We will be using the MongoDB Node.js driver for our Nuxt apps in this section and throughout the book in the upcoming chapters. Again, there are a few community MongoDB Node.js drivers, such as Mongoose (https://mongoosejs.com/) and Monk (https://automattic.github.io/monk/), if you feel like exploring outside the official drivers. But you should always start coding with the basic and official MongoDB driver directly before using any other layer of driver on top of the driver. So, let's start with the official MongoDB Node.js driver for our Nuxt apps in the following steps:

1. Install the MongoDB Node.js driver via `npm` in your project:

```
$ npm i mongodb
```

Note that the installation of Node.js packages may change over time, so you should always confirm the installation command lines with their official documentation if you are starting your project afresh. For installing the MongoDB Node.js driver, please visit https://www.npmjs.com/package/mongodb or https://github.com/mongodb/node-mongodb-native.

2. Create an `api` sub-directory with a `index.ts` file and a `[id].ts` file, as well as a `utils` sub-directory with a `mongo.ts` file in the `/pages/` directory as follows:

```
server
├── api
│   ├── index.ts
│   └── [id].ts
└── utils
    ├── ...
    └── mongo.ts
```

3. Create a **`.env`** file in the project root with the following variables and values for the MongoDB driver to connect to the MongoDB server and your MongoDB database:

~~~~
```bash
// .env
VITE_DB_HOST=mongodb://127.0.0.1:27017
VITE_DB_DBNAME=advanced-nuxtjs-course
```
~~~~

4. Create an exported **`connect`** async function with the MongoDB database details from the **`.env`** file for connecting to the MongoDB server in **`/server/utils/mongo.ts`**:

~~~~
```js
// server/utils/mongo.ts
import { MongoClient, ObjectId as objectId } from ‘mongodb’

const url = import.meta.env.VITE_DB_HOST
const dbName = import.meta.env.VITE_DB_DBNAME

export async function connect () {
  const client = new MongoClient(url)

  await client.connect()
  console.log(‘🚀 Connected successfully to MongoDB server’)

  const db = client.db(dbName)
  return { client, db }
}
```
~~~~

5. Create an exported **`close`** function for closing the MongoDB server connection in **`/server/utils/mongo.ts`**, and also export the **`ObjectId`** function as a constant as follows:

~~~~
```js
// server/utils/mongo.ts
import { MongoClient, ObjectId as objectId } from ‘mongodb’
...

export function close (client) {
  client.close()
  console.log(‘🚀 Disconnected from MongoDB server’)
~~~~

```
}

export const ObjectId = objectId
```

The `ObjectId` method is used to parse an ID string value into the BSON `ObjectId` type. You will need this method very often when filtering documents by the document ID generated by MongoDB. For more information about this method, please visit https://www.mongodb.com/docs/v7.0/reference/method/ObjectId/.

6. Use the `connect` async function to connect to list all user documents from the `users` collection with `find`, and then close the connection with the `close` function before returning the documents in `/server/api/users/index.ts`:

```js
// server/api/users/index.ts
export default eventHandler(async () => {
  const { client, db } = await connect()

  const collectionUsers = db.collection('users')
  const docs = await collectionUsers.find().toArray()

  close(client)
  return docs
})
```

7. Use `connect` to connect to find a user document with `findOne` and an ID from the request URL, and then close the connection with `close` before returning the document in `/server/api/users/[id].ts`:

```js
// server/api/users/[id].ts
export default eventHandler(async event => {
  const id = event.context.params.id
  const { client, db } = await connect()

  const collectionUsers = db.collection('users')
  const _id = new ObjectId(id)
  const doc = await collectionUsers.findOne({
    _id
```

```
    })

    close(client)
    return doc
  })
```

Notice that we need to parse the ID string from the request URL into the BSON **`ObjectId`** type for finding documents through the ID generated by MongoDB. For more information about the **`findOne`** method, please visit https://www.mongodb.com/docs/v7.0/reference/method/db.collection.findOne/.

8. Run the app on the **`dev`** environment:

```
$ npm run dev
```

You should see the following JSON response on your browser at **`/api/users`**:

```json
[
  {
    "_id": "64e0fdc9e3939a03c2dac6f2",
    "name": "John",
    "slug": "john",
    "email": "john@example.com",
    "createdAt": {
      "$timestamp": "7269088838306234369"
    }
  },
  {
    "_id": "64e0fdc9e3939a03c2dac6f3",
    "name": "Jane",
    "slug": "jane",
    "email": "jane@example.com",
    "createdAt": {
      "$timestamp": "7269088838306234370"
    }
  },
  {
    "_id": "64e0fdc9e3939a03c2dac6f4",
    "name": "Molly",
    "slug": "molly",
    "email": "molly@example.com",
```

~~~~
        "createdAt": {
          "$timestamp": "7269088838306234371"
        }
      }
    ]
    ```
~~~~

You can also request the JSON response of a specific user by its ID on your browser, for example, **`/api/users/64e0fdc9e3939a03c2dac6f2`**:

~~~~
```json
{
  "_id": "64e0fdc9e3939a03c2dac6f2",
  "name": "John",
  "slug": "john",
  "email": "john@example.com",
  "createdAt": {
    "$timestamp": "7269088838306234369"
  }
}
```
~~~~

Also, you should see the following information logged on your terminal for **`/api/users`**:

~~~~
```
New request: /api/users
🚀 Connected successfully to MongoDB server
🚀 Disconnected from MongoDB server
```
~~~~

The same for **`/api/users/64e0fdc9e3939a03c2dac6f2`**, you should see the following information logged on your terminal:

~~~~
```
New request: /api/users/64e0fdc9e3939a03c2dac6f2
🚀 Connected successfully to MongoDB server
🚀 Disconnected from MongoDB server
```
~~~~

We have used only a couple of methods and method options in the preceding steps and code for fetching our data from the MongoDB server. The method options may get more complicated when we want to filter the data deeper or when we need to paginate our data. But you just really need to use the official MongoDB documentation to help you through when things get more complicated. The documentation you need for your MongoDB driver to work with your data is the same as the documentation for the MongoDB Shell that you should follow to work with your data in the previous section.

Furthermore, you will likely need a Graphic User Interface (GUI) to browse and manage your database, collections, and documents. Again, it is recommended to use the official MongoDB GUI – Compass (https://www.mongodb.com/products/compass). You just need to download and install it on your machine. Then start connecting to your MongoDB server and browsing your databases and documents. There are commercial and free GUI options you can pick from, such as Studio 3T (https://studio3t.com/), when you want to explore outside the official MongoDB GUI.

MongoDB and Redis are both great choices for modern NoSQL database management systems for Nuxt apps. Keep in mind that MongoDB is an on-disk database system (by default), whereas Redis is an in-memory database system. You can read more about their differences at https://www.mongodb.com/compare/mongodb-vs-redis. We will use MongoDB more often in the remaining chapters, so you will discover more about it. Before that, let's look at another great alternative to manage and store our data for Nuxt apps by using Markdown documents in the next section. So, let's go and discover this option!

You can find the example app for this topic in `` `/1.nuxt/2.signle-domain/2.mongodb/` `` in the GitHub repository of this book.

# Managing Data with the Nuxt Content Module

Advanced databases like Redis and MongoDB require external and remote servers for themselves separately. However, if you are inclined towards the idea of storing data all in one place and locally in your Nuxt project, Markdown documents could be a good option for managing your app content – if you are comfortable with writing Markdown syntax and YML in your content data. In this section, we will use the Nuxt Content module to explore this alternative.

## Using Nuxt Content as Data Storage

Using Markdown documents to store content data for your Nuxt apps is very easy with the Nuxt Content module. The great thing about using Markdown documents is that it doesn't need another database server like MongoDB server to be installed on your machine. You simply have to keep your Markdown documents in the root directory of your Nuxt app. And you just need some basic Markdown syntax/MDC Syntax (https://www.markdownguide.org/basic-syntax/) and YML for front-matter to get started with Nuxt Content, which is built with additional features on top, such as MarkDown Components (https://content.nuxtjs.org/guide/writing/mdc). So, let's find out in the following steps:

1. Install **`@nuxt/content`** via **`npm`** in your project:

```
$ npm i -D @nuxt/content
```

Note that the installation of Node.js packages may change over time, so you should always confirm the installation command lines with their official documentation if you start your project afresh. For installing Nuxt Content, please visit https://content.nuxtjs.org/get-started.

2. Add **`@nuxt/content`** in **`/nuxt.config.ts`**:

```js
// nuxt.config.ts
export default defineNuxtConfig({
  modules: ['@nuxt/content']
})
```

3. Create an **`images`** sub-directory with some images in the **`/assets/`** directory:

```
assets
└── images
    ├── R0000096.jpg
    ├── ...
    └── R0009300.jpg
```

4. Create a `content` directory with an `index.md` file in the project root and a `blog` sub-directory with two `.md` files, `post-1.md` and `post-2.md`, as follows:

```
content
├── index.md
└── blog
    ├── post-1.md
    └── post-2.md
```

5. Create `index.vue`, `blog.vue`, and a `blog` sub-directory with `index.vue` and `[slug].vue` in the `/pages/` directory as follows:

```
pages
├── index.vue
├── blog.vue
└── blog
    ├── index.vue
    └── [slug].vue
```

6. Add the metadata (title, description, and images) on the front matter using YML, followed by a "`Lorem ipsum...`" dummy content body in `/content/index.md` as follows:

```md
// content/index.md
---
title: Welcome
description: “”
carousel:
  - filename: R0001844.jpg
    title: Post 1
    link: /blog/post-1
  - filename: R0000261.jpg
    title: Post 2
    link: /blog/post-2
---

Lorem ipsum dolor...
```

All the information on this page will become the data for our home page later on.

7. Add title, description, and images using YML, followed by a "`Lorem ipsum...`" dummy content body in `` `/content/blog/post-1.md` `` as follows:

````
```md
// content/blog/post-1.md
---
title: Post 1
description: “”
thumbnail:
  filename: R0001844.jpg
  title: Sample
carousel:
  - filename: R0001844.jpg
    title: Sample
attachments:
  - filename: R0003515.jpg
    title: Sample
  - filename: R0009300.jpg
    title: Sample
---

(Post 1) Lorem ipsum dolor sit amet...
```
````

8. Add title, description, and images using YML, followed by a "`Lorem ipsum...`" dummy content body in `` `/content/blog/post-2.md` `` as follows:

````
```md
// content/blog/post-1.md
---
title: Post 2
description: “”
thumbnail:
  filename: R0000261.jpg
  title: Sample
carousel:
  - filename: R0000261.jpg
    title: Sample
attachments:
  - filename: R0000096.jpg
    title: Sample
  - filename: R0002116.jpg
    title: Sample
````
````

```
---

(Post 1) Lorem ipsum dolor sit amet...
```

9. Use **`useAsyncData`**, **`queryContent`**, and **`findOne`** to query and fetch the data from **`/content/index.md`** in **`/pages/index.ts`**:

```js
// pages/index.ts
<script setup>
const { data } = await useAsyncData(‘home’, () => queryCon-
tent(‘/’).findOne())
</script>
```

The **`queryContent`** function is a built-in function from Nuxt Content. It is auto-imported by Nuxt to build queries using chained functions, such as **`findOne`**. For more information about **`queryContent`**, please visit https://content.nuxtjs.org/guide/displaying/querying.

10. Display the YML data (title and images) and use **`<ContentRenderer>`** to render the "`Lorem ipsum...`" dummy content (body) in **`/pages/index.ts`** as follows:

```html
// pages/index.ts
<template>
  <h1>
    {{ data.title }}
  </h1>
  <ul v-if=”data.carousel”>
    <li v-for=”image in data.carousel”>
      <nuxt-link :to=”image.link”>
        <img
          :src=”useAsset(image.filename)”
          :title=”image.title”
        />
      </nuxt-link>
    </li>
  </ul>
  <ContentRenderer :value=”data” />
</template>
```

The `<ContentRenderer>` component is one of the built-in components from Nuxt Content. It is used to render the body of a Markdown document that is returned by `queryContent` in a rich-text format. For more information about this component, please visit https://content.nuxtjs.org/guide/displaying/rendering#contentrenderer.

11. Assign `useRoute` to a `route` constant in `/pages/blog.vue`:

    ```js
    // pages/blog.vue
    <script setup>
    const route = useRoute()
    </script>
    ```

12. Use the `route` constant to conditionally show the `Blog` title in `/pages/blog.vue`:

    ```html
    // pages/blog.vue
    <template>
      <h2 v-if="!route.params.slug">
        Blog
      </h2>
      <NuxtPage />
    </template>
    ```

In the preceding markups, we didn't want to show the Blog title when rendering the child blog post in the `<NuxtPage>` component.

13. Use `queryContent` with `only` and `find` to query and fetch all the posts from the `/blog/` sub-directory in the `/content/` directory as a list in `/pages/blog/index.vue`:

    ```js
    // pages/blog/index.vue
    <script setup>
    const blog = await queryContent('blog')
      .only(['_path', 'title', 'thumbnail'])
      .find()
    </script>
    ```

The **`only`** chained function is used to select specific keys from the YML part in a Markdown document. The **`_path`** key is a reserved key auto-generated by Nuxt Content, and we can use it as a slug to form a URL. On the other hand, the **`find`** chained function is used to fetch all documents from a folder in a list. For more information about them, please visit https://content.nuxtjs.org/api/composables/query-content#onlykeys and https://content.nuxtjs.org/api/composables/query-content#find.

14. Loop and display the list in **`/pages/blog/index.vue`** as follows:

```html
// pages/blog/index.vue
<template>
  <ul v-if=”blog”>
    <li v-for=”post in blog” :key=”post._path”>
      <h3>
        <NuxtLink :to=”post._path”>
          {{ post.title }}
        </NuxtLink>
      </h3>
      <NuxtLink :to=”post._path”>
        <img
          :alt=”post.thumbnail.title”
          :src=”useAsset(post.thumbnail.filename)”
        />
      </NuxtLink>
    </li>
  </ul>
</template>
```

15. Use **`useAsyncData`**, **`queryContent`**, **`where`**, and **`findOne`** to query and fetch the data from **`/content/index.md`** in **`/pages/blog/[slug].vue`**:

```js
// pages/blog/[slug].vue
<script setup>
const { path } = useRoute()
const { data: post } = await useAsyncData(`content-${path}`,
() => {
  return queryContent().where({ _path: path }).findOne()
})
</script>
```

The `where` chained function is used to filter results with specific keys. In the preceding code, we use the `_path` key to locate the specific Markdown document requested via `slug`. For more information about this function, please visit https://content.nuxtjs.org/api/composables/query-content#wherequery.

16. Display the YML data (title and images) and use `<ContentRenderer>` to render the Markdown body in `/pages/blog/[slug].vue` as follows:

```html
// pages/blog/[slug].vue
<template>
  <div v-if="post">
    <h2>
      {{ post.title }}
    </h2>
    <ContentRenderer :value="post" />
    <ul>
      <li v-for="image in post.carousel">
        <img
          :alt="image.title"
          :src="useAsset(image.filename)"
        />
      </li>
    </ul>
    <ul>
      <li v-for="image in post.attachments">
        <img
          :alt="image.title"
          :src="useAsset(image.filename)"
        />
      </li>
    </ul>
  </div>
</template>
```

17. Run the app on the `dev` environment:

```
$ npm run dev
```

You should see the title, images, and body you set on `/content/index.md` displayed successfully on `localhost:3000`. Also, you should see the blog list is looped and displayed successfully on `/blog`. Lastly, you should see the data you set on the blog posts in Markdown documents is displayed successfully on /`blog/post-1` and `/blog/post-2`.

Nuxt Content is a great choice if you like the simplicity of using Markdown documents for storing data for your Nuxt apps. With Nuxt Content, you don't need any other Node.js package to translate and convert your Markdown syntax into HTML tags. You even can write Vue components, span texts, attributes, and more using MDC Syntax in your Markdown content body. However, it may be more suitable for developers if you want to utilize all the features of Nuxt Content, and therefore more complicated syntaxes are involved. Also, it can get very complicated when there are too many different metadata to manage in the frontmatter, which makes it more difficult for non-developers.

Although Markdown documents can be a turn-off for non-developers, you can use a WYSIWYG Markdown editor with a content management system (CMS), such as WordPress, to lift this barrier. There are tons of WYSIWYG Markdown editors and CMS available for you to explore, whether they are commercial or open source. With a WYSIWYG Markdown editor, you don't need to know the Markdown syntax; instead, you can just write your content in the WYSIWYG editor, and it will transform your content to the Markdown code. Alternatively, you can build a simple CMS yourself and integrate with a WYSIWYG Markdown editor, such as Milkdown (https://milkdown.dev/), to read and write your Markdown content in the `/content/` directory. You can check out the Milkdown integration with Nuxt from the example list at https://github.com/Milkdown/examples. But the decision to continue exploring further with Markdown is now left to you. We will now conclude this chapter and explore other areas in the upcoming chapters, both within and for Nuxt.

You can find the example app for this topic in `/1.nuxt/2.signle-domain/3.nuxt-content/` in the GitHub repository of this book.

Conclusion

In this chapter, you have learned to create APIs with Nuxt internally with Nitro by creating server routes, server middleware, server plugins, and server utility functions in the `/server/` directory. You have stored and managed your API's data in the in-memory data storage from Nitro and Unstorage, an on-disk database from MongoDB, and Markdown documents with Nuxt Content for your Nuxt app. Also, you have used the Node.js MongoDB driver to query data from the MongoDB server and database. Lastly, you have learned that all APIs in this chapter were created within the Nuxt project using Nitro, which is essentially powered by UnJS h3.

In the next chapter, you will discover how to create APIs outside the Nuxt project by just using Vite, Node.js HTTP API, and the `` `find-my-way` `` HTTP router. You will use them to create Hot Module Replacement (HMR) Node.js web servers (or we can also call them **apps**) with MySQL and MongoDB. You will learn how to enable CORS in the HMR Node.js apps for serving APIs to your Nuxt app. You will also create a real-time Nuxt app with RethinkDB and manage your app data with the RethinkDB database, Socket.IO, and the HMR Node.js app. So, let's go discover them!

CHAPTER 7

Managing Data with Node.js Apps for Nuxt

Introduction

Welcome to *Chapter* 7. In this chapter, you will create Hot Module Replacement (HMR) Node.js HTTP servers with Vite, the Node.js HTTP module, the Node.js File System module, and the `` `find-my-way` `` HTTP router. You will use the HMR Node.js app with MariaDB database, MongoDB database, and RethinkDB to manage the data for your Nuxt apps. You will also learn to enable CORS in HMR Node.js apps for your Nuxt app to connect and fetch data through HTTP requests. Lastly, you will create a real-time Nuxt app with RethinkDB, Socket.IO, and the HMR Node.js HTTP server.

Structure

The topics that will be covered in this chapter are as follows:

- Creating HMR Node.js HTTP Servers with Vite and the Node.js HTTP Module
- Managing Data with MariaDB
- Managing Data with MongoDB
- Managing Real-time Data with RethinkDB

Creating HMR Node.js HTTP Servers with Vite and the Node.js HTTP Module

Nitro and UnJS h3 are frameworks to help us to build web servers, much like the other popular frameworks such as Express (https://expressjs.com/), Koa (https://koajs.com/), and Fastify (https://fastify.io/). These frameworks, in one way or another, are built on top of the Node.js HTTP module, which is tucked inside somewhere deep in them. These frameworks are usually opinionated, and you need to follow the way they work. They change over time and you need to adapt. Some get more popular and maintained, while some get less popular and may be deprecated at some point. In such cases, you need to migrate to another new framework and start to adapt again. However, one infrastructure that will outlive them is the Node.js HTTP module. It is just a Node.js built-in module that helps you to build a minimal web server for receiving HTTP requests and giving HTTP responses. Nothing else on top, such as an HTTP router and Hot Module Replacement (HMR), which allows for the ability to push file updates without restarting the web server. However, all of these can be resolved with Node.js community packages or tools, such as **`find-my-way`** (https://github.com/delvedor/find-my-way) for the HTTP router, Vite (https://vitejs.dev/) for HMR. Hence, in this section, we will explore how to build an HTTP web server with the Node.js HTTP module along with other Node.js community packages. In our Node.js HTTP server, we want to add Hot HMR for development, and we also want to auto-import functions and utilities. Lastly, we also want our web server to be able to serve assets such as images, fonts, and text files. So, let's find out!

Creating a Node.js HTTP Web Server: HMR, Routers, and CORS

Vite is a frontend tool that helps you to develop your client-side apps out of the box. However, if you want to use it on the server side, then you will need to use the **`vite-plugin-node`** plugin. This allows us to make use of Vite's features during development, such as Hot HMR and ES6 modules (ESM). However, still, the nature of Vite is built for frontend single-page apps (SPA) and lacks an HTTP router. So, we will need an HTTP router to create API routes in our web server. For that, we can use a **`find-my-way`** Node.js package. Lastly, we will also need to have Cross-Origin Resource Sharing (CORS) enabled in our web server so that a cross-origin website can send HTTP requests and receive responses from us. For that, we can use the HTTP response object from the Node.js **`http`** module.

So, let's find out how you can use all these stuffs together to build a Node.js HTTP server in the following steps:

1. Install `vite` and `vite-plugin-node` as development dependencies only via `npm` on your terminal:

```
$ npm i -D vite
$ npm i -D vite-plugin-node
```

Note that the installation of Node.js packages may change over time, so you should always confirm the installation command lines with their official documentation if you start your project afresh. For `vite-plugin-node`, please check it out at https://github.com/axe-me/vite-plugin-node.

You also can use `npm create` to automate the process of scaffolding a new Vite project as follows:

```
$ npm create vite@latest
```

But again, the installation of a new Vite project may change over time, so you should always confirm the installation command lines with their official documentation if you start your project afresh. For more information about installing a Vite project using `npm create`, please visit https://github.com/axe-me/vite-plugin-node.

2. Install `find-my-way` to help us build a fast HTTP router via `npm` on your terminal:

```
$ npm i find-my-way
```

Note that these Node.js packages may change over time, so you should always confirm the installation command lines with their official documentation at https://github.com/delvedor/find-my-way.

3. Create a `package.json` and a `vite.config.ts` in your project root with a src directory that contains a `app.ts` and a `router.ts`:

```
├── package.json
├── vite.config.ts
└── src
    ├── app.ts
    └── router.ts
```

4. Create a `.env` file in your project root with the following variables for development:

```
// .env
VITE_APP_HOST=localhost
VITE_APP_PORT=5000
```

5. Create a `.env.production` file in your project root with the following variables for production:

```
// .env.production
VITE_APP_HOST=example.com
VITE_APP_PORT=5000
```

6. Import `resolve`, `defineConfig`, `loadEnv`, and `VitePluginNode` to configure your project as follows:

```js
// vite.config.ts
import { resolve } from 'path'
import { defineConfig, loadEnv } from 'vite'
import { VitePluginNode } from 'vite-plugin-node'

export default defineConfig(({ command, mode }) => {
  const env = loadEnv(mode, process.cwd(), '')
  return {
    server: {
      port: env.VITE_APP_PORT
```

```
      },
      resolve: {
        alias: {
          ‘@’: resolve(__dirname, ‘./src’)
        },
      },
      plugins: [
        ...VitePluginNode({
          adapter: ‘express’,
          appPath: ‘./src/app.ts’,
        })
      ],
    }
  })
```

In the preceding configuration, the `resolve` function from the Node.js `path` module is used to create a `@` for the `/src` path. The `loadEnv` function from Vite is used to access the Node.js environment variables, which include the ones from our custom `.env` files. Lastly, `VitePluginNode` is used to create HMR on our Vite project. We need to set the app load path and the adapter for this plugin. While this plugin supports Express, Koa, Nest, and Fastify apps out of the box, we need to tell `VitePluginNode` about the web server framework we use to create our app. The Node.js HTTP app works the same as the Express app. So, we can set Express as our app.

7. Import the Node.js `http` module to create your web server as follows:

```js
// src/app.ts
import http from ‘http’

const requestListener: http.RequestListener = (req, res) => {
  res.statusCode = 200
  res.setHeader(‘Content-Type’, ‘application/json’)
}

if (import.meta.env.PROD) {
  const host = import.meta.env.VITE_APP_HOST || ‘127.0.0.1’
  const port = import.meta.env.VITE_APP_PORT || ‘5000’
  const server = http.createServer(requestListener)
  server.listen(port, () => {
    console.log(`🚀 Server ready at ${host}:${port}`)
  })
}
```

````
export const viteNodeApp = requestListener
```
````

In the preceding code, we have created a function (a request listener) in the `requestListener` constant for listening to the HTTP request and returning the HTTP response to the request. This function is then passed to the `createServer` method from the Node.js `http` module to create an HTTP Server object, which is our HTTP server (or web server). Also, we have set the status code to **200** and the header content type to `application/json` by default in the HTTP response of our app. We only pass our app to `viteNodeApp` for HMR during development. While in production, our app will be executed and listened to on either the `5000` port or the port number we set in the `.env-production` file. For more information about the Node.js `http` module, please visit https://nodejs.org/api/http.html.

8. Import `findmyway` to create your app router and routes as follows:

````
```js
// src/router.ts
import findmyway from 'find-my-way'
const router = findmyway()

router.on('GET', '/', (req, res) => {
  res.end('{"message":"hello world"}')
})
router.on('GET', '/:test', (req, res, params) => {
  res.end(JSON.stringify(params))
})

export default router
```
````

In the preceding code, we have created the `/` route to return a **"hello world"** JSON in our HTTP response object. The `/:test` route is used to demonstrate how we can use `find-my-way` to take parameters from the HTTP request by using a **:** mark. The parameter key in the preceding example is `test`, which contains the value of the parameter.

9. Create a `/hello` route and use ***** to catch all unmatched routes as `404`:

````
```js
// src/router.ts
````

```
...
router.on('GET', '/hello', (req, res, params) => {
  res.end('{"winter":"is here"}')
})

router.on('GET', '*', (req, res) => {
  res.statusCode = 404
  res.end('{"message":"page not found!"}')
})
```

In the preceding code, we have created the `/hello` route to return a **"{"winter":"is here"}"** JSON in our HTTP response object. This demonstrates that we can use this pattern to create other API routes such as `/about`, `/contact`, `/users`, and so on. Then, lastly, we use `*` to catch any other unmatched routes as a 404 HTTP response. Notice that we set `404` to override the default HTTP status code, which is `200`.

10. Import the preceding routes into `/src/app.ts` and enable CORS as follows:

```js
// src/app.ts
import http from 'http'
import router from '@/router'

const requestListener: http.RequestListener = (req, res) => {
  res.setHeader('Access-Control-Allow-Origin', '*')
  res.setHeader('Access-Control-Allow-Methods', 'GET, POST,
OPTIONS, PUT, PATCH, DELETE')
  res.setHeader('Access-Control-Allow-Headers',
'X-Requested-With, Content-Type')
  res.setHeader('Access-Control-Allow-Credentials', true)

  res.statusCode = 200
  res.setHeader('Content-Type', 'application/json')

  if (req.method === 'OPTIONS') {
    res.end()
  } else {
    router.lookup(req, res)
  }
}
```

In the preceding code, we use `` `setHeader` `` to set which remote website can send requests to our API, what request methods they can send, and whether cookies are acceptable or not. The `` `*` `` value is used to allow any website to connect. You can set it to allow a specific website only if you prefer for production. You also can limit the request methods if you want to do that, but the `` `OPTIONS` `` method must be included for CORS. It is an HTTP method used by browsers to send it to our web server to find out the supported HTTP methods before sending the actual request information. Lastly, our APIs only can be started and served after passing the CORS requirements. We also need to make sure that our APIs are not running during the `` `OPTIONS` `` request.

11. Add the following npm scripts in `` `/package.json` ``:

````
```json
// package.json
"scripts": {
  "dev": "vite",
  "build": "vite build",
  "start": "node dist/app.js"
},
```
````

The `` `dev` `` command line is used to start the dev server. The `` `build` `` command line is used to build the app for production. The `` `start` `` command line is used to start the production app, which is built and exported to the `` `/dis/` `` directory. For more information about the command lines from Vite, please visit https://vitejs.dev/guide/cli.html.

12. Run the app on the `` `dev` `` environment:

````
```
$ npm run dev
```
````

You should see the following JSON response on `` `localhost:5000` `` on your browser screen:

````
```json
{"message":"hello world"}
```
````

You should see the following JSON response on `localhost:5000/xyz`:

````
```json
{"test":"xyz"}
```
````

And you should see the following JSON response on `localhost:5000/hello`:

````
```json
{“winter”:“is here”}
```
````

Then, finally, you should see the `404` JSON response on unmatched routes, for example, `localhost:5000/xyz/abc` and `localhost:5000/hello/xyz`:

````
```json
{“message”:”page not found!”}
```
````

In the preceding steps and lines, you have used Vite, `vite-plugin-node`, `find-my-way`, and the HTTP response object only from the Node.js `http` module to create an HMR web server with CORS enabled during development. Then, finally, during production, we simply let the Node.js HTTP module take over completely to create the web server for us, as HMR is no longer needed in the production app. And then, there you go, you now have an HTTP server that can be used as a backend API to manage your data and serve the Nuxt app. However, there is more we can do to improve this web server for development, such as auto-importing functions and utilities. So, let's find out how you can add compsables and utilities to your web server and auto-import them!

Adding and Auto-Importing Composables and Utilities

It is surprising to auto-import files from specific directories during development just through the help of an `unimport` Node.js package. It is the package used by Nuxt internally as well for auto-importing composables, functions, and so on. So, let's find out how you can use this package in your Node.js HTTP server in the following steps:

1. Install `unimport` as a development dependency only via `npm` on your terminal:

```
$ npm i -D unimport
```

Again, the installation of this Node.js package may change over time, so you should always confirm the installation command lines with their official documentation at https://github.com/unjs/unimport.

2. Create a **`composables`** sub-directory with a **`use-hello.ts`** file and a **`utils`** sub-directory with a **`hello.ts`** file in the **`/src/`** directory:

```bash
src
├── ...
├── composables
│   └── use-hello.ts
└── utils
    └── hello.ts
```

3. Import **`unimport`** and configure your project to auto-import files from **`/src/composables`** and **`/src/utils`** as follows:

```js
// vite.config.ts
...
import Unimport from 'unimport/unplugin'

export default defineConfig(({ command, mode }) => {
  ...
  return {
    ...
    plugins: [
      ...
      Unimport.vite({
        dirs: [
          './src/composables/**',
          './src/utils/**'
        ]
      })
    ],
  }
```

```
})
```

4. Create and export a `useHello` composable function in `/src/composables/use-hello.ts`:

```js
// src/composables/use-hello.ts
export default (text = null) => {
  const message = text ?? 'Hello'
  return {
    message
  }
}
```

5. Create and export a `hello` utility function in `/src/utils/hello.ts`:

```js
// src/utils/hello.ts
export default () => {
  return 'Hello World!'
}
```

6. Use `useHello` and `hello` anywhere in `/src`, for example:

```js
// src/router.ts
router.on('GET', '/hello', (req, res, params) => {
  const { message } = useHello()
  console.log('message from composables =', message)
  console.log('message from utils =', hello())
  res.end('{"winter":"is here"}')
})
```

7. Run the app on the `dev` environment:

```

$ npm run dev
```

You should see the following logs on your terminal when requesting the `` `/hello` `` route on `` `localhost:5000` ``:

```
message from composables = Hello
message from utils = Hello World!
```

There you go. You have just improved your development experience by auto-importing files from the `` `/composables/` `` and `` `/utils/` `` directories. You may have probably noticed that adding and creating composable and util functions in this HTTP web server is the same as how you add them in a Nuxt project. Besides auto-importing functions from specific directories, you also can use `` `unimport` `` to auto-import Node.js modules and packages, such as `` `fs` `` and `` `find-my-way` ``. However, it is not recommended to import everything in your project. Because it is always better to import the dependencies of our code explicitly for better debugging and maintenance.

Serving Assets with the Node.js File System Module

Most of the time, you will need to serve assets when using an HTTP web server to manage and serve data independently. For example, you might want to serve plain-text files and images. Then, the Nuxt app can fetch these files remotely via HTTP requests. For that, we can use the Node.js File System module (https://nodejs.org/api/fs.html), also called the `` `node:fs` `` module, to read the asset file and return the file data for the HTTP response object. So, let's find out how you can use this Node.js module in our web server in the following steps:

1. Create a `` `public` `` directory in your project root directory with the sub-directories and files:

```
├── package.json
├── ...
└── public
    ├── R0003515.jpg
    ├── fixtures
    │   └── hello.txt
    └── 世界
        └── R0003515.jpg
```

2. Import the Node.js `fs` module to read and serve the public assets on `/public/*` with the router:

````
```js
// src/router.ts
import fs from ‘fs’
import router from ‘@/router’

router.on(‘GET’, ‘/public/*’, (req, res) => {
  fs.readFile(`./${decodeURIComponent(req.url)}`, (err, data)
  => {
    res.setHeader(‘Content-Type’, ‘text/plain’)
    res.end(data)
  })
})
...
```
````

In the preceding code, the `readFile` method from `fs` is used to read the asset data of the requested asset from the URL. Then, we need to override the default content type of `application/json` to `text/plain` for responding asset data in the response object. The `decodeURIComponent` method is used to decode non-English characters in the URL. For more information about this method, please visit https://developer.mozilla.org/en-US/docs/Web/JavaScript/Reference/Global_Objects/decodeURIComponent.

3. Add an if-condition block in the `/public/*` route to handle requests on non-existent assets:

````
```js
// src/router.ts
router.on(‘GET’, ‘/public/*’, (req, res) => {
  fs.readFile(`./${decodeURIComponent(req.url)}`, (err, data)
  => {
    if (err) {
      res.statusCode = 404
      res.end(JSON.stringify({
        message: ‘File not found or you made an invalid
        request.’,
        data: err
      }))
      return
    }
````
````

```
        ...
      })
    })
```

In the preceding code, we need to override the default `200` HTTP status code to `404` in the response object for the requested asset that is not found in the `/public/` directory. Then, we end the HTTP response object with JSON data that contains the not-found message and the error data from `readFile`.

4. Run the app on the `dev` environment:

```
$ npm run dev
```

You should see the assets from the `/public/` directory are displayed successfully on your browser, for example:

- `http://localhost:5000/public/R0003515.jpg`
- `http://localhost:5000/public/世界/R0003515.jpg`
- `http://localhost:5000/public/fixtures/hello.txt`

Then, you will get the following JSON output on your browser for the non-existent asset, for example, `localhost:5000/public/a123.jpg`:

```json
{"message":"File not found or you made an invalid
request.","data":{"errno":-2,"code":"ENOENT","syscall":"open",
"path":".//public/a123.jpg"}}
```

There you go. In the preceding steps and lines, you have turned Node.js into a file server to serve assets for the public successfully. Now, besides storing the data of your Nuxt app remotely, you also can organize certain assets and store them remotely in the same Node.js HTTP server where you fetch the data. However, bear in mind that this will cause more HTTP requests to be made if you have to fetch tons of remote assets. To resolve such a situation, you can use a limit and offset on your data fetching to reduce the HTTPS request on the remote assets.

Finally, we have a Node.js HTTP server that has an HTTP router, HMR, auto-import, and CORS support. It is also a file server that we can serve assets from. We can be independent from Nuxt completely for serving server APIs.

Remember, we used the `/server/` directory for serving APIs in the previous chapter by using the Nitro Server Engine in Nuxt? It is good to separate our API (server) from the Nuxt app (client) so that we can keep our Nuxt project as thin as possible. We wouldn't want to mix up the client and server package dependency in one single project. If we do that, it can make our code harder to debug and maintain in the long term. It can lead to confusion and catastrophes. We want to avoid all that in the future. So, from now on, we will focus on the independent and standalone Node.js HTTP server for serving APIs and managing our data for Nuxt apps. There are benefits to having a standalone API that you will discover along the way in this book. For example, you will find out how easy it is to integrate with database systems without restrictions, such as MariaDB (or MySQL), MongoDB, and RethinkDB. So, let's find out the integration with MariaDB in the next section!

You can find the example app for this topic in `/2.native/1.starter/` in the GitHub repository of this book.

Managing Data with MariaDB

MariaDB, an open-source forked from MySQL, was created in 2009. It is backward-compatible with MySQL and is an improved version of MySQL. It supports the same features as MySQL, so you can use them interchangeably without issues. For example, you can run WordPress with MySQL or MariaDB as its database system with no issues at all. MySQL and MariaDB are usually known to work with PHP and an Apache server. However, in this section, let's find out how you can use MariaDB in the Node.js HTTP server and manage data for our Nuxt app.

Using MariaDB as Data Storage: MariaDB Server and MariaDB Client

Whether you use MySQL or MariaDB as your database system, you still can use MySQL queries for both systems. And whether you install MariaDB afresh on Linux, Windows, or OS, you should always confirm the installation command lines from the official documentation at https://mariadb.org/download/. This is just because the installation command lines may change over time.

If you are going to install MariaDB on Linux, you can choose a distribution from **MariaDB Server Repositories** at https://mariadb.org/download/?t=repo-config. Assuming that you have installed the MariaDB server successfully on your machine, then you can start creating and manipulating your database, collections, and documents in the following steps:

1. Connect to MariaDB Server via MariaDB Client with your password on your terminal:

```
$ mysql -u root -p
```

You should see the following output on your terminal when you have logged in successfully:

```
Welcome to the MariaDB monitor.  Commands end with ; or \g.
Your MariaDB connection id is 12
Server version: 10.6.12-MariaDB-0ubuntu0.22.04.1-log Ubuntu
22.04

Copyright (c) 2000, 2018, Oracle, MariaDB Corporation Ab and
others.

Type 'help;' or '\h' for help. Type '\c' to clear the current
input statement.

MariaDB [(none)]>
```

For more information about MariaDB Client, please visit https://mariadb.com/docs/skysql-previous-release/connect/clients/mariadb-client/.

2. List all the existing databases in your MySQL server:

```
MariaDB [(none)]> SHOW DATABASES;
+-----------------------------------+
| Database                          |
+-----------------------------------+
| advanced-nuxtjs-course            |
| information_schema                |
| mysql                             |
| performance_schema                |
| sys                               |
+-----------------------------------+
```

```
5 rows in set (0.001 sec)
```

If you install MariaDB from scratch, then you should see the following default databases used by MariaDB:

```
+--------------------+
| Database           |
+--------------------+
| information_schema |
| mysql              |
| performance_schema |
| sys                |
+--------------------+
4 rows in set (0.00 sec)
```

3. Create the **advanced-nuxtjs-course** database (if it has not existed yet) with the `CREATE DATABASE` statement:

```
MariaDB [(none)]> CREATE DATABASE advanced-nuxtjs-course;
Query OK, 1 row affected (0.01 sec)
```

4. Select the **advanced-nuxtjs-course** database:

```
MariaDB [(none)]> USE advanced-nuxtjs-course
Reading table information for completion of table and column
names
You can turn off this feature to get a quicker startup with -A

Database changed
MariaDB [advanced-nuxtjs-course]>
```

5. Create a **users** table with the `CREATE TABLE` statement:

```
MariaDB [advanced-nuxtjs-course]> CREATE TABLE users
(
```

```
    id              varchar(255) NOT NULL,
    name            varchar(255) NOT NULL,
    slug            varchar(255) NOT NULL,
    created_on      varchar(255) NOT NULL,
    updated_on      varchar(255) NOT NULL,
    PRIMARY KEY     (id),
    UNIQUE          (slug)
);
Query OK, 0 rows affected (0.013 sec)
```

6. Check if the **users** table has been created with the `` `SHOW TABLES` `` statement:

```
MariaDB [advanced-nuxtjs-course]> SHOW TABLES;
+-----------------------------------+
| Tables_in_advanced-nuxtjs-course |
+-----------------------------------+
| users                             |
+-----------------------------------+
1 row in set (0.000 sec)
```

7. Shows the information of the **users** table with the `` `DESCRIBE` `` statement:

```
MariaDB [advanced-nuxtjs-course]> DESCRIBE users;
+------------+--------------+------+-----+---------+-------+
| Field      | Type         | Null | Key | Default | Extra |
+------------+--------------+------+-----+---------+-------+
| id         | varchar(255) | NO   | PRI | NULL    |       |
| name       | varchar(255) | NO   |     | NULL    |       |
| slug       | varchar(255) | NO   | UNI | NULL    |       |
| created_on | varchar(255) | NO   |     | NULL    |       |
| updated_on | varchar(255) | NO   |     | NULL    |       |
+------------+--------------+------+-----+---------+-------+
5 rows in set (0.002 sec)
```

8. Add records into the **users** table with the `` `INSERT...VALUES` `` statement:

```
    MariaDB [advanced-nuxtjs-course]> INSERT INTO users ( id,
name, slug, created_on, updated_on ) VALUES
```

```
  ( 1, 'Sandy', 'sandy', 0, 0 ),
  ( 2, 'Casey', 'casey', 0, 0 ),
  ( 3, 'Charlie', 'charlie', 0, 0 );
Query OK, 3 rows affected (0.001 sec)
Records: 3  Duplicates: 0  Warnings: 0
```

9. Retrieve the records from the **users** table with the `` `SELECT` `` statement and `` `*` `` to match all columns:

```
MariaDB [advanced-nuxtjs-course]> SELECT * FROM users;
+----+---------+---------+------------+------------+
| id | name    | slug    | created_on | updated_on |
+----+---------+---------+------------+------------+
| 3  | Charlie | charlie | 0          | 0          |
| 2  | Casey   | casey   | 0          | 0          |
| 1  | Sandy   | sandy   | 0          | 0          |
+----+---------+---------+------------+------------+
3 rows in set (0.001 sec)
```

10. Delete all rows from the **users** table with the `` `TRUNCATE TABLE` `` statement:

```
MariaDB [advanced-nuxtjs-course]> TRUNCATE TABLE user;
Query OK, 0 rows affected (0.001 sec)
```

11. Exit **MariaDB** Client with the `` `QUIT` `` statement:

```
MariaDB [advanced-nuxtjs-course]> QUIT;
Bye
```

Just like MySQL, MariaDB has tons of SQL statements for us to work with our data. We only have used a few of them in the preceding steps and code. You can check out the rest of the available SQL statements at https://mariadb.com/kb/en/sql-statements/. Since MariaDB and MySQL are highly compatible with each other, you also can use the MySQL Reference Manual from MySQL at https://dev.mysql.com/doc/refman/8.0/en/sql-statements.html to work with your data in MariaDB if you prefer.

Fetching Data from MariaDB: MariaDB Drivers and MariaDB GUI

To connect with the MariaDB server from a Node.js app, you can either use a MySQL Node.js driver or a MariaDB Node.js connector (https://mariadb.com/kb/en/nodejs-connector/). We will use the official MariaDB Node.js connector from MariaDB to connect with our database. But MariaDB Server still maintains high levels of compatibility with MySQL. Hence, you can use any MySQL Node.js driver to connect with the MariaDB server, such as **`mysql`** (https://github.com/mysqljs/mysql) and **`mysql2`** (https://github.com/sidorares/node-mysql2), if you feel like exploring outside the MariaDB connector. However, you should always start coding with the official MariaDB driver (or **connector)** directly before using any other drivers. So, let's start with the official MariaDB Node.js driver for our Nuxt apps in the following steps:

1. Install the MariaDB Node.js connector via **`npm`** in your project:

```
$ npm i mariadb
```

Note that the preceding driver may change over time, so you should always confirm with their official documentation at https://mariadb.com/kb/en/nodejs-connector/ or https://github.com/mariadb-corporation/mariadb-connector-nodejs. MariaDB also provides the connector in other scripting languages, which you can check out at https://mariadb.com/kb/en/connectors/.

2. Create **a `composables`**, a **`utils`**, and a **`routes`** sub-directories in the **`/src/`** directory, as well as two **`.ts`** files in the **`/routes/`** sub-directory for abstracting the callback function from each API route into these separate files as follows:

```
src
├── composables
├── utils
└── routes
    ├── index.ts
    └── users
        └── index.ts
```

3. Create a `.env` file in the project root with the following variables and values for the database and the app:

````
```bash
// .env
# Set database env variables:
VITE_DB_HOST=localhost
VITE_DB_DBNAME=advanced-nuxtjs-course
VITE_DB_USER=root
VITE_DB_PASSWORD=tklau

# Set app env variables:
VITE_APP_HOST=localhost
VITE_APP_PORT=5000
VITE_CROSS_ORIGIN=http://localhost:3000
```
````

4. Create a `use-mariadb.ts` file in `/src/composables/` to export a connection pooling from the driver in an async function with the database details from the `.env` file for connecting the database server:

````
```js
// src/composables/use-mariadb.ts
import mariadb from 'mariadb'

const pool = mariadb.createPool({
  connectionLimit: 10,
  host: import.meta.env.VITE_DB_HOST,
  user: import.meta.env.VITE_DB_USER,
  password: import.meta.env.VITE_DB_PASSWORD,
  database: import.meta.env.VITE_DB_DBNAME
})

export default async () => {
  let connection
  try {
    connection = await pool.getConnection()
  } catch (err) {
    throw err
  }

  return {
    pool: connection
  }
````
````

```
}
```

5. Create an `index` callback function for the main route of our app in `/src/routes/index.t`:

```js
// src/routes/index.ts
export default (req, res) => {
  return {
    statusCode: 200,
    data: {
      message: ‘Hello World!’
    }
  }
}
```

We would want to return the callback data with an HTTP status code in each of our callback functions in the `/src/routes/` directory. However, this process can be tedious and repetitive. So, it would be better to abstract and tuck away the repetitive lines and logic. Then, we just need to focus on working out the data and pass it a function as follows:

```js
// src/routes/index.ts
export default ctxHandler(ctx => {
  return {
    message: ctx.message
  }
})
```

In the preceding idea and code, we create our callback function in a `ctxHandler` function. In this callback function, we work out the data for the HTTP request. The `ctxHandler` function then does the rest of the repetitive cosmetic work for us.

6. Create a `ctx-handler.ts` file in `/src/utils/` for the `ctxHandler` function as follows:

```js
// src/utils/ctx-handler.ts
export default (callback) => {
```

```js
  return async ctx => {
    let data = null
    let statusCode = 200
    try {
      data = await callback(ctx)
    } catch (e) {
      statusCode = e.statusCode || 500
      data = {
        name: e.name,
        message: e.message,
        stack: e.stack
      }
    }
    data = JSON.stringify(data)

    return {
      statusCode,
      data
    }
  }
}
```

This `ctxHandler` function takes `callback` and `ctx` from a **caller**. It executes `callback` with `ctx` to get the callback returned data, which it then **stringifies** before returning the HTTP status code and the **stringified** data to the caller. In this `ctxHandler` function, we also need to catch any error from `callback`, work out the error information, and return it to the caller.

It is worth knowing that JSON has its limitations, for example, it doesn't serialize `BigInt` values by default. So, using `JSON.stringify` on a `BigInt` value will get a `TypeError` result. However, this can be resolved by converting the `BigInt` value to a string using a `replacer` function as follows:

```js
// src/utils/ctx-handler.ts
const replacer = (key, value) =>
  typeof value === "bigint" ? value.toString() : value

export default (callback) => {
  return async ctx => {
    ...
    data = JSON.stringify(data, replacer)
    ...
  }
```

````
}
```
````

7. Import the **`index`** callback function for the **/** main route in **`/src/router.ts`**:

````
```js
// src/router.ts
import index from ‘@/routes/index’

router.on(‘GET’, ‘/’, async (req, res) => {
  const ctx = {
    req,
    message: ‘Hello World!!’
  }
  const { data, statusCode } = await index(ctx)
  res.statusCode = statusCode
  res.end(data)
})
```
````

Notice that we tuck the HTTP request object into the **`ctx`** constant with a **`Hello World`** message. You can add any other properties and data into this **`ctx`** constant. We then pass it to the **`index`** callback. We get **`data`** and **`statusCode`** from the **`index`** callback and set them to the HTTP response object.

8. Create a **`users`** callback function for the **`/users`** route of our app in **`/src/routes/users/index.ts`**:

````
```js
// src/routes/users/index.ts
export default ctxHandler(async () => {
  const { pool } = await useMariadb()
  const query = ‘SELECT `id`, `name`, `slug`, `created_on`,
`updated_on` FROM `users`’;

  const rows = await pool.query(query)
  pool.end()

  return rows
})
```
````

Notice that you can only write a single line of the SQL query. This can cause lengthy and readability issues on longer queries. And that can be difficult to
````

read, debug, and maintain over time. So, it is better if we can write the query in a more readable template/ string literal as follows:

````
```js
// src/routes/users/index.ts
...
const query = toSql(`
  SELECT
    ‘id’,
    ‘name’,
    ‘slug’,
    ‘created_on’,
    ‘updated_on’
  FROM ‘users’
`)
```
````

To achieve that, we will need to create a `` `toSql` `` function in `` `/src/utils/` `` to help us to convert 'to` for SQL query so that we can use the string literal to write a readable SQL query in it:

````
```js
// src/utils/to-sql.ts
export default (str) => {
  if (!str) {
    return
  }
  return str.replace(/\’/g, ‘\`’)
}
```
````

9. Import the '**users**' callback function for the '**/users**' API route in '**/src/router.ts**':

````
```js
// src/router.ts
import users from ‘@/routes/users/index’

router.on(‘GET’, ‘/users’, async (req, res) => {
  const ctx = { req }
  const { data, statusCode } = await users(ctx)
  res.statusCode = statusCode
  res.end(data)
````
````

```
})
```

10. Run the app on the `dev` environment:

```
$ npm run dev
```

You should see the following JSON response on your browser at `localhost:5000` for the main route of our app:

```json
{"message":"Hello World!!"}
```

You should see the JSON response of a list of users, which you have injected in the previous section through MariaDB Client, on your browser on `localhost:5000/users` for the `/users` API route:

```json
[{"id":"1","name":"Sandy","slug":"sandy","created_
on":"0","updated_on":"0"},{"id":"2","name":"Casey","slug":
"casey","created_on":"0","updated_
on":"0"},{"id":"3","name":"Charlie","slug":"charlie",
"created_on":"0","updated_on":"0"}]
```

11. Create a `.env` file in your Nuxt project root with the following variables and values for the app and the cross-origin API:

```
// .env
APP_BASE_URL=http://localhost:3000
API_BASE_URL=http://localhost:5000
```

Note that `localhost:3000` is your Nuxt app, while `localhost:5000` is the cross-origin API.

12. Store the value of the `API_BASE_URL` env variable to an `apiBaseUrl` key in `runtimeConfig` in `nuxt.config.ts`:

```js
// nuxt.config.ts
export default defineNuxtConfig({
  runtimeConfig: {
    public: {
      apiBaseUrl: process.env.API_BASE_URL
    }
  }
})
```

13. Create a `use-f3tch.ts` file in the `/composable/` directory in your Nuxt project to export a custom fetch composable by customizing the Nuxt `useFetch` API with `hash` from `ohash` as follows:

```js
// composables/use-f3tch.ts
import { hash } from ‘ohash’

export default (path, options = {}) => {
  const runtimeConfig = useRuntimeConfig()
  const key = options && options.key ? {
    key: hash(Date.now())
  } : {}

  return useFetch(path, {
    ...options,
    ...key,
    baseURL: options.baseURL ?? runtimeConfig.pub-
    lic[‘apiBaseUrl’],
    async onResponse({ request, response, options }) {
      response._data = response._data.data ?? response._data
    },
    async onResponseError({ response }) {
      return new Promise((resolve, reject) => {
        response.ok ? resolve() : reject({
          statusCode: response.statusCode || 500,
          name: response._data.name || ‘Error’,
          message: response._data.message,
          stack: response._data.stack,
          data: response._data
        })
      })
    }
  })
```

```
}
```

This custom `fetch` composable, `useF3tch`, is used to fetch data from the cross-origin API by default if `baseURL` is not provided through `options`. A unique key can be set by ourselves through `hash` from `ohash` if `key` is set to `true` in `option`, to prevent the default `useFetch` API from generating keys automatically for us.

This custom `useF3tch` composable also does the following things:

- **Intercept the response data**: Because our cross-origin API response data is stored in the **data** key, we intercept the response data to read the data from this key if it exists.
- **Intercept the response error data**: We use the `onResponseError` interceptor to modify the Nuxt error object so that it contains the error data from cross-origin API instead.

14. Use `useF3tch` in the `<script>` block to fetch the list of users from the cross-origin API:

```js
// pages/users.vue
<script setup>
const { data: users, error } = await useF3tch('/users')
</script>
```

15. Display the data of each user in the `<template>` block:

```html
// pages/users.vue
<template>
  <error-boundary v-bind:error="error">
    <h2>
      Users
    </h2>
    <ul>
      <li v-for="user in users" v-bind:key="user.id">
        {{ user.name }}
      </li>
    </ul>
  </error-boundary>
</template>
```

16. Run the app on the `dev` environment:

```
$ npm run dev
```

You should see all the users are fetched from the cross-origin API and displayed successfully on your browser at `localhost:3000/users`.

There you go. You have successfully queried the data from the MariaDB server using the MariaDB driver and created the API route in a standalone Node.js HTTP server for the Nuxt app to fetch data from. The communication between two separate cross-origin apps is possible also because we have CORS enabled on our Node.js HTTP server, which is used as an API to serve and store data. Note that we have used only a minimal SQL statement to query and select data from the MariaDB server in the preceding steps. The SQL statement can get very complicated when we want to filter the data deeper or when we need to paginate our data. But you just really need to use any SQL reference to help you through when things get more complicated, for example, the SQL Statements https://mariadb.com/kb/en/sql-statements/ from MariaDB.

Furthermore, you will likely need a GUI or a graphical client to browse and manage your database, collections, and documents. Again, since MariaDB and MySQL are highly compatible, you can use a MySQL GUI, for example, Adminer https://www.adminer.org/. It is just a file written in PHP. You just need to download and place it on a server that supports PHP, such as Apache. Access it from your browser and start connecting to your MariaDB server with your MariaDB server credentials. You also can use any GUI listed on MariaDB website at https://mariadb.com/kb/en/graphical-and-enhanced-clients/ or https://mariadb.com/kb/en/applications-supporting-mariadb/.

Injecting Data with UUID and Timestamp

You have successfully queried data from the MariaDB server and database in the API. But what about injecting data? How do we read the incoming data from the HTTP body before injecting it into the database? We are going to look into these in this section. Also, we will want to inject each piece of data with a UUID and a timestamp instead of the arbitrary values we have done in the previous section in MariaDB Shell. So, let's find out in the following steps:

1. Create a **`normalize-body.ts`** file in **`/src/utils/`** for parsing the HTTP request body from the **`PATCH`**, **`POST`**, **`PUT`**, and **`DELETE`** methods as follows:

```js
// src/utils/normalize-body.ts
export default async (req) => {
  let body = []
  const requestMethods = [‘PATCH’, ‘POST’, ‘PUT’, ‘DELETE’]
  if (requestMethods.includes(req.method)) {
    for await (const chunk of req) {
      body += chunk
    }

    if (req.headers[‘content-type’]?.includes(‘application/
    json’)) {
      body = JSON.parse(body)
    }
  }

  return body
}
```

Notice that we only parse the body if the content type is set in the request headers and this content type must be **`application/json`**.

2. Create a **`create-error.ts`** file in **`/src/utils/`** for creating and throwing a new **`Error`** object as follows:

```js
// src/utils/create-error.ts
export default (options = {}) => {
  const error = new Error(options.message)
  error.statusCode = options.statusCode
  error.name = options.name
  throw error
}
```

3. Create a **`userCreate`** callback function for the **`/users/create`** route of our app in **`/src/routes/users/create/index.ts`**:

```js
// src/routes/users/create/index.ts
```

```
export default ctxHandler(async ctx => {
  const body = await normalizeBody(ctx.req)

  if (body.name === undefined) {
    createError({
      statusCode: 500,
      message: ‘name is undefined’
    })
  }

  if (body.slug === undefined) {
    createError({
      statusCode: 500,
      message: ‘slug is undefined’
    })
  }

  if (body.name === ‘’) {
    createError({
      statusCode: 400,
      message: ‘name is required’
    })
  }

  if (body.slug === ‘’) {
    createError({
      statusCode: 400,
      message: ‘slug is required’
    })
  }
})
```

In this callback, the body is parsed through the **`normalizeBody`** util. We want to validate **`name`** and **`slug`** so that none of them is undefined nor empty in the body data; otherwise, errors will be created and thrown through the **`createError`** util.

4. Import **`crypto`** from Node.js to help us generate a UUID for each new user when the request has passed the validation:

```js
// src/routes/users/create/index.ts
import crypto from ‘crypto’

export default ctxHandler(async ctx => {
  const { pool } = await useMariadb()
```

```
  const body = await normalizeBody(ctx.req)
  ...

  const timestamp = Date.now()
  const user = {
    id: crypto.randomUUID(),
    name: body.name,
    slug: body.slug,
    createdAt: timestamp,
    updatedAt: timestamp
  }

  const query = buildSql(`
    INSERT INTO ‘users’(
      ‘id’,
      ‘name’,
      ‘slug’,
      ‘created_on’,
      ‘updated_on’
      ) VALUES (
      “${user.id}”,
      “${user.name}”,
      “${user.slug}”,
      “${user.createdAt}”,
      “${user.updatedAt}”
    )
  `)

  const result = await pool.query(query)
  pool.end()

  return result
})
```

Notice that we also use `Date.now` to help us to create a timestamp for each new valid user.

5. Import the `userCreate` callback function for the `/users/create` API route in `/src/router.ts`:

```js
// src/router.ts
import userCreate from ‘@/routes/users/create’

router.on(‘POST’, ‘/users/create’, async (req, res) => {
```

```
  const ctx = { req }
  const { data, statusCode } = await userCreate(ctx)
  res.statusCode = statusCode
  res.end(data)
})
```

6. Run the app on the `dev` environment:

```
$ npm run dev
```

7. Add a new user via `curl` on your terminal:

```
$ curl -X POST http://localhost:5000/users/create \
 -H “Content-Type: application/json” \
 -d ‘{“name”: “John”, “slug”: “john”}’
```

You should see the following result on your terminal when a new user is added to the database successfully:

```js
{"affectedRows":1,"insertId":"0","warningStatus":0}
```

You should see UUID and timestamps are included to the new user data in the JSON response on your browser at `localhost:5000/users`, for example:

```json
[{"id":"4a999878-4bd4-4d63-8f02-bf363273bb5a","name":
"John","slug":"john","created_on":"1693318660044","updated_
on":"1693318660044"}]
```

There you go. Now you have the API route for injecting and storing data to the MariaDB data. This means you can send data from your Nuxt app through an HTTP request to the `/users/create` API route. So, you just need a form to collect data on any page and then send the data over. This form is left for you to create on a page in the `/pages/` directory as you should be familiar with form creations in Vue, which will not be covered in Nuxt in this book. However, you can find the form for sending data to the API in the example app in **`/1.nuxt/3.cross-domains/1.connect-native/2.mongodb/`**.

As you can see, we have managed to integrate MariaDB with our Node.js HTTP server and develop the server app separately without having to think about the client app, the Nuxt app, or look at it. At the same time, we can develop our Nuxt app without having to think about the server app. All we need between them is the API routes. The Node.js web app provides them and the Nuxt app consumes them remotely. Furthermore, in this section, you have discovered another data storage for your Nuxt app if you ever want to use an SQL database system and an RDBMS (Relational Database Management System). In the next section, you will find out how to integrate MongoDB, which you have learned in the previous chapter, with the Node.js HTTP server. So, let's get to it!

You can find the example apps for this topic in **`/2.native/2.mysql/`** and **`/1.nuxt/3.cross-domains/1.connect-native/1.mysql/`** in the GitHub repository of this book.

Managing Data with MongoDB

You should have been familiar with MongoDB if you have followed the previous chapters in this book. In *Chapter* 6, *Managing Data with Nitro Server Engine in Nuxt*, you have already learned how to query and fetch data. Remember, we created the server API in the built-in Nitro web server in Nuxt in *Chapter* 6. We built the server APIs and fetched data in the same Nuxt project and app. However, in this section, we are going to separate the server API from the Nuxt app. You will find how easy it is to un-pluck the MongoDB connection and the API routes from the Nuxt project in *Chapter* 6 and migrate them over to the standalone Node.js HTTP server.

Fetching Data from MongoDB: Cross-origin Resource Sharing (CORS)

Assuming you have already created the MongoDB database and injected documents into the database through MongoDB Shell, just as we did in *Chapter* 6. What is left to do now is to add the MongoDB driver in our Node.js HTTP server, establish the database connection, create the API routes, and then fetch the data from the Nuxt app through HTTP requests. So, let's find out in the following steps:

1. Install the MongoDB Node.js driver via `npm` in your project:

```
$ npm i mongodb
```

2. Create a `composables` and a `routes` sub-directories in the `/src/` directory, as well as three `.ts` files in the `/routes/` sub-directory for abstracting the callback function from each API route into these separate files as follows:

```
src
├── composables
│   └── use-mongo.ts
└── routes
    ├── index.ts
    └── users
        ├── index.ts
        └── id.ts
```

3. Create a `.env` file in the project root with the following variables and values for the database and the app:

```bash
// .env
# Set database env variables:
VITE_DB_HOST=mongodb://127.0.0.1:27017
VITE_DB_DBNAME=advanced-nuxtjs-course

# Set app env variables:
VITE_APP_HOST=localhost
VITE_APP_PORT=5000
VITE_CROSS_ORIGIN=http://localhost:3000
```

4. Create a `connect` async function and a `close` function with the MongoDB database details from the `.env` file for connecting to the MongoDB server in `/src/composables/use-mongo.ts`:

```js
// src/composables/use-mongo.ts
```

```
import { MongoClient, ObjectId } from ‘mongodb’

const url = import.meta.env.VITE_DB_HOST
const dbName = import.meta.env.VITE_DB_DBNAME

async function connect () {
  const client = new MongoClient(url)
  await client.connect()
  console.log(‘🚀 Connected successfully to MongoDB server’)

  const db = client.db(dbName)
  return { client, db }
}

function close (client) {
  client.close()
  console.log(‘🚀 Disconnected from MongoDB server’)
}
```

5. Create an exported `default` function containing the `connect` async function and the `close` function, as well as the `ObjectId` function in an object as follows:

```js
// src/composables/use-mongo.ts
...
export default () => {
  return {
    ObjectId,
    connect,
    close
  }
}
```

6. Create a `users` callback function for the `/users` route of our app in `/src/routes/users/index.ts`:

```js
// src/routes/users/index.ts
export default handleCtx(async () => {
  const { connect, close } = useMongo()
  const { client, db } = await connect()
```

```
  const collectionUsers = db.collection('users')
  const docs = await collectionUsers.find().toArray()

  close(client)
  return docs
})
```

Notice that `useMongo` is used to connect to the MongoDB database and find the user documents. We then need to close the connection before returning the found documents.

7. Create a `userById` callback function for the `/users/:id` route of our app in `/src/routes/users/id.ts`:

```js
// src/routes/users/id.ts
export default handleCtx(async ctx => {
  const { connect, close, ObjectId } = useMongo()
  const id = ctx.params.id

  const { client, db } = await connect()
  const collectionUsers = db.collection('users')

  const _id = new ObjectId(id)
  const doc = await collectionUsers.findOne({
    _id
  })

  close(client)
  if (!doc) {
    createError({
      statusCode: 404,
      message: `user with id of "${ctx.params.id}" not found`
    })
  }
  return doc
})
```

Notice that we want to throw a `404` error HTTP response when the requested user is not found in our database.

8. Import the `users` callback function for the `/users` API route in `/src/router.ts`:

```js
// src/router.ts
import users from ‘@/routes/users/index’

router.on(‘GET’, ‘/users’, async (req, res) => {
  const ctx = { req }
  const { data, statusCode } = await users(ctx)
  res.statusCode = statusCode
  res.end(data)
})
```

9. Import the `userById` callback function for the `/users/:id` API route in `/src/router.ts`:

```js
// src/router.ts
import userById from ‘@/routes/users/id’

router.on(‘GET’, ‘/users/:id’, async (req, res, params) => {
  const ctx = { req, params }
  const { data, statusCode } = await userById(ctx)
  res.statusCode = statusCode
  res.end(data)
})
```

10. Run the app on the `dev` environment:

```
$ npm run dev
```

You should see the following JSON response on your browser at `localhost:5000` for the main route of our app:

```json
{“message”:”Hello World!!”}
```

You should see the JSON response of a list of users on your browser on **`localhost:5000/users`** for the **`/users`** API route:

```json
[{“_id”:”64e0fdc9e3939a03c2dac6f2”,”name”:”John”,”slug”:
”john”,”email”:”john@example.com”,”createdAt”:{“$timesta
mp”:”7269088838306234369”}},{“_id”:”64e0fdc9e3939a03
c2dac6f3”,”name”:”Jane”,”slug”:”jane”,”email”:”jane@example.
com”,”createdAt”:{“$timestamp”:”7269088838306234370”}},
{“_id”:”64e0fdc9e3939a03c2dac6f4”,”name”:”Molly”,”slug”:
”molly”,”email”:”molly@example.com”,”createdAt”:
{“$timestamp”:”7269088838306234371”}}]
```

You should see the JSON response of a user on your browser for the **`/users/[id]`** API route, for example, **`localhost:5000/users/64e0fdc9e3939a03c2dac6f2`**:

```json
{“_id”:”64e0fdc9e3939a03c2dac6f2”,”name”:”John”,
”slug”:”john”,”email”:”john@example.com”,”createdAt”:
{“$timestamp”:”7269088838306234369”}}
```

11. Create a **`.env`** file in your Nuxt project root with the following variables and values for the app and the cross-origin API:

```
// .env
APP_BASE_URL=http://localhost:3000
API_BASE_URL=http://localhost:5000
```

Note that **`localhost:3000`** is your Nuxt app, while **`localhost:5000`** is the cross-origin API.

12. Use **`useF3tch`** in the **`<script>`** block to fetch the list of users from the cross-origin API:

```js
// pages/users.vue
<script setup>
const { data: users, error } = await useF3tch(‘/users’)
</script>
```

13. Display the data of each user in the `<template>` block:

```html
// pages/users.vue
<template>
  <error-boundary v-bind:error=”error”>
    <h2>
      Users
    </h2>
    <ul>
      <li v-for=”user in users” v-bind:key=”user._id”>
        <NuxtLink :to=”`/users/${user._id}`”>
          {{ user.name }}
        </NuxtLink>
      </li>
    </ul>
  </error-boundary>
</template>
```

14. Use `useF3tch` in the `<script>` block to fetch a user from the cross-origin API:

```js
// pages/users/[id].vue
<script setup>
const route = useRoute()
const id = route.params.id
const { data: user, error } = await useF3tch(`/users/${id}`)
</script>
```

15. Display the user data in the `<template>` block:

```html
// pages/users/[id].vue
<template>
  <div v-if=”user”>
    <h2>
      {{ user.name }}
    </h2>
    <p>Email:
      {{ user.email }}
    </p>
```

```
    <p>Created On:
      {{ useDate(user.createdAt) }}
    </p>
  </div>
</template>
```

16. Run the app on the `dev` environment:

```
$ npm run dev
```

You should see all the users are fetched from the cross-origin API and displayed successfully on your browser at `localhost:3000/users`. Also, you should see a user is fetched from the cross-origin API and displayed successfully on your browser at `localhost:3000/users/64e0fdc9e3939a03c2dac6f2`, for example.

There you go. You have successfully queried the data from the MongoDB server using the MongoDB driver and created the API route in a standalone Node.js HTTP server for the Nuxt app to fetch data from. Again, the communication between two separate cross-origin apps is possible also because we have CORS enabled on our Node.js HTTP server. Also, you can see that the code in the Node.js HTTP server in this section is almost identical to the code in the Nitro web server in *Chapter 6* for querying data from MongoDB.

As you can see, just like MariaDB in the previous section, we have managed to integrate MongoDB with our Node.js HTTP server and develop the server app separately without having to think about the client app, the Nuxt app, or looki at it. At the same time, we can develop our Nuxt app without having to think about the server app. All we need between them is the API routes. The Node.js web app provides them and the Nuxt app consumes them remotely.

MongoDB is a great and popular choice for a NoSQL database management system, but if you need a real-time NoSQL database management system, you will need to configure MongoDB and it is not easy. However, if you want a real-time NoSQL database management system out of the box, zero-configuration, then RethinkDB might be a better option for you. So, let's find out how you can add RethinkDB to our Node.js HTTP server and turn Nuxt into a real-time app in the next section.

You can find the rest of the CRUD API routes for injecting, updating, and deleting documents for this topic in `/2.native/3.mongodb/` in the GitHub repository of this book. You also can find the rest of the Nuxt pages with forms for injecting, updating, and deleting data through HTTP requests for this topic in `` `/1.nuxt/3.cross-domains/1.connect-native/2.mongodb/` `` in the same GitHub repository of this book.

Managing Real-time Data with RethinkDB

RethinkDB provides change feeds on its database tables out of the box. However, RethinkDB is a database, and by itself alone, it is not sufficient to make our Nuxt app perform in real-time. We will need Socket.IO to help us complete the process of making real-time apps on both the server and client sides. In this section, we will look into these two awesome technologies and merge them with the Node.js HTTP server and the Nuxt app. You will learn to use RethinkDB Query Language (ReQL) to create API routes for querying, injecting, updating, and deleting the RethinkDB database documents. And then, in the end, you will be able to turn your Nuxt app into a real-time app. So, let's find out!

Creating Real-time Nuxt Apps with RethinkDB and Socket.IO: Cross-origin Resource Sharing (CORS)

Similar to MongoDB and MariaDB, if we want to use RethinkDB as the database for our Nuxt app, we will need to install the RethinkDB server on our machine. And then we will need a RethinkDB driver to connect with the RethinkDB server and database. If you are installing the RethinkDB server afresh, you should always use the guide from the RethinkDB official documentation at https://rethinkdb.com/docs/install/. From there, you can choose the official RethinkDB package for your OS, whether it is Ubuntu or MacOS.

It is almost the same with Socket.IO, even though it is not a database system, we will need a Socket.IO driver on the server side and another driver on the client side to work as a bridge to broadcast and receive the change events from the database for our Nuxt app. Assuming that you have successfully installed the RethinkDB server on your machine, you can start creating and manipulating your database, tables, and documents. At the same time, you can broadcast and receive the change events with Socket.IO and the Nuxt app. So, let's find out in the following steps:

1. Install the official RethinkDB client Node.js driver and **`socket.io`** for the server side via **`npm`** in your project:

    ```
    $ npm i rethinkdb
    $ npm i socket.io
    ```

Note that the preceding Node.js packages may change over time, so you should always confirm with their official documentation at https://rethinkdb.com/docs/install-drivers/ and https://socket.io/docs/v4/server-installation/.

2. Create a **`composables`** with a **`use-rethink.ts`** file, a **`routes`** sub-directories with a **`users`** sub-directory, and **`.ts`** files, in the **`/src/`** directory, as follows:

    ```
    src
    ├── composables
    │   └── use-rethink.ts
    └── routes
        ├── index.ts
        └── users
            ├── index.ts
            └── slug.ts
    ```

In the **`/users/`** directory, create the following sub-directories **`.ts`** files for abstracting the callback function from each API route into these separate files:

```
users
├── ...
├── create
│   └── index.ts
├── delete
│   └── index.ts
└── update
    └── index.ts
```

3. Create a `.env` file in the project root with the following variables and values for the database and the app:

````
```bash
// .env
# Set database env variables:
VITE_DB_HOST=localhost
VITE_DB_DBNAME=advanced-nuxtjs-course
VITE_DB_PORT=28015

# Set app env variables:
VITE_APP_HOST=localhost
VITE_APP_PORT=5000
VITE_CROSS_ORIGIN=http://localhost:3000
```
````

4. Create a `connect` async function and a `change` async function with the database details from the `.env` file for connecting to the RethinkDB server in `/src/composables/use-rethink.ts`:

````
```js
// src/composables/use-rethink.ts
import rdb from ‘rethinkdb’

const connect = async () => {
  const connection = await rdb.connect({
    host: import.meta.env.VITE_DB_HOST,
    port: import.meta.env.VITE_DB_PORT,
    db: import.meta.env.VITE_DB_DBNAME
  })
  return connection
}

async function change (io, tableName, eventName) {
  try {
    const connection = await connect()
    const cursor = await rdb.table(tableName)
      .changes()
      .run(connection)

    cursor.each(function (err, row) {
      if (err) {
        throw err
      }
      console.log(JSON.stringify(row, null, 2))
````
````

```js
        io.emit(eventName, row)
      })
    } catch (err) {
      console.error(err)
    }
  }
```

For more information about connecting the RethinkDB server, please visit https://rethinkdb.com/api/javascript/connect/.

5. Create an exported **`default`** function containing the **`connect`** async function and the **`changes`** async function in an object as follows:

```js
// src/composables/use-rethink.ts
...
export default () => {
  return {
    connect,
    change
  }
}
```

6. Create the HTTP production server by integrating with the Socket.IO server and listen to the change feed of the **`users`** table from the RethinkDB database:

```js
// src/app.ts
...
import { Server as SocketServer } from ‘socket.io’
const { change } = useRethink()

if (import.meta.env.PROD) {
  const host = import.meta.env.VITE_APP_HOST || ‘127.0.0.1’
  const port = import.meta.env.VITE_APP_PORT || ‘5000’
  const server = http.createServer(requestListener)

  const io = new SocketServer(server, {
    cors: {
      origin: import.meta.env.VITE_CROSS_ORIGIN
    }
  })
```

```
  change(io, 'users', 'users.changefeeds')

  server.listen(port, () => {
    console.log(`🚀 Server ready at ${host}:${port}`)
  })
}
```

Note that we only start the change feed after built for production. Also, the cross-origin domain must be explicitly defined in the Socket.IO settings. Additionally, you can add the following simple broadcasting and listening block for testing purposes:

```js
// src/app.ts
io.sockets.on('connection', socket => {
  console.log('a user connected: ' + socket.id)

  io.emit('emit.onserver', 'Hi client, what you up to?')
  console.log('Message to client: ' + socket.id)

  socket.on('emit.onclient', message => {
    console.log('Message from client, ' + socket.id + ': ' +
    message)
  })

  socket.on('disconnect', () => {
    console.log('user disconnected: ' + socket.id)
  })
})
```

For using Socket.IO on cross-origin domains, please visit https://socket.io/docs/v4/handling-cors/.

7. Create a `users` callback function for the `/users` route of our app in `/src/routes/users/index.ts`:

```js
// src/routes/users/index.ts
import rdb from 'rethinkdb'

export default ctxHandler(async () => {
```

```
  const { connect } = useRethink()
  const db = await connect()

  const cursor = await rdb.table('users')
    .orderBy(rdb.desc('createdAt'))
    .run(db)
  const docs = await cursor.toArray()
  db.close()

  return docs
})
```

Notice that `useRethink` is used to connect to the RethinkDB database and find the user documents. We then need to close the connection before returning the found documents. Also, `rethinkdb` is imported as `rdb` so that we can use the RethinkDB query language (ReQL) to query the database. You can also add an if-condition block to throw a `500` error with the `createError` util if the table you want to query does not exist (recommended):

```js
const exists = await rdb.tableList().contains('users').
run(db)
if (exists === false) {
  createError({
    statusCode: 500,
    message: '"users" table does not exist'
  })
}
```

For more information on ReQL and the query functions we have used in this step (and the rest of the incoming steps), please visit https://www.rethinkdb.com/docs/guide/javascript/.

8. Create a `userBySlug` callback function for the `/users/:slug` route of our app in `/src/routes/users/slug.ts`:

```js
// src/routes/users/slug.ts
import rdb from 'rethinkdb'

export default ctxHandler(async () => {
```

```
    const { connect } = useRethink()
    const slug = ctx.params.slug
    const db = await connect()

    const searchQuery = {
      slug
    }
    const doc = await rdb.table('users')
      .filter(searchQuery)
      .nth(0)
      .default(null)
      .run(db)
    db.close()

    return doc
  })
  ```
```

Notice that we retrieve the RethinkDB the requested document (user) by using a **`filter`** ReQL command (method/ function), followed by **`nth`** (used to get the specific element in an array) and **`default`** (used to set a default value) commands.

Lastly, we should throw a **`404`** error HTTP response when the requested user is not found in our database right before returning the **`doc`** result:

```
  ```js
  if (!doc) {
    createError({
      statusCode: 404,
      message: `User "${slug}" not found`
    })
  }
  ```
```

For more information about the **`filter`** ReQL command, please visit https://rethinkdb.com/api/javascript/filter/; https://rethinkdb.com/api/javascript/nth for **`nth`** and https://rethinkdb.com/api/ruby/default/#wrapper for **`default`**.

9. Create a **`userCreate`** callback function for the **`/users/create`** route of our app in **`/src/routes/users/create/index.ts`**:

```
  ```js
  // src/routes/users/create/index.ts
```

```js
import rdb from ‘rethinkdb’

export default ctxHandler(async ctx => {
  const { connect } = useRethink()
  const body = await normalizeBody(ctx.req)

  const db = await connect()
  const timestamp = Date.now()
  const options = {
    name: body.name,
    slug: body.slug,
    createdAt: timestamp
  }

  const doc = await rdb.table(‘users’)
    .insert(options, { returnChanges: true })
    .run(db)
  db.close()

  return doc
})
```

Notice that we use an **`insert`** ReQL command to insert the new document. But before that, we should also check if the provided **`slug`** is taken after the **`body`** constant:

```js
const searchQuery = {
  slug: body.slug
}
const found = await rdb.table(‘users’)
  .filter(searchQuery)
  .nth(0)
  .default(null)
  .run(db)

if (found) {
  createError({
    statusCode: 400,
    message: `slug “${body.slug}” has been taken`
  })
}
```

Notice that the preceding query is the same as querying a requested document in the previous step. Lastly, we should throw a `500` if the injection fails before returning the `doc` result:

```js
if (doc.inserted !== 1) {
  createError({
    statusCode: 500,
    message: `Add user failed`
  })
}
```

For more information about inserting documents in RethinkDB, please visit https://rethinkdb.com/api/javascript/insert.

Also, note that the `inject`, `update`, `delete`, and `replace` commands in RethinkDB have a `returnChanges` option for us to return a **change** array consisting of old and new values on the document whether it is being injected, updated, or deleted. These old and new values then can be used on the client app.

10. Create a `userDeleteById` callback function for the `/users/delete/:id` route of our app in `/src/routes/users/delete/index.ts`:

```js
// src/routes/users/delete/index.ts
import rdb from 'rethinkdb'

export default ctxHandler(async ctx => {
  const { connect } = useRethink()
  const id = ctx.params.id
  const db = await connect()

  const doc = await rdb.table('users')
    .get(id)
    .delete()
    .run(db)
  db.close()

  return doc
})
```

Notice that we use a `get` and a `delete` ReQL commands to get the document first and then delete it. But before that, we should also check if the user exists or not by using the `get` command with an ID:

```js
const found = await rdb.table(‘users’)
  .get(id)
  .run(db)
if (!found) {
  createError({
    statusCode: 404,
    message: `User “${id}” does not exist`
  })
}
```

Lastly, we should throw a `500` if the deletion fails before returning the `doc` result:

```js
if (doc.deleted !== 1) {
  createError({
    statusCode: 500,
    message: `Delete user failed`
  })
}
```

For more information about deleting documents in RethinkDB, please visit https://rethinkdb.com/api/javascript/delete/. For more information about selecting a document using the `get` command, please visit https://rethinkdb.com/api/java/get/#wrapper.

11. Create a `userUpdateById` callback function for the `/users/update/:id` route of our app in `/src/routes/users/update/index.ts`:

```js
// src/routes/users/update/index.ts
import rdb from ‘rethinkdb’

export default ctxHandler(async ctx => {
  const { connect } = useRethink()
  const id = ctx.params.id
  const body = await normalizeBody(ctx.req)
  const db = await connect()
```

```
    const currentDocument = await rdb.table('users')
      .get(id)
      .run(db)

    const timestamp = Date.now()
    const updateQuery = {
      name: body.name,
      slug: body.slug,
      updatedAt: timestamp
    }

    const options = { ...currentDocument, ...updateQuery }
    const doc = await rdb.table('users')
      .get(id)
      .update(options, { returnChanges: true })
      .run(db)
    db.close()

    return doc
  })
```

Notice that we retrieve the data of the existing document first using the `get` command to merge the existing data with the updated data, and then update the document with an `update` ReQL command. But before that, we should also check to make sure that the new provided `slug` is not taken by other existing documents by filtering the documents (`eq` as in **equal)** except the document we want to update (`ne` as in **not equal**). If it is taken, we want to throw a `400` error:

```js
const found = await rdb.table('users')
  .filter(
    rdb.row('slug').eq(body.slug)
  )
  .filter(
    rdb.row('id').ne(id)
  )
  .nth(0)
  .default(null)
  .run(db)
if (found) {
  createError({
    statusCode: 400,
    message: `slug "${body.slug}" has been taken`
  })
```

```
}
```

Lastly, we should throw a `500` if the update fails before returning the `doc` result:

```js
if (doc.replaced !== 1) {
  createError({
    statusCode: 500,
    message: `Update user failed`
  })
}
```

For more information about updating documents in RethinkDB, please visit https://rethinkdb.com/api/javascript/update/; https://rethinkdb.com/api/java/eq/#wrapper for `eq` and https://rethinkdb.com/api/javascript/ne/#wrapper for `ne`.

12. Import the `users` callback function for the `/users` API route in `/src/router.ts`:

```js
// src/router.ts
import users from '@/routes/users/index'

router.on('GET', '/users', async (req, res) => {
  const ctx = { req }
  const { data, statusCode } = await users(ctx)
  res.statusCode = statusCode
  res.end(data)
})
```

13. Import the `userBySlug` callback function for the `/users/:slug` API route in `/src/router.ts`:

```js
// src/router.ts
import userBySlug from '@/routes/users/slug'

router.on('GET', '/users/:slug', async (req, res, params) => {
  const ctx = { req, params }
```

```js
  const { data, statusCode } = await userBySlug(ctx)
  res.statusCode = statusCode
  res.end(data)
})
```

14. Import the **`userCreate`** callback function for the **`/users/create`** API route in **`/src/router.ts`**:

```js
// src/router.ts
import userCreate from ‘@/routes/users/create’

router.on(‘POST’, ‘/users/create’, async (req, res) => {
  const ctx = { req }
  const { data, statusCode } = await userCreate(ctx)
  res.statusCode = statusCode
  res.end(data)
})
```

15. Import the **`userDeleteById`** callback function for the **`/users/delete/:id`** API route in **`/src/router.ts`**:

```js
// src/router.ts
import userDeleteById from ‘@/routes/users/delete’

router.on(‘DELETE’, ‘/users/delete/:id’, async (req, res,
params) => {
  const ctx = { req, params }
  const { data, statusCode } = await userDeleteById(ctx)
  res.statusCode = statusCode
  res.end(data)
})
```

16. Import the **`userUpdateById`** callback function for the **`/users/update/:id`** API route in **`/src/router.ts`**:

```js
// src/router.ts
import userUpdateById from ‘@/routes/users/update’
```

```
router.on('PUT', '/users/update/:id', async (req, res,
params) => {
  const ctx = { req, params }
  const { data, statusCode } = await userUpdateById(ctx)
  res.statusCode = statusCode
  res.end(data)
})
```

17. Run the app on the `dev` environment for development:

```
$ npm run dev
```

You should see the following JSON response on your browser at `localhost:5000` for the main route of our app:

```json
{"message":"Hello World!!"}
```

You should see an empty **[]** JSON response on `localhost:5000/users` for the `/users` API route when the database is started afresh with no user in the `users` table yet.

18. Build and start the app for broadcasting to and listening on the client for the `users` table:

```
$ npm run build
$ npm run start
```

If you insert a new user to the database on the `/users/create` API route with `curl` on a separate terminal as follows:

```
$ curl -X POST http://localhost:5000/users/create \
 -H "Content-Type: application/json" \
 -d '{"name": "John", "slug": "john"}'
```

You should get the following result on your second terminal if the injection is successful:

```js
{“changes”:[{“new_val”:{“createdAt”:1693486800077,”id”:
”f9a95fad-9413-4a4c-8fb3-99b53fc15812”,”name”:”John”,”slug”:
”john”},”old_val”:null}],”deleted”:0,”errors”:0,”generated_
keys”:[“f9a95fad-9413-4a4c-8fb3-99b53fc15812”],”inserted”:1,”
replaced”:0,”skipped”:0,”unchanged”:0}
```

You should get the following live change feed to appear on your first terminal:

```js
{
  “new_val”: {
    “createdAt”: 1693486800077,
    “id”: “f9a95fad-9413-4a4c-8fb3-99b53fc15812”,
    “name”: “John”,
    “slug”: “john”
  },
  “old_val”: null
}
```

Then, you should see the JSON response of a list of users on your browser on **`localhost:5000/users`** for the **`/users`** API route:

```json
[{“createdAt”:1693486800077,”id”:”f9a95fad-9413-4a4c-8fb3-99b
53fc15812”,”name”:”John”,”slug”:”john”}]
```

You should see the JSON response of a user on your browser for the **`/users/:slug`** API route, for example, **`localhost:5000/users/john`**:

```json
{“createdAt”:1693486800077,”id”:”f9a95fad-9413-4a4c-8fb3-99b5
3fc15812”,”name”:”John”,”slug”:”john”}
```

19. Install `socket.io` for the client side via `npm` in your Nuxt project:

```
$ npm i socket.io-client
```

Note that the Socket.IO client Node.js packages may change over time, so you should always confirm with their official documentation at https://socket.io/docs/v4/client-installation/.

20. Create a `.env` file in your Nuxt project root with the following variables and values for the app and the cross-origin API:

```
// .env
APP_BASE_URL=http://localhost:3000
API_BASE_URL=http://localhost:5000
```

Note that `localhost:3000` is your Nuxt app, while `localhost:5000` is the cross-origin API.

21. Use `useF3tch` in the `<script>` block to fetch the list of users from the cross-origin API:

```js
// pages/users.vue
<script setup>
const { data: users, error } = await useF3tch(‘/users’)
</script>
```

22. Display the data of each user in the `<template>` block:

```html
// pages/users.vue
<template>
  <error-boundary v-bind:error=”error”>
    <h2>
      Users
    </h2>
    <ul>
      <li v-for=”user in users” v-bind:key=”user.id”>
```

```
      {{ user.name }}
    </li>
  </ul>
</error-boundary>
</template>
```

23. Add the following lines for listening on the change feed on the **`users`** table from the RethinkDB database and server:

```js
// pages/users.vue
<script setup>
import io from 'socket.io-client'
const runtimeConfig = useRuntimeConfig()
const socket = io(runtimeConfig.public['apiBaseUrl'])
...
socket.on('users.changefeeds', data => {
  if (data.new_val === undefined && data.old_val === undefined) {
    return
  }

  if(data.old_val === null && data.new_val !== null) {
    users.value.unshift(data.new_val)
  }

  if(data.new_val === null && data.old_val !== null) {
    var id = data.old_val.id
    var index = users.value.map(el => {
      return el.id
    }).indexOf(id)
    users.value.splice(index, 1)
  }

  if(data.new_val !== null && data.old_val !== null) {
    var id = data.new_val.id
    var index = users.value.findIndex(item => item.id === id)
    users.value.splice(index, 1, data.new_val)
  }
})
</script>
```

In the preceding code, when we receive data from the server, we just use **`unshift`** to prepend the new user at the beginning of the array; **`splice`**, `map`, and `indexOf` to pop off the deleted user; `splice` and `findIndex` for the updated user. These are just JavaScript native methods.

24. Run the app on the `dev` environment:

```
$ npm run dev
```

You should see all the users are fetched from the cross-origin API and displayed successfully on your browser at `localhost:3000/users`. If you insert a new user to the database on the `localhost:5000/users/create` API route with `curl` on a separate terminal as follows:

```
$ curl -X POST http://localhost:5000/users/create \
 -H “Content-Type: application/json” \
 -d ‘{“name”: “Jane”, “slug”: “jane”}’
```

You should see the newly added user appear on the user list at `localhost:3000/users` immediately without refreshing your browser. It is the same with the event of updating a user on the `localhost:5000/users/update/:id` API route with `curl` on the separate terminal. For example:

```
    $ curl -X PUT http://localhost:5000/users/update/f9a95
fad-9413-4a4c-8fb3-99b53fc15812 \
     -H “Content-Type: application/json” \
     -d ‘{“name”: “Johnny”, “slug”: “john”}’
```

You should see the targeted user is updated on the user list at `localhost:3000/users` immediately without refreshing your browser. Lastly, it is also the same with the event of deleting a user on the `localhost:5000/users/delete/:id` API route with `curl` on the separate terminal. For example:

```
    $ curl -X DELETE http://localhost:5000/users/delete/f9a95
fad-9413-4a4c-8fb3-99b53fc15812
```

You should see the deleted user disappear on the user list at `` `localhost:3000/users` `` immediately without refreshing your browser.

There you go. You have successfully created a real-time Nuxt app with RethinkDB and Socket.IO just in a number of preceding steps and lines. You have managed to inject, query, update, and delete the data in the RethinkDB database through the standalone Node.js HTTP server. On top of that, you have managed to listen to the change event of injecting, updating, and deleting data in real-time. And then with the help of Socket.IO, you are able to broadcast the real-time events to be picked up by the Nuxt app. Well done!

You may have noticed that we also can use RethinkDB as a non-real-time database management system if we just ignore the change feeds from RethinkDB. We can remove the Socket.IO layer from our Node.js HTTP server and Nuxt app. And also remove the `` `returnChanges` `` option in the `` `inject` ``, `` `update` ``, `` `delete` ``, and `` `replace` `` ReQL commands. Then, we can use RethinkDB as a standard data storage. So, we can think of RethinkDB as a **win-win** database system. We can use its real-time feature anytime out of the box. We can also use it as a standard database anytime. It is the best of both worlds and also it is always good to know there is another database system available out there for us when we need one.

You can find the example apps for this topic in `` `/2.native/4.rethinkdb/` `` and `` `/1.nuxt/3.cross-domains/1.connect-native/3.rethinkdb/` `` in the GitHub repository of this book.

Conclusion

In this chapter, you have managed to separate server APIs from your Nuxt project and Nuxt app by creating a standalone HMR Node.js HTTP server with the Node.js HTTP module, Vite, `` `vite-plugin-node` ``, and `` `find-my-way` ``. Also, you have used the Node.js File System module to turn your Node.js HTTP server into a file server for serving assets, such as images and text files. You have also learned to enable CORS in the Node.js HTTP server through the setting in the HTTP response object, in order to allow the Nuxt app to connect remotely and fetch data on the HTTP requests. With the standalone Node.js HTTP server, you have been able to manage data with MySQL database, MongoDB database, and RethinkDB for your Nuxt app. Finally, you have created a real-time Nuxt app with RethinkDB, Socket.IO, and the HMR Node.js app.

In the next chapter, you will learn to manage data for your Nuxt app in a different language – PHP. You will work with WordPress REST API and Carbon Fields (WordPress custom fields library) to create a server API to serve data for your Nuxt app. Also, you will create custom fields with Carbon Fields to manage the SEO and Open Graph meta information dynamically and create a framework-agnostic PHP app that complies with PHP Standards Recommendations (PSR) to manage data for your Nuxt app.

CHAPTER 8

Managing Database with PHP Apps for Nuxt

Introduction

Welcome to *Chapter* 8. In this chapter, you will use WordPress to manage data for your Nuxt app. You will use the WordPress REST API layer to create custom API routes for your Nuxt app to fetch data from. You will create a PHP app that implements PHP Standards Recommendations (PSR) to manage data for your Nuxt app. Lastly, you will learn to manage the SEO and Open Graph metadata using WordPress and Carbon Fields. You will also learn to use Carbon Fields to create custom fields in WordPress for managing the metadata.

Structure

The topics that will be covered in this chapter are as follows:

- Managing Data with WordPress
- Managing Data with PHP PSR Apps
- Managing Metadata with WordPress for SEO and Open Graph

Managing Data with WordPress

Besides using Node.js and JavaScript to create a server app, you may want to use other server-side scripting languages, such as PHP. In most cases, you will need a content management system (CMS) to manage your data. One of the best

CMS options today in the PHP world is WordPress. Even though WordPress is a general-purpose CMS that can help you to build an entire website with layouts and pages just like those in Nuxt apps, WordPress also shipped with a REST API layer that you can use to create API routes to interact with the database, such as fetching data of a page. So, in this section, we are going to leverage the WordPress REST API for managing the data for Nuxt apps. Let's find out!

Creating Headless WordPress REST APIs

Creating a custom REST API with WordPress is very easy. You just need to use an `add_action` function, a `rest_api_init` hook, and a callback. In this section, we will use them to create a REST API for us to fetch the `page` type post from the database and feed the page in our Nuxt app. Besides the `page` type post, you will also learn to create a custom post type and its REST API for our Nuxt app. So, let's find out in the following steps:

1. Create a new theme called `headlessapi-v1` in your WordPress `/themes/` directory with the following files and an `inc` folder:

```
themes
└── headlessapi-v1
    ├── index.php
    ├── functions.php
    ├── header.php
    ├── footer.php
    └── inc
```

2. Create a `custom-post-types` folder with a `project.php` file in the `/inc/` directory:

```
inc
├── ...
└── custom-post-types
    └── project.php
```

3. Create an `` `apis` `` folder with the following files and sub-folders in the `` `/inc/` `` directory:

```
inc
├── ...
└── apis
    ├── commons.php
    ├── page
    │   └── get
    │       └── one.php
    └── project
        ├── get
        │   └── one.php
        └── post
            └── many.php
```

4. Open the HTML tags with the WordPress functions in `` `/headlessapi-v1/header.php` `` as follows:

```php
// headlessapi-v1/header.php
<!doctype html>
<html <?php language_attributes(); ?>>
<head>
  <meta charset="<?php bloginfo( 'charset' ); ?>" />
  <meta name="viewport" content="width=device-width, ini-
  tial-scale=1" />
  <?php wp_head(); ?>
</head>

<body <?php body_class(); ?>>
<?php wp_body_open(); ?>
```

5. Close the HTML tags with a `` `wp_footer` `` WordPress function in `` `/headlessapi-v1/footer.php` `` as follows:

```php
// headlessapi-v1/footer.php
<?php wp_footer(); ?>
</body>
```

```
</html>
```

6. Create a **Hello World** greeting page with the WordPress functions in **`/headlessapi-v1/index.php`** as follows:

```php
// headlessapi-v1/index.php
get_header(); ?>

<main>
  <h1><?php the_title(); ?></h1>
  <p>Hello World</p>
</main>

<?php get_footer();
```

7. Use **`add_action`** and **`register_post_type`** WordPress functions to create and register a custom **`project`** post type in **`/headlessapi-v1/inc/custom-post-types/project.php`**:

```php
// headlessapi-v1/inc/custom-post-types/project.php
add_action(‘init’, ‘create_project_post_type’);
function create_project_post_type () {
    $args = [
        ‘labels’ => [
            ‘name’ => __(‘Project (Pages)’),
            ‘singular_name’ => __(‘Project’),
            ‘all_items’ => ‘All Projects’
        ],
        ‘public’ => true,
        ‘show_ui’ => true,
        ‘capability_type’ => ‘page’,
        ‘hierarchical’ => true,
        ‘query_var’ => true,
        ‘menu_icon’ => ‘dashicons-star-filled’,
        ‘supports’ => [
            ‘title’,
            ‘editor’,
            ‘excerpt’,
            ‘thumbnail’,
            ‘page-attributes’,
        ]
```

```
        ];
        register_post_type(‘project’, $args);
    }
```

8. Use **`add_action`** and **`register_taxonomy`** WordPress functions to create and register a custom **`project-category`** taxonomy for **`project`** type pages only in **`/headlessapi-v1/inc/custom-post-types/project.php`**:

    ```php
    // headlessapi-v1/inc/custom-post-types/project.php
    add_action(‘init’, ‘create_project_categories’);
    function create_project_categories() {
        $args = [
            ‘label’ => __(‘Categories’),
            ‘has_archive’ =>  true,
            ‘hierarchical’ => true,
            ‘rewrite’ => [
                ‘slug’ => ‘project’,
                ‘with_front’ => false
            ],
        ];
        $postTypes = [‘project’];
        $taxonomy = ‘project-category’;
        register_taxonomy($taxonomy, $postTypes, $args);
    }
    ```

This is optional but good to have it to allow **`project`** type pages to be queried through specific taxonomies.

9. Create a global prefix namespace for all your API endpoints in **`/headlessapi-v1/inc/apis/commons.php`**:

    ```php
    // headlessapi-v1/inc/apis/commons.php
    $namespace = ‘api/v1/’;
    ```

10. Create a **`/wp-json/api/v1/page/[slug]`** API endpoint with **`add_action`** and **`register_rest_route`** WordPress functions to query single **`page`** type pages in **`/headlessapi-v1/inc/apis/page/get/one.php`**:

```php
// headlessapi-v1/inc/apis/page/get/one.php
add_action('rest_api_init', function () use ($namespace) {
    $route = 'page/(?P<slug>[a-zA-Z0-9-]+)';
    $args = [
        'methods' => 'GET',
        'callback' => 'fetch_page',
    ];
    register_rest_route($namespace, $route, $args);
});

function fetch_page($data) {
    $post = get_page_by_path($data['slug'], OBJECT, 'page');
    if (!count((array)$post)) {
        return [];
    }

    $post->featured_image = get_the_post_thumbnail_url
    ($post->ID);
    return $post;
}
```

Notice that we use `**get_page_by_path**` and `**get_the_post_thumbnail_url**` WordPress functions in our **fetch_page** function to help us to query single `**page**` type pages and their thumbnail images.

11. Create a `**/wp-json/api/v1/projects**` API endpoint with `**add_action**` and `**register_rest_route**` WordPress functions to query a list of `**project**` type pages in `**/headlessapi-v1/inc/apis/project/post/many.php**`:

```php
// headlessapi-v1/inc/apis/project/post/many.php
add_action('rest_api_init', function () use ($namespace) {
    $route = 'projects/';
    $args = [
        'methods' => 'POST',
        'callback' => 'fetch_projects',
    ];
    register_rest_route($namespace, $route, $args);
});

function fetch_projects($data) {
    $paged = $data['page_number'] ? $data['page_number'] : 1;
    $posts_per_page = $data['posts_per_page'] ? $data['posts_
```

```
    per_page'] : 6;
    $count_only = $data['count_only'] ? $data['count_only'] :
    false;
    $post_type = 'project';

    $args = [
        'post_type' => $post_type,
        'post_status' => ['publish'],
        'posts_per_page' => $posts_per_page,
        'paged' => $paged,
        'orderby' => 'date'
    ];
    $posts = get_posts($args);
    if (empty($posts)) {
        return [];
    }

    $total = wp_count_posts($post_type);
    if ($count_only) {
        return $total->publish;
    }
    $total_max_pages = ceil($total->publish / $posts_per_
    page);
    foreach ($posts as &$post) {
        $post->thumbnail = get_the_post_thumbnail_url
        ($post->ID, $size = 'thumbnail');
        $post->categories = get_the_terms($post->ID,
        'project-category');
    }

    return [
        'items' => $posts,
        'total_pages' => $total_max_pages,
        'current_page' => (int) $paged,
        'next_page' => (int) $paged === (int) $total_max_
        pages ? null : $paged + 1,
        'prev_page' => (int) $paged === 1 ? null
        : $paged - 1,
    ];
}
```

Notice that we use `**get_posts**`, `**wp_count_posts**`, `**get_the_post_thumbnail_url**`, and `**get_the_terms**` WordPress functions in our `**fetch_projects**` function to help us to query lists of `**project**` type pages, their thumbnail images, and their categories/taxonomies. Also, we use a `ceil` PHP function to help us compute the information for creating a pagination.

12. Create a `/wp-json/api/v1/project/[slug]` API endpoint with `add_action` and `register_rest_route` WordPress functions to query single `project` type pages in `/headlessapi-v1/inc/apis/project/get/one.php`:

```php
// headlessapi-v1/inc/apis/project/get/one.php
add_action(‘rest_api_init’, function () use ($namespace) {
    $route = ‘project/(?P<slug>[a-zA-Z0-9-]+)’;
    $args = [
        ‘methods’ => ‘GET’,
        ‘callback’ => ‘fetch_project’,
    ];
    register_rest_route($namespace, $route, $args);
});

function fetch_project($data) {
    $post = get_page_by_path($data[‘slug’], OBJECT,
    ‘project’);

    if (!count((array)$post)) {
        return [];
    }

    $post->post_content = wpautop($post->post_content);
    $post->categories = get_the_terms($post->ID,
    ‘project-category’);

    return $post;
}
```

Notice that we use `get_page_by_path`, `wpautop`, and `get_the_terms` WordPress functions in our `fetch_project` function to help us to query single project pages and their categories/ taxonomies.

13. Include all the files of your custom post types and API endpoints in `/headlessapi-v1/functions.php`:

```php
// headlessapi-v1/functions.php
...
// Include custom post types.
```

```
include 'inc/custom-post-type/project.php';

// Include APIs.
include 'inc/apis/commons.php';
include 'inc/apis/project/post/many.php';
include 'inc/apis/project/get/one.php';
include 'inc/apis/page/get/one.php';
```

14. Run the WordPress app with the PHP built-in web server for development at `` `0.0.0.0:4000` ``:

```
$ cd /path/to/your/wordpress/
$ php -S 0.0.0.0:4000
```

You should see the `` `Hello World` `` greeting page `` `localhost:5000` `` on your browser as follows:

```
Home
Hello World
```

You should see the following JSON response on `` `/wp-json/api/v1/page/[slug]` `` on your browser, for example, `` `/wp-json/api/v1/page/about` ``:

```json
{"ID":179,"post_author":"1","post_date":"2022-03-10
12:42:34","post_date_gmt":"2022-03-10 12:42:34","post_
content":"About Lorem ipsum dolor sit amet, consectetur
adipiscing elit, sed do eiusmod tempor incididunt ut labore et
dolore magna aliqua. Ut enim ad minim veniam, quis
nostrud exercitation ullamco laboris nisi ut aliquip ex ea
commodo consequat. Duis aute irure dolor in reprehenderit in
voluptate velit esse cillum dolore eu fugiat nulla pariatur.
 Excepteur sint occaecat cupidatat non proident, sunt in
culpa qui officia deserunt mollit anim id est laborum.","post_
title":"About","post_excerpt":"","post_status":
"publish","comment_status":"closed","ping_status":
"closed","post_password":"","post_name":"about",
"to_ping":"","pinged":"","post_modified":"2022-07-23
18:42:09","post_modified_gmt":"2022-07-23 17:42:09","post_
```

~~~~
content_filtered”:””,”post_parent”:0,”guid”:”http:\/\/
localhost:4000\/?page_id=179”,”menu_order”:0,”post_
type”:”page”,”post_mime_type”:””,”comment_count”:”0”,
”filter”:”raw”,”featured_image”:”http:\/\/localhost:4000\/
wp-content\/uploads\/2022\/03\/Whitsands-Bay-03.jpg”}
    ```
~~~~


Open a new terminal and query a list of project pages on `/wp-json/api/v1/projects`:

~~~~
    ```
    curl -d “page_number=1&posts_per_page=6” -X POST
http://localhost:4000/wp-json/api/v1/projects
    ```
~~~~

You should see the following JSON response on your terminal:


~~~~
    ```json
    {“items”:[{“ID”:99,”post_author”:”1”,”post_date”
:”2022-03-08 14:12:06”,”post_date_gmt”:
”2022-03-08 14:12:06”,”post_content”:”hello world”,
”post_title”:”Project Lorem ipsum dolor sit consectetuer
10”,”post_excerpt”:””,”post_status”:”publish”,
”comment_status”:”open”,”ping_status”:”closed”,”post_
password”:””,”post_name”:”project-lorem-ipsum-dolor-sit-consec-
tetuer-10”,”to_ping”:””,”pinged”:””,”post_modified”:”2023-02-16
07:14:21”,”post_modified_gmt”:”2023-02-16 07:14:21”,”post_
content_filtered”:””,”post_parent”:0,”guid”:”http:\/\/
localhost:4000\/?post_type=project&#038;p=99”,”menu_
order”:0,”post_type”:”project”,”post_mime_type”:””,”comment_
count”:”0”,”filter”:”raw”,”excerpt”:”<p>Excerpt 10 Lorem ipsum
dolor sitamet, consectetur adipiscing elit, sed do eiusmod
tempor incididunt utlabore et dolore magna aliqua.<\/
p>\n”,”thumbnail”:”http:\/\/localhost:4000\/wp-content\/uploa
ds\/2022\/03\/122117647_642328129764202_7538735420254885246_
n-1-150x150.jpeg”,”categories”:false},...],”total_pages”:2,
”current_page”:1,”next_page”:2,”prev_page”:null}
    ```
~~~~


Lastly, you should see the following example JSON response on `/wp-json/api/v1/project/[slug]` on your browser, for example, `/wp-json/api/v1/project/project-lorem-ipsum-dolor-sit-consectetuer-10`:

```
```json
{"ID":99,"post_author":"1","post_date":"2022-03-08 14:12:06","post_date_gmt":"2022-03-08 14:12:06","post_content":"<p>hello world<\/p>\n","post_title":"Project Lorem ipsum dolor sit consectetuer 10","post_excerpt":"","post_status":"publish","comment_status":"open","ping_status":"closed","post_password":"","post_name":"project-lorem-ipsum-dolor-sit-consectetuer-10","to_ping":"","pinged":"","post_modified":"2023-02-16 07:14:21","post_modified_gmt":"2023-02-16 07:14:21","post_content_filtered":"","post_parent":0,"guid":"http:\/\/localhost:4000\/?post_type=project&p=99","menu_order":0,"post_type":"project","post_mime_type":"","comment_count":"0","filter":"raw","categories":false}
```
```

There you go. You have made use of WordPress to create REST APIs for us to fetch data from the database as JSON objects. You can use WordPress to manage your data and assets, such as images, without having to create a CMS on your own to support your Nuxt apps. Now, let's find out how you can use the REST APIs you have created in your Nuxt app in the next section.

# Connecting Nuxt Apps with WordPress REST APIs

We have the API routes ready. All we need to do is create pages in the Nuxt app to consume these APIs. We will reuse some of the code you have learned in the previous chapter, Managing Data with Node.js Apps for Nuxt, notably the `` `useF3tch` `` custom fetch composable. You will see our Nuxt app doesn't need to know what server-side app we used to manage our data. And we also don't need to worry about the `` `/server/` `` directory getting bloated over time once we have plucked it off our Nuxt project. Let's connect your Nuxt app with the WordPress REST APIs in the following steps:

1. Create the following sub-folders and Vue pages in the `` `/pages/` `` directory:

```
```
pages
├── index.php
├── projects.vue
└── projects
    ├── index.vue
    ├── [slug].vue
```
```

```
    └── pages
        └── [number].vue
```

2. Create a `projects` sub-folder with an `items-with-pager.vue` component in the `/components/` directory:

    ```
    components
    ├── ...
    └── projects
        └── items-with-pager.vue
    ```

3. Create a `.env` file in your Nuxt project root with the following variables and values for the app and the cross-origin API:

    ```
    // .env
    APP_BASE_URL=http://localhost:3000
    API_BASE_URL=http://localhost:4000
    ```

Note that `localhost:3000` is your Nuxt app, while `localhost:4000` is the cross-origin API (WordPress).

4. Use `useF3tch` in the `<script>` block to fetch the list of project pages from the cross-origin WordPress API in `/components/projects/items-with-pager.vue`:

    ```js
    // components/projects/items-with-pager.vue
    <script setup>
    const route = useRoute()
    const number = route.params.number
    const query = {
      posts_per_page: 6,
      page_number: number === undefined ? 1 : parseInt(number)
    }
    const { data, refresh, error } = await useF3tch('/wp-json/
    api/v1/projects/', {
      method: 'POST',
      body: query
    })
    ```

````
refresh()
</script>
```
````

Notice that we use the **`useF3tch`** custom fetch composable that you have learned in *Chapter 7: Managing Data with Node.js Apps for Nuxt*. Also, note that a **`refresh`** function must be used to refresh the data during data fetching each time; otherwise, the data on the next pages will always stay the same. For more information on refreshing data during data fetching, please visit https://nuxt.com/docs/getting-started/data-fetching#refreshing-data.

5. Display the data of each project and create the pagination navigation in the **`&lt;template&gt;`** block:

````
```html
// components/projects/items-with-pager.vue
<template>
  <div v-if=”data”>
    <ul>
      <li v-if=”data.prev_page”>
        <NuxtLink :to=”’/projects/pages/’ + data.prev_page”>
          Previous
        </NuxtLink>
      </li>
      <li>
        <p v-if=”data.current_page && data.total_pages”>
          {{ data.current_page }} of {{ data.total_pages }}
        </p>
      </li>
      <li v-if=”data.next_page”>
        <NuxtLink :to=”’/projects/pages/’ + data.next_page”>
          Next
        </NuxtLink>
      </li>
    </ul>
    <ul>
      <li v-for=”post in data.items” :key=”post.ID”>
        <h3>
          <NuxtLink :to=”`/projects/${post.post_name}`”>
            {{ post.post_title }}
          </NuxtLink>
        </h3>
        <div
          v-html=”post.excerpt”
        />
````

```
          <img
            :alt=”post.post_title”
            :src=”useAsset(post.thumbnail)”
          />
        </li>
      </ul>
    </div>
</template>
```

6. Use `useF3tch` in the `<script>` block to fetch the Home page data from **the** `/wp-json/api/v1/page/home` API endpoint:

```js
// pages/index.vue
<script setup>
const { data: post } = await useF3tch(`/wp-json/api/v1/page/
home`)
</script>
```

7. Display the data in the `<template>` block if you want to; otherwise, we can just print a `Hello World` static message:

```html
// pages/index.vue
<template>
  <p>
    Hello World!
  </p>
</template>
```

8. Fetch the `Projects` page data in the `<script>` block from `/wp-json/api/v1/page/projects`:

```js
// pages/projects.vue
<script setup>
const route = useRoute()
const { data: post, error } = await useF3tch(`/wp-json/api/
v1/page/projects`)
</script>
```

9. Display the data in the **`<template>`** block if you want to; otherwise, we can just print a **`Projects`** heading:

```html
// pages/projects.vue
<template>
  <div v-if=”!error”>
    <h2 v-if=”!route.params.slug”>
      Projects
    </h2>
    <NuxtPage :page-key=”route.path” />
  </div>
</template>
```

Notice that we use a **`<NuxtPage>`** component to create a children's page in this **Projects** page.

10. Use the **`<projects-items-with-pager>`** component to fetch and display the list of project pages in the **`<template>`** block in **`/pages/projects/index.vue`**:

```html
// pages/projects/index.vue
<template>
  <projects-items-with-pager />
</template>
```

11. Reuse the **`<projects-items-with-pager>`** component to fetch and display the list of project pages in the **`<template>`** block in **`pages/projects/pages/[number].vue`**:

```html
// pages/projects/pages/[number].vue
<template>
  <projects-items-with-pager />
</template>
```

12. Fetch single project pages with `useF3tch` in the `<script>` block from the cross-origin API:

```js
// pages/projects/[slug].vue
<script setup>
const route = useRoute()
const slug = route.params.slug
const { data: post, error } = await useF3tch(`/wp-json/api/
v1/project/${slug}`)
</script>
```

13. Display the data in the `<template>` block:

```html
// pages/projects/[slug].vue
<template>
  <div v-if=”post”>
    <h2>
      {{ post.post_title }}
    </h2>
    <div
      v-html=”post.post_content”
    />
  </div>
</template>
```

14. Run the Nuxt app on the `dev` environment:

```
$ npm run dev
```

You should get a list of projects fetched from the cross-origin API and displayed successfully on your browser at `localhost:3000/projects`. If you click the Next button, you should see your current URL is changed to `localhost:3000/projects/pages/2` and the second list of projects is fetched successfully. You can click to see individual projects, for example, `localhost:3000/projects/sample-12`, and you should see the data of this page is fetched successfully from your WordPress site.

There you go. You have connected the Nuxt app with WordPress just through the `` `.env` `` file in the Nuxt project and the REST APIs from WordPress. By doing this, we can keep our Nuxt project thin and lightweight to make future maintenance easier.

Out in the real world in a large project, we can't build a website or app with Nuxt alone without a database and a CMS to manage the data for our Nuxt app. WordPress' CMS provides everything we need out of the box to manage our data. All you need to do is some customization and configurations, just as what you have just learned in this section.

For more information on WordPress REST API, please visit https://developer.wordpress.org/rest-api/.

For more information about the built-in WordPress functions we have covered in this section, please visit https://developer.wordpress.org/reference/.

You can find the example apps for this topic in `` `/3.php/1.wordpress/` `` and `` `/1.nuxt/3.cross-domains/2.connect-php/1.wordpress/` `` in the GitHub repository of this book.

Managing Data with PHP PSR Apps

Of course, you can build a custom PHP app to manage the data for your Nuxt app without WordPress. If there is any reason for doing this, we can use some PHP-recommended standards to help us shape and develop the app. The PHP Framework Interop Group (PHP-FIG), https://www.php-fig.org/, has provided a great list of recommended PHP standards that we can definitely benefit from and are strongly encouraged to implement. We don't need to use all of the recommended standards to scaffold the PHP app we need. In fact, we only need three of them. So, let's find out how to use them in this section!

Scaffolding PHP PSR Apps: PSR-4, PSR-7, PSR-15, and CORS

We can use standards from PHP-FIG – PHP Standards Recommendations (PSR), to help us create a PHP app just like the Node.js app in *Chapter 7: Managing Data with Node.js Apps for Nuxt*, which has the following important features:

- HTTP request and response objects that receive HTTP requests and send HTTP responses (PSR-7 HTTP messages).
- A router that allows us to create HTTP routes (PSR-7 routing/dispatcher).

- Middleware interface that allows us to stack middleware (PSR-15 middleware implementation).

Besides PSR-7 and PSR-15, we also want to implement the PSR-4 autoloading standard for autoloading classes from file paths. Lastly, we want to enable CORS in our PHP app so that the remote client can send HTTP requests to and receive HTTP responses from the app without being blocked by the browser. So, let's find out in the following steps:

1. Install **`laminas-diactoros`**, **`laminas-httphandlerrunner`**, **`laminas-stratigility`**, and **`league/route`** via **`composer`** and terminal in your project root:

```
$ composer install laminas/laminas-diactoros
$ composer install laminas/laminas-httphandlerrunner
$ composer install laminas/laminas-stratigility
$ composer install league/route
```

The preceding PHP packages can be summarized as follows:

- **`laminas-diactoros`** (https://docs.laminas.dev/laminas-diactoros/) implements PSR-7 HTTP messages.
- **`laminas-httphandlerrunner`** (https://docs.laminas.dev/laminas-httphandlerrunner/) implements PSR-15 HTTP request handling and HTTP response emitting.
- **`laminas-stratigility`** (https://docs.laminas.dev/laminas-stratigility/) implements PSR-15 middleware creation and dispatch.
- **`league/route`** (https://route.thephpleague.com/) implements PSR-7 routing and dispatcher.

2. Create the following folders, sub-folders, and files in your project root as follows:

```
├── composer.json
├── public
│   └── index.php
└── src
    ├── middleware.php
    ├── router.php
    ├── config
    ├── middleware
    │
```

```
        ├── config
        ├── modules
        ├── routes
        └── utils
```

3. Add the PSR-4 autoload details in `/composer.json` as follows:

```json
// composer.json
{
  "require": {
    //...
  },
  "autoload": {
    "files": [
      "src/utils/get-files.php"
    ],
    "psr-4": {
      "NameA\\": [
        "src/",
        "src/modules/",
        "src/routes/"
      ]
    }
  }
}
```

The preceding configuration will help us to autoload files from the `/modules/` and `/utils/` sub-directories in `/src`.

4. Create the `/` and `404` routes with `league/route` in `/src/router.php`:

```php
// src/router.php
use Psr\Http\Message\ServerRequestInterface;
use Psr\Http\Message\ResponseInterface;
use Laminas\Diactoros\Response\JsonResponse;

$router->get('/', function (ServerRequestInterface $request) :
ResponseInterface {
    return new JsonResponse('Hello world!');
});
```

```
    $router->map('GET', '/{routes:.+}', function (Server
RequestInterface $request) : ResponseInterface {
        throw new League\Route\Http\Exception\NotFoundException;
    });
    ```
```

In the preceding routes, **/** will respond with a JSON **Hello world!** message. On the other hand `` `/{routes:.+}` `` will catch all other routes and respond with `` `NotFoundException` `` from League.

5. Import the routes and dispatch them in `` `/public/index.php` ``:

````
```php
// public/index.php
chdir(dirname(__DIR__) . '/src');
require_once '../vendor/autoload.php';

$request = Laminas\Diactoros\ServerRequestFactory::
fromGlobals(
    $_SERVER, $_GET, $_POST, $_COOKIE, $_FILES
);

$router = new League\Route\Router;
try {
    require './router.php';
    $response = $router->dispatch($request);
} catch(Exception $exception) {
    $statusCode = method_exists($exception, 'getStatusCode') ?
        (int) $exception->getStatusCode() :
        (int) $exception->getCode();

    $statusCode = ($statusCode >= 100) && ($statusCode <=
    599) ? $statusCode : 500;
    $data = [
        "statusCode" => $statusCode,
        "message" => $exception->getMessage()
    ];

    $response = new Laminas\Diactoros\Response\
    JsonResponse($data, $statusCode);
}

(new Laminas\HttpHandlerRunner\Emitter\
SapiEmitter)->emit($response);
```
````
````

In the preceding code, we want to catch the `NotFoundException` exception and other errors, such as 400, 404, and 500 errors, in a try-catch block, so that we can design a custom JSON for the HTTP response. Lastly, we need to emit the HTTP response to the browser using `SapiEmitter`.

6. Run the PSR app with the PHP built-in web server for development at `0.0.0.0:8181`:

```
$ php -S 0.0.0.0:8181 -t public
```

You should see the following JSON text response on `0.0.0.0:8181`:

```
"Hello world!"
```

On the other hand, you should get the following 404 JSON response if you type in any route, for example, `0.0.0.0:8181/xyz`:

```
{"statusCode":404,"message":"Not Found"}
```

7. Add the CORS details in `/src/config/cors.php` as follows:

```php
// src/config/cors.php
return [
    'origin' => 'http://localhost:3000',
    'methods' => 'GET, POST, PUT, DELETE, PATCH, OPTIONS',
    'headers.allow' => 'X-Requested-With, Content-Type,
Accept, Origin, Authorization'
];
```

8. Create a `cors.php` middleware in the `/middleware/` directory, import the CORS details, and set them to the router as follows:

~~~
```php
// src/middleware/cors.php
use Psr\Http\Message\ResponseInterface;
use Psr\Http\Message\ServerRequestInterface;
use function Laminas\Stratigility\middleware;

$router->map('OPTIONS', '/{routes:.+}', function
(ServerRequestInterface $request) : ResponseInterface {
    $response = new Laminas\Diactoros\Response;
    return $response;
});

$router->middleware(middleware(function ($request, $handler) {
    $cors = require './config/cors.php';
    $response = $handler->handle($request);
    return $response
        ->withHeader('Access-Control-Allow-Origin',
        $cors['origin'])
        ->withHeader('Access-Control-Allow-Headers',
        $cors['headers.allow'])
        ->withHeader('Access-Control-Allow-Methods',
        $cors['methods'])
        ;
}));
```
~~~

Notice that we will also need to map the **`OPTIONS`** HTTP request, which comes from the **`PUT`**, **`DELETE`**, and **`PATCH`** HTTP methods, to enable CORS for the remote Nuxt app to connect.

9. Import the CORS middleware in **`/src/middleware.php`**:

~~~
```php
// src/middleware.php
require './middleware/cors.php';
```
~~~

10. Import the all middleware in **`/public/index.php`**:

~~~
```php
// public/index.php
...
try {
~~~

```
        require './middleware.php';
        ...
    } catch(Exception $exception) {
        ...
        $cors = require './config/cors.php';
        $response = new Laminas\Diactoros\Response\Json
Response($data, $statusCode, [
            'Access-Control-Allow-Origin' => [ $cors['origin'] ]
        ]);
    }
```

Notice that we also need to import the CORS details and set them to the HTTP error response in the error block so that our Nuxt app will receive the error response without any CORS issue.

There you go. You have successfully created a PHP app with these four PHP packages that implement PSRs. You can use other PHP packages that you prefer as long as they comply with PSRs. You even can create your own packages as long as you follow the PSRs as well. So, it doesn't matter which packages you use, the PHP app stays the same unaffected. If a package is deprecated, we can always get another package to replace it without breaking our app. Hence, you can see the real benefit of PSR implementations for maintaining your PHP app in the long run.

# Managing Data with the PSR App and MySQL: MySQL driver, UUID, and Timestamp

We have scaffolded the PHP app. Now what we need to do is create the API routes for managing our data. We will use the `catfan/medoo` driver to interact with our database and the `ramsey/uuid` package to generate UUIDs for each new row that we are going to inject into the database. So, let's find out how to use them to add, select, update, and delete data in the following steps:

1. Install `catfan/medoo` and `ramsey/uuid` via `composer` in your project:

```
$ composer install catfan/medoo
$ composer install ramsey/uuid
```

2. Create a `**mysql.php**` in the `**/config/**` directory with the following connection details of your MariaDB/ MySQL database:

```php
// src/config/mysql.php
$name = ‘advanced-nuxtjs-course’;
$username = ‘root’;
$password = ‘tklau’;
$host = ‘localhost’;

return [
    ‘type’ => ‘mysql’,
    ‘options’ => [
        ‘PDO::MYSQL_ATTR_INIT_COMMAND’ => ‘SET NAMES
        \’UTF8\’’
    ],
    ‘dsn’ => ‘mysql:dbname=’ . $name . ‘;host=’ . $host,
    ‘host’ => $host,
    ‘name’ => $name,
    ‘username’ => $username,
    ‘password’ => $password,
];
```

3. Create a `**routes.php**` in the `**/config/**` directory with the following details of folder names that you are going to create in `**/src/routes**`:

```php
// src/config/routes.php
return [
    ‘Home’,
    ‘User’
];
```

4. Create a `**getFiles**` function to scan files in a directory in `**/src/utils/get-files.php**`:

```php
// src/utils/get-files.php
namespace NameA\Util;

function getFiles(string $directory): array {
    $files = array_diff(scandir($directory), [‘.’, ‘..’]);
```

```
        $allFiles = [];

        foreach ($files as $file) {
            $fullPath = $directory . DIRECTORY_SEPARATOR . $file;
            is_dir($fullPath) ?
                array_push($allFiles, ...getFiles($fullPath)) :
                array_push($allFiles, $fullPath);
        }

        return $allFiles;
    }
```

5. Import the **`getFiles`** function to loop the directories that you set in **`/src/config/routes.php`** and import files from them automatically:

```php
// src/router.php
use function NameA\Util\getFiles;

$routes = require 'config/routes.php';
foreach ($routes as $route) {
    $directory = './routes/' . $route . '/entries';
    $files = getFiles($directory);
    foreach ($files as $file) {
        require $file;
    }
}
```

6. Create a **`MySQL.php`** file in the **`/modules/`** directory and create a **`MySQL`** connection object with MySQL details as follows:

```php
// src/modules/Database/MySQL.php
namespace NameA\Database;

class MySQL
{
    protected $connection;

    public function __construct()
    {
        $dbconfig = require './config/mysql.php';
        $this->connection = new \Medoo\Medoo([
```

```
            ‘database_type’ => ‘mysql’,
            ‘database_name’ => $dbconfig[‘name’],
            ‘server’ => $dbconfig[‘host’],
            ‘username’ => $dbconfig[‘username’],
            ‘password’ => $dbconfig[‘password’]
        ]);
    }

    public function connect()
    {
        return $this->connection;
    }
}
```

7. Create a `Base.php` file in the `/User/` directory with an abstract class to construct the database object from `/src/modules/Database/MySQL.php`:

```php
// src/routes/User/Base.php
namespace NameA\User;

use Medoo\Medoo;

abstract class Base
{
    protected $database;

    public function __construct(
        Medoo $database
    ) {
        $this->database = $database;
    }
}
```

8. Create a `NameA\User\Fetch\Users` class in a `User.php` file in the `/User/` directory for fetching all users as follows:

```php
// src/routes/User/Fetch/Users.php
namespace NameA\User\Fetch;

use NameA\User\Base;
```

```
class Users extends Base
{
    public function fetch()
    {
        $columns = [
            'id',
            'name',
            'slug',
            'created_on',
            'updated_on',
        ];

        return $this->database->select('users', $columns);
    }
}
```

Notice that we import `**/src/routes/User/Base.php**` and extend it in this object class. After that, we can fetch rows from our database using the `**select**` method from Medoo. For more information about the `**select**` method for retrieving a row in the database, please visit https://medoo.in/api/select.

9. Create a `**NameA\User\Fetch\User**` class in a `**User.php**` file in the `**/User/**` directory for fetching a user as follows:

```php
// src/routes/User/Fetch/User.php
namespace NameA\User\Fetch;

use NameA\User\Base;

class User extends Base
{
    public function fetch(array $routeParams)
    {
        $columns = [
            'id',
            'name',
            'slug',
            'created_on',
            'updated_on',
        ];

        $data = $this->database->get('users', $columns, [
            "slug" => $routeParams['slug']
```

```
        ]);

        if ($data === NULL) {
            throw new \Exception('No user found', 404);
        }

        return $data;
    }
}
```

Notice that we use a `get` method to fetch a row from the database. Then we want to throw a 404 exception when the requested user is not found in the database. For more information about the `get` method for retrieving a row in the database, please visit https://medoo.in/api/get.

10. Create a `NameA\User\Create\User` class in a `User.php` file in the `/User/` directory for creating a new user as follows:

```php
// src/routes/User/Create/User.php
namespace NameA\User\Create;

use Psr\Http\Message\ServerRequestInterface;
use Ramsey\Uuid\Uuid;

use NameA\User\Base;

class User extends Base
{
    public function create(ServerRequestInterface $request)
    {
        $params = $request->getParsedBody();
        $name = $params['name'];
        $slug = $params['slug'];
        // validation...

        $date = new \DateTime();
        $createdOn = $date->getTimestamp();

        $uuid3 = Uuid::uuid3(Uuid::NAMESPACE_DNS, $slug);
        $id = $uuid3->toString();

        $model = new \stdClass;
        $model->id = $id;
        $model->name = $name;
```

~~~
        $model->slug = $slug;
        $model->created_on = $createdOn;

        $result = $this->database->insert(‘users’, [
            ‘id’ => $model->id,
            ‘name’ => $model->name,
            ‘slug’ => $model->slug,
            ‘created_on’ => $model->created_on,
            ‘updated_on’ => $model->created_on
        ]);

        if ($result->rowCount() === 0) {
            throw new \Exception(‘Insert row failed’, 500);
        }

        return $model;
    }
}
```
~~~

In the preceding code, we get the data in parameters from the parsed body and use **`Ramsey\Uuid\Uuid`** to generate a UUID for us before injecting the data into our database. Then we want to throw a 500 exception when the row injection fails. For more information about the **`insert`** method for injecting a row into the database, please visit https://medoo.in/api/insert.

11. Create a **`NameA\User\Update\User`** class in a **`User.php`** file in the **`/User/`** directory for updating an existing user as follows:

~~~
```php
// src/routes/User/Update/User.php
namespace NameA\User\Update;

use Psr\Http\Message\ServerRequestInterface;

use NameA\User\Base;

class User extends Base
{
    public function update(ServerRequestInterface $request)
    {
        parse_str(file_get_contents(‘php://input’), $params);
        $id = $params[‘id’];
        $name = $params[‘name’];
        $slug = $params[‘slug’];
~~~

```
        // validation...

        $date = new \DateTime();
        $updatedOn = $date->getTimestamp();

        $model = new \stdClass;
        $model->id = $id;
        $model->name = $name;
        $model->slug = $slug;
        $model->updated_on = $updatedOn;

        $result = $this->database->update("users", [
            "name" => $model->name,
            "slug" => $model->slug,
            'updated_on' => $model->updated_on
        ], [
            "id" => $model->id
        ]);

        if ($result->rowCount() === 0) {
            throw new \Exception('Update row failed', 500);
        }

        return $model;
    }
}
```

In the preceding code, we get the data in parameters from the parsed body before updating the data into our database. Then we want to throw a 500 exception when the row update fails. For more information about the `update` method for updating a row in the database, please visit https://medoo.in/api/update.

12. Create a `NameA\User\Delete\User` class in a `User.php` file in the `/User/` directory for deleting an existing user as follows:

```php
// src/routes/User/Delete/User.php
namespace NameA\User\Delete;

use Psr\Http\Message\ServerRequestInterface;

use NameA\User\Base;

class User extends Base
{
```

```
        public function delete(ServerRequestInterface $request)
        {
            parse_str(file_get_contents('php://input'), $params);
            $id = $params['id'];
            if (!$id) {
                throw new \Exception('$id is empty', 400);
            }

            $model = new \stdClass;
            $model->id = $id;

            $result = $this->database->delete("users", [
                "id" => $model->id
            ]);

            if ($result->rowCount() === 0) {
                throw new \Exception('Delete row failed', 500);
            }

            return $model;
        }
    }
    ```
```

In the preceding code, we get the data in parameters from the parsed body before deleting the row from our database. Then we want to throw a 500 exception when the row deletion fails. For more information about the `**delete**` method for updating a row in the database, please visit https://medoo.in/api/delete.

13. Create a `**1.fetch**` folder with a `**1.users.php**` file in `**/src/routes/User/entries/**` and create a `**/users**` Get method route with the `**NameA\User\Fetch\Users**` class to send the MySQL query result in the HTTP JSON response as follows:

```
    ```php
    // src/routes/User/entries/1.fetch/1.users.php
    use Psr\Http\Message\ResponseInterface;
    use Psr\Http\Message\ServerRequestInterface;
    use Laminas\Diactoros\Response\JsonResponse;

    use NameA\Database\MySQL;
    use NameA\User\Fetch\Users;

    $router->get('/users', function (ServerRequestInterface
$request) : ResponseInterface {
```

```php
        $connection = (new MySQL())->connect();
        $rows = (new Users($connection))->fetch();

        return new JsonResponse($rows);
    });
```

14. Create a **`2.user.php`** file in **`/User/entries/1.fetch`** and create a **`/user/{slug}`** Get method route with the **`NameA\User\Fetch\User`** class to send the MySQL query result in the HTTP JSON response as follows:

    ```php
    // src/routes/User/entries/1.fetch/2.user.php
    use Psr\Http\Message\ResponseInterface;
    use Psr\Http\Message\ServerRequestInterface;
    use Laminas\Diactoros\Response\JsonResponse;

    use NameA\Database\MySQL;
    use NameA\User\Fetch\User;

    $router->get('/users/{slug}', function (ServerRequest
    Interface $request, array $args) : ResponseInterface {
        $connection = (new MySQL())->connect();
        $row = (new User($connection))->fetch($args);

        return new JsonResponse($row);
    });
    ```

15. Create a **`2.create`** folder with a **`user.php`** file in **`/src/routes/User/entries/`** and create a **/user** POST method route with the **`NameA\User\Create\User`** class to send the MySQL injection result in the HTTP JSON response as follows:

    ```php
    // src/routes/User/entries/2.create/user.php
    use Psr\Http\Message\ResponseInterface;
    use Psr\Http\Message\ServerRequestInterface;
    use Laminas\Diactoros\Response\JsonResponse;

    use NameA\Database\MySQL;
    use NameA\User\Create\User;

    $router->post('/user', function (ServerRequestInterface
    ```

````
$request, array $args) : ResponseInterface {
        $connection = (new MySQL())->connect();
        $result = (new User($connection))->create($request);

        return new JsonResponse($result);
    });
    ```
````

16. Create a `3.update` folder with a `user.php` file in `/src/routes/User/entries/` and create a `/user` PUT method route with the `NameA\User\Update\User` class to send the MySQL update result in the HTTP JSON response as follows:

````
    ```php
    // src/routes/User/entries/3.update/user.php
    use Psr\Http\Message\ResponseInterface;
    use Psr\Http\Message\ServerRequestInterface;
    use Laminas\Diactoros\Response\JsonResponse;

    use NameA\Database\MySQL;
    use NameA\User\Update\User;

    $router->put('/user', function (ServerRequestInterface
$request, array $args) : ResponseInterface {
        $connection = (new MySQL())->connect();
        $result = (new User($connection))->update($request);

        return new JsonResponse($result);
    });
    ```
````

17. Create a `4.delete` folder with a `user.php` file in `/src/routes/User/entries/` and create a `/user` DELETE method route with the `NameA\User\Delete\User` class to send the MySQL deletion result in the HTTP JSON response as follows:

````
    ```php
    // src/routes/User/entries/4.delete/user.php
    use Psr\Http\Message\ResponseInterface;
    use Psr\Http\Message\ServerRequestInterface;
    use Laminas\Diactoros\Response\JsonResponse;

    use NameA\Database\MySQL;
    use NameA\User\Delete\User as DeleteUser;
````

```
    $router->delete('/user', function (ServerRequestInterface
$request, array $args) : ResponseInterface {
        $connection = (new MySQL())->connect();
        $result = (new DeleteUser($connection))->delete
($request);

        return new JsonResponse($result);
    });
```

18. Run the PSR app with the PHP built-in web server for development at `0.0.0.0:8181`:

```
$ php -S 0.0.0.0:8181 -t public
```

Open a new terminal and add a new user row to the database using `curl`. For example:

```
$ curl -d "name=John&slug=john" -X POST http://0.0.0.0:8181/
user
```

You should get the following JSON response on your terminal:

```json
{"id":"caeaa633-bbb2-3ce3-878d-085da9e61a19","name":
"John","slug":"john","created_on":1695554719}
```

Update an existing user row in the database using `curl`. For example:

```
$ curl -d "name=Johnny&slug=johnny&id=caeaa633-bbb2-3ce3-878d
-085da9e61a19" -X PUT http://localhost:8181/user
```

You should get the following JSON response on your terminal:

```
    ```json
    {"id":"caeaa633-bbb2-3ce3-878d-085da9e61a19","name":
"Johnny","slug":"johnny","updated_on":1695554822}
    ```
```

You should get the following example JSON response if you fetch all users from the database on your browser at `` `/localhost:8181/users` ``:

```
    ```json
    [{"id":"caeaa633-bbb2-3ce3-878d-085da9e61a19","name":
"Johnny","slug":"johnny","created_on":"1695554719","updated_
on":"1695554822"}]
    ```
```

You should get the following JSON response if you fetch a user, for example, `` `/localhost:8181/users/johnny` ``:

```
    ```json
    {"id":"caeaa633-bbb2-3ce3-878d-085da9e61a19","name":
"Johnny","slug":"johnny","created_on":"1695554719","updated_
on":"1695554822"}
    ```
```

Finally, delete an existing user in the database using `` `curl` `` on a separate terminal. For example:

```
    ```
    $ curl -d "id=caeaa633-bbb2-3ce3-878d-085da9e61a19" -X DELETE
http://localhost:8181/user
    ```
```

You should get the following JSON response on your terminal:

```
    ```json
    {"id":"caeaa633-bbb2-3ce3-878d-085da9e61a19"}
    ```
```

19. Create a `.env` file in your Nuxt project root with the following variables and values for the app and the cross-origin API:

    ```
    // .env
    APP_BASE_URL=http://localhost:3000
    API_BASE_URL=http://localhost:8181
    ```

Note that `localhost:3000` is your Nuxt app, while `localhost:8181` is the cross-origin API.

20. Use `useF3tch` in the `<script>` block to fetch the list of users from the cross-origin API:

    ```js
    // pages/users.vue
    <script setup>
    const { data: users, error } = await useF3tch('/users')
    </script>
    ```

21. Display the data of each user in the `<template>` block:

    ```html
    // pages/users.vue
    <template>
      <error-boundary v-bind:error="error">
        <h2>
          Users
        </h2>
        <ul>
          <li v-for="user in users" v-bind:key="user.id">
            {{ user.name }}
          </li>
        </ul>
      </error-boundary>
    </template>
    ```

22. Run the Nuxt app on the `dev` environment:

    ```
    $ npm run dev
    ```

You should see all the users are fetched from the cross-origin API and displayed successfully on your browser at `localhost:3000/users`.

Well done! You have managed to create API routes for managing data in the PHP PSR app with `catfan/medoo` and `ramsey/uuid`. Then you just need a `.env` file to connect your Nuxt app with the PHP app remotely without any CORS issues. You can see that making the connection between two separate apps in this section is the same as the Nuxt app and WordPress in the previous section. And once again, by doing this, you have managed to keep your Nuxt project and app thin and lightweight.

PHP code and apps can get very messy, unreadable, and even unmaintainable over time if we are not guided by certain standard rules and recommendations. You wouldn't enjoy maintaining someone else' messy code. Even though it is not mandatory that we comply with the recommended standards set by PHP-FIG, you should pick up at least some of them if you want to collaborate with other developers on large projects.

You can find the example apps for this topic in `/3.php/2.psr/` and `/1.nuxt/3.cross-domains/2.connect-php/2.psr/` in the GitHub repository of this book.

Managing Metadata with WordPress for SEO and Open Graph

Besides managing data for the `<body>` tag in the HTML document of our pages, we must also manage the metadata in the `<head>` tag in the HTML document of the pages in our Nuxt app. It is the same with the `<body>` data, the `<head>` metadata must be stored and fetched. It is important for a website to have metadata rendered as `<meta>` tags for Search Engine Optimization (SEO) and Open Graph (OG) social sharing. We can use the CMS from WordPress to manage the SEO and OG metadata for us, but WordPress doesn't provide the input fields out of the box for us to store the data. So, we must create custom fields for storing the metadata, and we can use Carbon Fields (https://carbonfields.net/), a WordPress custom fields library, to help us do that. So, let's find out how you can use this awesome library to complement WordPress in this section.

Managing SEO and Open Graph Metadata with WordPress and Carbon Fields

Using Carbon Fields to help us create custom fields in WordPress can increase our productivity as we don't have to create them from scratch. It also helps us avoid tons of custom field plugins and add-ons that eventually could make our WordPress site bloated and unmaintainable in the long run. It might be a bit of a learning curve in learning Carbon Fields and using it to create custom fields. But once you have got the hang of it, you will find your joy in creating custom fields is finally found! You can use Carbon Fields to create any kind of custom fields you need for managing your WordPress data, such as image field and repeater field (it is called "complex" in Carbon Fields). It is limitless! However, in this section, we will focus on the custom fields for the SEO and OG metadata. So, let's find out in the following steps:

1. Install **`htmlburger/carbon-fields`** and **`htmlburger/carbon-field-number`** via **`composer`** on your terminal:

```
$ composer install htmlburger/carbon-fields
$ composer install htmlburger/carbon-field-number
```

The **`htmlburger/carbon-field-number`** package is optional but it is good to have it for adding a **`number`** field type to Carbon Fields. For more information about this package, please visit https://github.com/htmlburger/carbon-field-number.

2. Create a **`metaboxes`** folder and the following **`fields`** sub-folder with a **`metainfo.php`** file in **`/inc/`** directory:

```
inc
├── ...
└── metaboxes
    └── carbon-fields
        ├── ...
        └── fields
            ├── ...
            ├── metainfo.php
            └── theme-options.php
```

3. Create a `**utils**` folder with a `**metainfo.php**` file in the `**/inc/**` directory:

````
```
inc
├── ...
└── utils
    ├── ...
    └── metainfo.php
```
````

4. Create a `**siteinfo.php**` file in the existing `**apis**` folder in the `**/inc/**` directory:

````
```
inc
├── ...
└── apis
    ├── ...
    └── siteinfo.php
```
````

5. Use `**Container**` and `**Field**` from Carbon Fields to create custom fields for adding SEO and OG meta information to a post **individually/locally** in your WordPress in `**/headlessapi-v1/inc/metaboxes/carbon-fields/fields/metainfo.php**` as follows:

````
```php
// headlessapi-v1/inc/metaboxes/carbon-fields/fields/metainfo.
php
use Carbon_Fields\Container;
use Carbon_Fields\Field;

add_action('carbon_fields_register_fields', 'crb_attach_post_
meta_seo_contents');
function crb_attach_post_meta_seo_contents() {
    Container::make('post_meta', __('Meta Contents'))
        ->add_tab(__('SEO Meta'), [
            Field::make('textarea', 'seo_meta_title',
            __('Title'))
                ->set_width(33.3)
                ->set_rows(8),
            Field::make('textarea', 'seo_meta_description',
            __('Description'))
                ->set_width(33.3)
````
````

```
                ->set_rows(8),
            Field::make('textarea', 'seo_meta_keywords',
            __('Keywords'))
                ->set_width(33.3)
                ->set_rows(8),
        ])
        ->add_tab(__('Social Meta'), [
            Field::make('textarea', 'social_meta_title',
            __('Title'))
                ->set_width(33.3)
                ->set_rows(8),
            Field::make('textarea', 'social_meta_
description', __('Description'))
                ->set_width(33.3)
                ->set_rows(8),
            Field::make('image', 'social_meta_image',
__('Image'))
                ->set_width(33.3)
                ->set_value_type('url'),
        ])
        ;
}
```

The preceding code creates two tabs on the post in your WordPress:

- The **SEO Meta** tab creates custom input fields for adding the SEO meta content of title, description, and keywords.
- The **Social Meta** tab creates custom input fields for adding the OG meta content of the title, description, and image.

6. Use `Container` and `Field` from Carbon Fields to create custom fields (Theme Options) for adding SEO and OG meta information to your WordPress site **globally** in `/headlessapi-v1/inc/metaboxes/carbon-fields/theme-options`.php as follows:

```php
// headlessapi-v1/inc/metaboxes/carbon-fields/theme-options.
php
use Carbon_Fields\Container;
use Carbon_Fields\Field;

add_action('carbon_fields_register_fields', 'crb_attach_theme_
options');
function crb_attach_theme_options() {
    $basic_options_container = Container::make('theme_
```

```
options', __('Basic Options'))
            ->add_tab(__('General Settings'), [
                ...
                Field::make('textarea', 'description',
                 __('Description'))
                    ->set_width(50)
                    ->set_rows(8),
                Field::make('textarea', 'keywords',
                __('Keywords'))
                    ->set_width(50)
                    ->set_rows(8),
                Field::make('text', 'tagline', 'Tagline')
                    ->set_width(50),
            ])
            ;
        Container::make('theme_options', __('Social Options'))
            ->set_page_parent($basic_options_container)
            ->add_tab(__('Open Graph'), [
                Field::make('complex', 'open_graph', '')
                    ->set_duplicate_groups_allowed(false)
                    ->add_fields([
                        ...
                        Field::make('image', 'og_image',
'og:image')
                            ->set_value_type('url')
                    ])
            ])
            ;

    }
```

The preceding code creates two option groups on the Theme Options in your WordPress:

- The **`Basic Options`** option group creates custom input fields for adding a tagline and SEO meta information of your site globally. Of course, there are other site-related custom input fields you can add to this group, such as company name, telephone number, and more, but we only focus on the SEO custom fields in this section.
- The **`Social Options`** option group creates custom input fields for adding the OG meta information of your site globally. Of course, there are more custom OG input fields you can add to this group, such as Facebook app ID, image width, image height, and more, but in this section, we only focus on the image custom field that is used to contain the URL of your OG image.

7. Create a `create_post_title` function for creating the data of the `<title>` tag of a post in `/headlessapi-v1/inc/utils/metainfo.php`:

```php
// headlessapi-v1/inc/utils/metainfo.php
function create_post_title($id = null) {
    $post_title = get_the_title($id);
    if (is_tax()) {
        $term_slug = get_query_var('term');
        $term_taxonomy = get_query_var('taxonomy');
        $term = get_term_by('slug', $term_slug, $term_
        taxonomy);
        $post_title = $term->name;
    }

    $home_id = (int)get_option('page_on_front');
    $site_title = get_bloginfo('title', 'display');
    $site_tagline = carbon_get_theme_option('tagline');

    $page_title = $post_title . ' | ' . $site_title;
    if ($id === $home_id) {
        $page_title = $site_title . ' | ' . $site_tagline;
    }
    return $page_title;
}
```

The preceding function is used to create the title text for the `<title>` tag in a post in the following default formats:

- **[`site title`] | [`tagline`]** for the Home page only. The `tagline` data is retrieved from the custom `tagline` Carbon Fields' Theme Options, instead of the default `tagline` field from WordPress. However, you can use the WordPress default `tagline` field for storing and retrieving the tagline of your site if you prefer.
- **[`post title or term name`] | [`site title`]** for a post and category page that is accessible by the public user. However, this default format can be overridden if a specific preferred title is set in the `seo_meta_title` custom field on the post.

The `get_the_title` WordPress function is used to retrieve the post title. We also use `get_option`, `get_query_var`, and `get_term_by` from WordPress to help us to retrieve data. For more information about these functions, please visit https://developer.wordpress.org/reference/functions/.

8. Create a **`create_post_meta`** function for retrieving the SEO and Open Graph metadata of a post using **`carbon_get_post_meta`** from Carbon Fields in **`/headlessapi-v1/inc/utils/metainfo.php`**:

```php
// headlessapi-v1/inc/utils/metainfo.php
function create_post_meta($id, $type = 'article') {
    $meta_title = carbon_get_post_meta($id, 'seo_meta
    _title');
    $meta_description = carbon_get_post_meta($id, 'seo_meta
    _description');
    $meta_keywords = carbon_get_post_meta($id, 'seo_meta
    _keywords');
    $social_title = carbon_get_post_meta($id, 'social_meta
    _title');
    $social_description = carbon_get_post_meta($id, 'social
    _meta_description');
    $social_image = carbon_get_post_meta($id, 'social_meta
    _image');

    $open_graph = carbon_get_theme_option('open_graph')[0];
    if (!$meta_title) {
        $meta_title = create_post_title($id);
    }
    if (!$meta_description) {
        $meta_description = carbon_get_theme_option
        ('description');
    }
    if (!$meta_keywords) {
        $meta_keywords = carbon_get_theme_option('keywords');
    }
    if (!$social_title) {
        $social_title = $meta_title;
    }
    if (!$social_description) {
        $social_description = $meta_description;
    }
    if (!$social_image) {
        $social_image = $open_graph['og_image'];
    }

    return [
        'title' => $meta_title,
        'description' => $meta_description,
        'keywords' => $meta_keywords,
        'og' => [
```

```
                'title' => $social_title,
                'description' => $social_description,
                'type' => $type,
                'image' => $social_image
            ]
        ];
    }
```

The preceding code retrieves the metadata from the custom fields in Carbon Fields' Theme Options by default. If the metadata is set on a post individually, then the metadata from the post will override the default metadata from the Theme Options and the default title format from the `**create_post_title**` function.

9. Call `**create_post_meta**` in the `**fetch_page**` function to retrieve the SEO and OG metadata of a `**page**` type post in `**/headlessapi-v1/inc/apis/page/get/one.php**` as follows:

```php
// headlessapi-v1/inc/apis/page/get/one.php
add_action('rest_api_init', function () use ($namespace) {
    $route = 'page/(?P<slug>[a-zA-Z0-9-]+)';
    $args = [
        'methods' => 'GET',
        'callback' => 'fetch_page',
    ];
    register_rest_route($namespace, $route, $args);
});

function fetch_page($data) {
    $post = get_page_by_path($data['slug'], OBJECT, 'page');
    ...
    $post->head = create_post_meta($post->ID);

    return $post;
}
```

10. Call `**create_post_meta**` in the `**fetch_project**` function to retrieve the SEO and OG metadata of a `**project**` type post in `**/headlessapi-v1/inc/apis/project/get/one.php**` as follows:

```php
// headlessapi-v1/inc/apis/project/get/one.php
```

~~~
add_action('rest_api_init', function () use ($namespace) {
    $route = 'project/(?P<slug>[a-zA-Z0-9-]+)';
    $args = [
        'methods' => 'GET',
        'callback' => 'fetch_project',
    ];
    register_rest_route($namespace, $route, $args);
});

function fetch_project($data) {
    $post = get_page_by_path($data['slug'], OBJECT,
    'project');
    ...
    $post->head = create_post_meta($post->ID);
    ...

    return $post;
}
```
~~~

11. Create a `**/wp-json/api/v1/siteinfo**` API endpoint for retrieving the global metadata of your site from Theme Options in `**/headlessapi-v1/inc/apis/siteinfo.php**`

~~~
```php
// headlessapi-v1/inc/apis/siteinfo.php
add_action('rest_api_init', function () use ($namespace) {
    $route = 'siteinfo';
    $args = [
        'methods' => 'GET',
        'callback' => 'create_siteinfo',
    ];
    register_rest_route($namespace, $route, $args);
});

function create_siteinfo($data) {
    ...
    $open_graph = carbon_get_theme_option('open_graph');
    if ($open_graph) {
        $open_graph = reset($open_graph);
    }

    $siteinfo = [
        'title' => get_bloginfo('name'),
        'tagline' => carbon_get_theme_option('tagline'),
~~~

```
        ...
        'open_graph' => $open_graph,
        'social_profiles' => carbon_get_theme_option('social_
        profiles')
    ];
    return $siteinfo;
}
```

12. Load `Carbon Fields` and register the custom fields of `theme-options` and `metainfo` in `/headlessapi-v1/functions.php`:

```php
// headlessapi-v1/functions.php
use Carbon_Fields\Container;
use Carbon_Fields\Field;

add_action('after_setup_theme', 'crb_load');
function crb_load() {
    require_once('vendor/autoload.php');
    \Carbon_Fields\Carbon_Fields::boot();
}

include 'inc/metaboxes/carbon-fields/fields/theme-options.php';
include 'inc/metaboxes/carbon-fields/fields/metainfo.php';
...
include 'inc/apis/siteinfo.php';
```

13. Run the WordPress app with the PHP built-in web server for development at `0.0.0.0:4000`:

```
$ php -S 0.0.0.0:4000
```

14. Log into your WordPress at `/wp-admin` and start adding the SEO and OG data through the custom fields that you have just created.

After adding the SEO and OG data, you should see the following example JSON response, which has included the SEO and OG data, from `/wp-json/api/v1/siteinfo`, on your browser:

```json
{“title”:”Nuxt + WordPress”,”company”:””,”tagline”:”Awesome
Headless WordPress REST API”,”description”:”My awesome headless
WordPress REST API”,”keywords”:”wordpress, php, nuxt”,
”telephone”:””,”email”:””,”address”:””,”opening_hours”:””,
”copyright”:””,”credits”:null,”logo”:””,”logos”:[],
”favicon”:””,”open_graph”:{“_type”:”_”,”fb_app_
id”:”2740922996222837”,”og_type”:”article”,”og_image”:”http:\/\/
localhost:4000\/wp-content\/uploads\/2023\/02\/R0009300.jpg”,
”og_image_width”:”1200”,”og_image_height”:”1200”,”twitter_card”:
”summary_large_image”,”twitter_site”:”@lautiamkok”,”twitter_
creator”:”@lautiamkok”},”social_profiles”:[]}
```


On the other hand, you should see the SEO and OG data are injected into the JSON response into any post on your site, for example, `/wp-json/api/v1/project/project-lorem-ipsum-dolor-sit-consectetuer-10`:


```json
{“ID”:99,...,”post_name”:”project-lorem-ipsum-dolor-sit-
consectetuer-10”,...,”head”:{“title”:”Project Lorem ipsum
dolor sit consectetuer 10 | Mock API”,”description”:””,
”keywords”:””,”og”:{“title”:”Project Lorem ipsum dolor sit
consectetuer 10 | Mock API”,”description”:””,”type”:
”article”,”image”:”http:\/\/localhost:4000\/wp-content\/
uploads\/2022\/03\/Whitsands-Bay-03.jpg”}}}
```


15. Create a `.env` file in your Nuxt project root with the following variables and values for the app and the cross-origin API:

```
// .env
APP_BASE_URL=http://localhost:3000
API_BASE_URL=http://localhost:4000
```

Note that `localhost:3000` is your Nuxt app, while `localhost:4000` is the cross-origin API.

16. Fetch the general site info from `/wp-json/api/v1/siteinfo` and set it to the document `<head>` tag globally as a default with `useHead` in `app.vue` as follows:

````
```js
// app.vue
<script setup>
const { data, error } = await useF3tch(`/wp-json/api/v1/
siteinfo`)

if (!error.value) {
  const siteinfo = unref(data)
  siteinfo.url = import.meta.env.VITE_APP_BASE_URL
  useState(‘siteinfo’, () => siteinfo)

  useHead({
    title: ‘’,
    meta: [
      {
        name: ‘description’,
        content: siteinfo.description
      },
      {
        name: ‘keywords’,
        content: siteinfo.keywords
      },
      {
        property: ‘og:type’,
        content: siteinfo.open_graph.og_type
      },
      {
        property: ‘og:url’,
        content: siteinfo.url
      },
      {
        property: ‘og:title’,
        content: siteinfo.title
      },
      {
        property: ‘og:description’,
        content: siteinfo.description
      },
      {
        property: ‘og:image’,
        content: siteinfo.open_graph.og_image
      },
````
````

```
        {
          property: 'og:image:width',
          content: siteinfo.open_graph.og_image_width
        },
        {
          property: 'og:image:height',
          content: siteinfo.open_graph.og_image_height
        },
        {
          property: 'fb:app_id',
          content: siteinfo.open_graph.fb_app_id
        }
      ],
    })
  }
  </script>
```

Notice that we also use `useState` to set the site info globally so that it can be accessed and used by any component, such as a site navigation component, without re-fetching the same data.

17. Fetch the `page` type post data and override the default head in the `<script>` block, for example, in `/pages/index.vue`:

```js
// pages/index.vue
<script setup>
const { data: post } = await useF3tch(`/wp-json/api/v1/page/
home`)

if (post.value) {
  const head = unref(post).head
  useHead({
    title: head.title,
    meta: [
      {
        name: 'description',
        content: head.description
      },
      {
        property: 'og:title',
        content: head.og.title
      },
      {
        property: 'og:description',
```

```
          content: head.og.description
        },
        {
          property: 'og:image',
          content: head.og.image
        },
        {
          name: 'twitter:description',
          content: head.og.description
        },
      ],
    })
  }
  </script>
```

18. Fetch the `project` type post data and override the default head in the `<script>` block in `/pages/projects/[slug].vue`:

```js
// pages/projects/[slug].vue
<script setup>
const route = useRoute()
const slug = route.params.slug
const { data: post, error } = await useF3tch(`/wp-json/api/
v1/project/${slug}`)

if (post.value) {
  const head = unref(post).head
  useHead({
    title: head.title,
    meta: [
      {
        name: 'description',
        content: head.description
      },
      {
        name: 'keywords',
        content: head.keywords
      },
      {
        property: 'og:title',
        content: head.og.title
      },
      {
        property: 'og:description',
```

```
          content: head.og.description
        },
        {
          property: 'og:image',
          content: head.og.image
        },
        {
          name: 'twitter:description',
          content: head.og.description
        },
      ],
    })
  }
  </script>
```

19. Run the Nuxt app on the `dev` environment:

```
$ npm run dev
```

You should see the following `<title>` and `<meta>` tags rendered successfully in the HTML document `head` tag on your browser at `localhost:3000`.

```html
<head>
  <meta charset="utf-8">
  <meta name="viewport" content="width=device-width,
  initial-scale=1">
  <title>Nuxt + WordPress | Awesome Headless WordPress REST
  API</title>
  <meta name="description" content="My awesome headless
  WordPress REST API">
  <meta name="keywords" content="wordpress, php, nuxt">
  <meta property="og:type" content="article">
  <meta property="og:url" content="http://localhost:3000">
  <meta property="og:image:width" content="1200">
  <meta property="og:image:height" content="1200">
  <meta property="fb:app_id" content="2740922996222837">
  <meta property="og:title" content="Nuxt + WordPress |
  Awesome Headless WordPress REST API">
  <meta property="og:description" content="My awesome
  headless WordPress REST API">
  <meta property="og:image" content="http://localhost:4000/
```

```
wp-content/uploads/2023/02/R0009300.jpg">
    ...
  </head>
  ```
```

You should see the following `description`, `keywords`, and `og:image &lt;meta&gt;` tags that override the default ones on `/projects/sample-12`:

```
```html
<head>
  <meta charset="utf-8">
  <meta name="viewport" content="width=device-width, ini-
  tial-scale=1">
  <title>Sample 12</title>
  <meta name="description" content="My awesome Sample 12">
  <meta name="keywords" content="sample 12, wordpress, nuxt">
  ...
  <meta property="og:title" content="Sample 12 OG">
  <meta property="og:description" content="My awesome Sample
  12 OG">
  <meta property="og:image" content="http://localhost:4000/
  wp-content/uploads/2023/02/R0003515.jpg">
  ...
</head>
```
```

Notice that the title text in the preceding `&lt;title&gt;` tag also overrides the default format of **[`post title`] | [`site name`]** that is created by the `create_post_title` function in `/headlessapi-v1/inc/utils/metainfo.php`. Lastly, you should see the following `&lt;meta&gt;` tags on pages that do not override the default ones, for example, `/projects/sample-11`:

```
```html
<head>
<meta charset="utf-8">
  <meta name="viewport" content="width=device-width,
  initial-scale=1">
  <title>Sample 11 | Nuxt + WordPress</title>
  <meta name="description" content="My awesome headless
  WordPress REST API">
  <meta name="keywords" content="wordpress, php, nuxt">
  ...
  <meta property="og:title" content="Sample 11 | Nuxt +
  WordPress">
```

```
    <meta property="og:description" content="My awesome
    headless WordPress REST API">
    <meta property="og:image" content="http://localhost:4000/
    wp-content/uploads/2023/02/R0009300.jpg">
    ...
</head>
```

There you go. You have managed to manage your SEO and OG metadata with Carbon Fields and WordPress. Once you have your data populated in the database remotely, you just need to fetch via HTTP requests and use the `useHead` API to populate them in your Nuxt app through the `<script setup>` block. Then the `<meta>` and `<title>` tags with the SEO and OG info will be generated automatically for you in the HTML document on the client and server sides. We don't have to fiddle with the HTML tags and worry about them. That's sweet!

Our Nuxt pages aren't complete without metadata rendered into `<meta>` tags in the `<head>` tag. There is no way to manage the metadata in WordPress without custom fields. The `useHead` API generates the `<meta>` tags out of the box for us in our Nuxt app. Carbon Fields complements WordPress well and helps us create custom fields without having to fiddle with JavaScript. Hence, you must make use of them (`useHead` and Carbon Fields) to complete your Nuxt pages for SEO and OG social sharing.

You can find the example apps for this topic in `/2.native/2.mysql/` and `/1.nuxt/3.cross-domains/1.connect-native/1.mysql/` in the GitHub repository of this book.

Conclusion

In this chapter, you have managed to use WordPress to manage the data for your Nuxt app. You have learned to create custom post types in WordPress and have used the WordPress REST API layer to create API routes for your Nuxt to fetch the data from the database. Besides WordPress, you also learned to create a PHP PSR app to manage data for your Nuxt app. You have used PSR-4, PSR-7, PSR-15, and CORS to scaffold the PHP PSR app. You have learned that it is not mandatory to comply with the recommended PHP standards, but it is a good practice to use them for collaboration. Lastly, you have used Carbon Fields to create custom fields for managing SEO and OG metadata in WordPress. Then, finally, you have used the `useHead` API from Nuxt to render the metadata into `<meta>` tags, and you learned that it is important to have this meta information to complete your Nuxt pages.

In the next chapter, you will learn to use GraphQL to fetch data in your Nuxt app. You will create HMR GraphQL apps with Apollo Server, Node.js HTTP API, MongoDB, and WordPress. You will also use Gridsome and Markdown documents as the GraphQL server and database for your Nuxt app. So, let's discover them in the next exciting chapter!

CHAPTER 9

Building GraphQL Layers with MongoDB, WordPress, and GraphQL Tools for Nuxt

Introduction

Welcome to *Chapter* 9. In this chapter, you will be introduced to GraphQL. You will learn about GraphQL queries, schema, object types, resolvers, and GraphQL schema language by creating HMR Node.js HTTP GraphQL servers with GraphQL.js and GraphQL Tools. Also, you will learn to incorporate MongoDB with your GraphQL server and APIs, as well as bridging with WordPress for Nuxt apps. Lastly, you will fetch data from GraphQL servers using GraphQL queries in your Nuxt apps.

Structure

The topics that will be covered in this chapter are as follows:

- Introducing GraphQL and Understanding GraphQL Schema
- Creating GraphQL Servers with MongoDB and Node.js HTTP API
- Creating GraphQL Servers with WordPress and Node.js HTTP API

Introducing GraphQL and Understanding GraphQL Schema

GraphQL is an open-source query language, server-side runtime engine, and specification (technical standard). It is a data query and manipulation language, and to be specific, a client query language. The following is a good example of a GraphQL query:

```js
{
 planet(name: “earth”) {
   id
   age
   population
 }
}
```

The GraphQL query, like the one above, is used in an HTTP client such as a Nuxt or Vue app, which sends the query to the server for an exchange of a JSON response. For example:

```js
{
  “data”: {
    “planet”: {
      “id”: 3,
      “age”: “4543000000”,
      “population”: “7594000000”
    }
  }
}
```

As you can see from the data, you get the specific data for the fields (age, population) that you request and nothing more. This is what makes GraphQL distinctive – it gives the power to the client to request what they want precisely. But “what” is it in the server that returns the GraphQL response? It's a GraphQL API server.

GraphQL queries are sent by the client to a GraphQL API server over an HTTP endpoint via the POST method to the server as a “**string**”. The server extracts and processes the query string, and then just like any typical API server, the GraphQL API will fetch the data from a database or other services/ APIs and return it to the client in a JSON response.

So then, can we use a server like Express as a GraphQL API server? Yes and no. All qualified GraphQL servers must implement two core components specified in the GraphQL specification to validate the process and return the data: a **schema** and **resolvers**.

A GraphQL schema is a collection of type definitions that consist of objects that the client can request and the fields that the objects have. The GraphQL resolvers are functions attached to the fields that return the values when the client makes a query or mutation. For example, below is the type definitions for finding a planet:

```js
type Planet {
  id: Int
  name: String
  age: String
  population: String
}

type Query {
  planet(name: String): Planet
}
```

You can see from the types above that GraphQL uses a strongly typed schema – each field must be defined with a type, which can be a scalar type (which is a single value that can be an integer, boolean, or a string) or object type. The type **`Planet`** and **`Query`** are object types, while **`String`** and **`Int`** are scalar types. And each of the fields in the object types must be resolved with a function, for example:

```js
Planet: {
  id: (root, args, context, info) => root.id,
  name: (root, args, context, info) => root.name,
  age: (root, args, context, info) => root.age,
  population: (root, args, context, info) => root.population,
}

Query: {
```

```
  planet: (root, args, context, info) => {
    return planets.find(planet => planet.name === args.name)
  },
}
```

The example above is written in JavaScript, but a GraphQL server can be written in any programming language as long as you follow and implement what is outlined in the GraphQL specification at https://spec.graphql.org/. The following are some examples of GraphQL implementations in different languages:

- GraphQL.js (JavaScript) at https://github.com/graphql/graphql-js.
- graphql-php (PHP) at https://github.com/webonyx/graphql-php.
- Graphene (Python) at https://github.com/graphql-python/graphene.
- GraphQL Ruby (Ruby) at https://github.com/rmosolgo/graphql-ruby.

You are free to create a new implementation as long as you comply with the GraphQL specification, but we use GraphQL.js throughout this chapter. At this point of reading, you might have questions and doubts – what exactly is the type `Query` (or the query type) in the preceding example? Why do we need it? Let's find out and understand it in the next section by creating a low-level GraphQL API server.

Understanding GraphQL Schema and Resolvers by Creating Low-level GraphQL APIs with GraphQL.js Only

The example schema and resolvers for finding a planet in the previous section are presumed that we use the **GraphQL schema language** to help us create the **GraphQL schema** that is required by the GraphQL server. GraphQL schema language is a **shortcut** – a **shorthand notation** to construct your GraphQL schema and its type system. Before making use of this shorthand notation, we should take a look at how a GraphQL schema is built from the low-level objects and functions like `GraphQLObjectType`, `GraphQLString`, `GraphQLList`, and so on, from GraphQL.js that implements GraphQL specification. Let's install this following package and create a simple GraphQL API server with the HMR Node.js HTTP server that you have learned in *Chapter 7, Managing Data with Node.js Apps for Nuxt*, in the following steps:

1. Install GraphQL.js only via **`npm`** as the project dependency:

   ```
   $ npm i graphql
   ```

2. Import **`graphql`**, **`GraphQLSchema`**, and the following GraphQL object types in **`/src/app.ts`**:

   ```js
   // src/app.ts
   import http from 'http'

   + import {
   +  graphql,
   +  GraphQLSchema,
   +  GraphQLObjectType,
   +  GraphQLInt,
   +  GraphQLString,
   +  GraphQLList
   + } from 'graphql'
   ```

3. Create a static data of planets:

   ```js
   // src/app.ts
   const planets = [
     { id: 3, name: "earth", age: 4543000000, population:
     8045311447 },
     { id: 4, name: "mars", age: 4603000000, population: 0 }
   ]
   ```

4. Define a **`Planet`** object type and the object fields that the client can query:

   ```js
   // src/app.ts
   const Planet = new graphql.GraphQLObjectType({
     name: 'Planet',
     fields: {
     id: { ... },
     name: { ... },
   ```

```js
  age: { ... },
  population: { ... }
})
```

Note that it is a convention to capitalize the object type in the `name` field for the GraphQL schema creation.

5. Define types and how you want to resolve the value for each field:

```js
// src/app.ts
id: {
  type: graphql.GraphQLInt,
  resolve: (root, orgs, context, info) => root.id
},
name: {
  type: graphql.GraphQLString,
  resolve: (root, orgs, context, info) => root.name
},
age: {
  type: graphql.GraphQLString,
  resolve: (root, orgs, context, info) => root.age
},
population: {
  type: graphql.GraphQLString,
  resolve: (root, orgs, context, info) => root.population
}
```

Notice that every resolver function accepts the following four arguments:

- `root` – the object or value resolved from the parent object type (the `Planet` object type in this case).
- `args` – arguments that the field can receive if they are set.
- `context` – a mutable value that is shared across all the resolvers. We can create this context value and add general data that you want them to be shared such as authentication and database connection.
- `info` – a JavaScript object that holds the information about the current field such as its field name, return type, parent type (the `Planet` object type in this case), and the general schema details.

We can omit them if they are not needed for resolving the value for the current field.

6. Define a `Query` object type and the object fields that the client can query:

    ```js
    // src/app.ts
    const queryType = new graphql.GraphQLObjectType({
      name: 'Query',
      fields: {
        hello: { ... },
        planet: { ... }
      }
    })
    ```

Note that the `Query` object type must be defined in the type definition for receiving GraphQL queries from the client.

7. Define the type and resolve how you want to return the value for the `hello` field:

    ```js
    // src/app.ts
    hello: {
      type: graphql.GraphQLString,
      resolve: (root, args, context, info) => 'world'
    }
    ```

Notice that the resolver is just a JavaScript function and each field must have one resolver attached to the `resolve` property.

8. Define the type and resolve how you want to return the value for the `planet` field:

    ```js
    // src/app.ts
    planet: {
      type: Planet,
      args: {
        name: { type: graphql.GraphQLString }
      },
      resolve: (root, args, context, info) => {
        return planets.find(planet => planet.name === args.name)
      }
    ```

```
}
```

Notice that we pass the `Planet` object type that we created and stored in the `Planet` constant to the `planet` field in the `Query` object type so that the relationship between them can be established.

9. Construct a GraphQL schema instance with the required `query` field and the `Query` object type that you have just defined with the fields, types, arguments, and resolvers in it as follows:

```js
// src/app.ts
const schema = new GraphQLSchema({
  query: new GraphQLObjectType({
    name: ‘Query’,
    fields: {
      hello: {
        type: GraphQLString,
        resolve: (root, args, context, info) => ‘world’
      },
      planet: {
        type: Planet,
        args: {
          name: { type: GraphQLString }
        },
        resolve (root, args, context, info) {
          return planets.find(planet => planet.name === args.
          name)
        }
      }
    }
  })
})
```

Note that the `query` key must be provided as the GraphQL query root type So that our query can be chained down to the fields in the `Planet` object type. We can say that the `Planet` object type is a subtype or a child of the `Query` object type (the root type), and their relationship must be established in the parent object (the `Query`) by using the type field in the `planet` field.

10. Pass the preceding constructed GraphQL schema to a `graphql` instance in our `requestListener` async function and then pass it to

`VitePluginNode` for running our server on HMR for development as follows:

```js
// src/app.ts
const requestListener: http.RequestListener = async (req,
res) => {
  res.setHeader(‘Content-Type’, ‘application/json’)
  res.statusCode = 200

  if (req.method === ‘GET’) {
    res.end(‘{“message”:”GraphQL API is ready!”}’)
  } else if (
    req.method === ‘POST’ && (
      req.url === ‘/’ || req.url.startsWith(‘/graphql’)
    )
  ) {
    const source =  (await normalizeBody(req)).query
    const response = await graphql({
      schema,
      source
    })
    res.end(JSON.stringify(response))
  } else {
    res.statusCode = 404
    res.end(‘{“message”:”page not found!”}’)
  }
}

if (import.meta.env.PROD) { ... }

export const viteNodeApp = requestListener
```

Notice that the preceding code is just ordinary if-else condition blocks that you should be familiar with to run our GraphQL HMR server for receiving the HTTP requests and sending the HTTP responses. We just want to process the GraphQL requests and responses from the **`POST`** method on the `/` or **`/graphql`** route. Any other `POST` method route will respond with a “page not found!” JSON message. On the other hand, any **`GET`** method route will just print a “GraphQL API is ready!” JSON message. Also, at this top level, you can create a context that can be shared across resolvers, for example:

````
```js
// src/app.ts
...
const contextValue = {
  something: 'something to be shared'
}
const response = await graphql({
  ...
  contextValue
})
```
````

11. Run the app on the **`dev`** environment for development:

````
```

$ npm run dev
```
````

You should see the following JSON response on your browser at `localhost:5000` or on any `GET` route:

````
```json
{"message":"GraphQL API is ready!"}
```
````

12. Open a separate terminal and send the **`hello`** GraphQL query with **`curl`**:

````
```

$ curl --request POST \
  --header 'content-type: application/json' \
  --url http://localhost:5000/ \
  --data '{"query":"query { hello }"}'
```
````

You should get the following JSON response on the separate terminal:

````
```json
{"data":{"hello":"Hello world!"}}
```
````

Send the `` `greet` `` GraphQL query with "John" as the value for the `` `name` `` parameter via `` `curl` `` on the separate terminal as follows:

````
```
$ curl --request POST \
  --header 'content-type: application/json' \
  --url http://localhost:5000/ \
  --data '{"query":"query { greet (name: \"John\") }"}'
```
````

You should get the following JSON response on the separate terminal:

````
```json
{"data":{"greet":"Hello John"}}
```
````

Send the `` `planet` `` GraphQL query with "earth" as the value for the `` `name` `` parameter via `` `curl` `` on the separate terminal as follows:

````
```
$ curl --request POST \
  --header 'content-type: application/json' \
  --url http://localhost:5000/ \
  --data '{"query":"query { planet (name: \"earth\") { id,
name, age, population } }"}'
```
````

You should get the following JSON response on the separate terminal:

````
```json
{"data":{"planet":{"id":3,"name":"earth","age":"4543000000","
population":"8045311447"}}}
```
````

Well done! You have managed to create a basic GraphQL API server with the HMR Node.js HTTP server from the low-level approach. It is hoped that this can give you a full picture of how a GraphQL API server is created with the GraphQL schema and resolvers. Also, it is hoped that you can see the relationship between these two core components in GraphQL and the doubt and questions have been answered – what exactly is the `` `Query` `` type? Why do we need it? Do we need to have it in the schema? The answer is yes; the query (object) type is a root object type (usually called as root `` `Query` `` type) that must be provided in the GraphQL schema creation.

But you still might have some questions and complaints, particularly on the resolvers – surely you would find it tedious and dumb to define the resolvers in this section for the fields in the `Planet` object type because they do nothing much except return the values that are resolved from the query object. Is there any way to avoid this painful repetition? The answer is yes; you don't specify them for every field in your schema and this lies in the default resolver. But how do we do it? Let's find out in the next section.

Understanding GraphQL Default Resolvers by Creating GraphQL APIs with GraphQL.js and GraphQL Tools

When there is no resolver specified to a field, then by default this field will take the value from the property in the object resolved by the parent – if that object has the property name that matches the field name. So, the fields in the `Planet` object type from the previous section can be refactored as follows:

```js
fields: {
  id: { type: graphql.GraphQLInt },
  name: { type: graphql.GraphQLString },
  age: { type: graphql.GraphQLString },
  population: { type: graphql.GraphQLString }
}
```

The value for these fields will fall back to the properties in the object resolved by the parent (the query type) below accordingly under the hood:

```js
root.id
root.name
root.age
root.population
```

So, the other way around, when a resolver is specified explicitly to a field, then this resolver will always be used, even if the parent's resolver returns any value for that field. For example, let's specify a value explicitly to the ID field in the `Planet` object type as follows:

```js
fields: {
  id: {
    type: graphql.GraphQLInt,
    resolve: (root, orgs, context, info) => 2
  }
}
```

As we know, the default ID values for Earth and Mars are `3` and `4`, and they are resolved by the `Query` object type (the parent), as discussed in the previous section. But now these resolved values will never be used because they are overridden by the value in the ID's resolver above. So, whether you query Earth or Mars, for example:

```js
{
  planet (name: "mars") {
    id
  }
}
```

You will always get 2 in the JSON response:

```json
{
  "data": {
    "planet": {
      "id": 2
    }
  }
}
```

In the preceding code, you can see that it saves us from painful repetition – if you have tons of fields in an object type. Still, however, so far we have been using the most painful way to construct our schema by working with GraphQL.js only because we want to see and understand how a GraphQL schema is created from the low-level types. We probably would not want to take this long and winding road in real life, especially in a large project. We would prefer to use the GraphQL schema language to build the schema and resolvers for us. This is where GraphQL Tools comes in.

We can easily create a GraphQL.js GraphQLSchema instance from the GraphQL schema language using the `makeExecutableSchema` function from a Node.js package `@graphql-tools/schema` in GraphQL Tools. You can find out more information about GraphQL Tools at https://github.com/ardatan/graphql-tools or https://the-guild.dev/graphql/tools. It is a set of NPM packages for building GraphQL schema and resolvers in JavaScript. So let's find out how you can use GraphQL Tools to help us build GraphQL schema using GraphQL language in the following steps:

1. Install `@graphql-tools/schema` via `npm` in the existing project:

```
$ npm i @graphql-tools/schema
```

2. Import `makeExecutableSchema` from `@graphql-tools/schema`, remove the following GraphQL schema and types, except `graphql`, in `/src/app.ts`:

```js
// src/app.ts
import http from 'http'
import {
  graphql,
- GraphQLSchema,
- GraphQLObjectType,
- GraphQLInt,
- GraphQLString,
- GraphQLList
} from 'graphql'
+ import { makeExecutableSchema } from '@graphql-tools/
schema'
```

3. Create the following static data that hold the lists of authors and posts:

```js
// src/app.ts
const authors = [
  { id: 1, name: 'Jane' },
  { id: 2, name: 'John' },
  { id: 3, name: 'Molly' }
]
```

````
const posts = [
  { id: 1, title: 'Post 1', authorId: 1 },
  { id: 2, title: 'Post 2', authorId: 1 },
  { id: 3, title: 'Post 3', authorId: 2 },
  { id: 4, title: 'Post 4', authorId: 3 }
]
```
````

4. Define the **`Author`**, **`Post`**, and **`Query`** object types with the fields that the client can query:

````
```js
// src/app.ts
const typeDefs = `
  type Author {
   id: Int
   name: String
  }

  type Post {
   id: Int
   title: String
   author: Author
  }

  type Query {
    posts: [Post]
    post(id: Int): Post
  }
`
```
````

Note that we can shorthand the **`Author`**, **`Post`**, and **`Query`** object types as **`Author`** type, **`Post`** type, and **`Query`** type, respectively. It is just clearer to use "**object type**" to describe them because that is what they are. Remember that, apart from being an object type by nature, the **`Query`** type is also the root type in GraphQL schema creation.

Notice how we establish the relationship of **`Author`** with **`Post`** and **`Post`** with **`Query`** – the type for the author field is an **`Author`** type. The **`Author`** type has simple scalar types for its fields (**`id`**, **`name`**), while the `Post` type has simple scalar types (**`id`**, **`title`**), and the `Author` type (author) for its field. The `Query` type has the `Post` type for its only field – posts, but it is a list of
````

posts, so we must use the type modifier to wrap the `Post` type with open and closed square brackets to indicate that this posts field will resolve with an array of `Post` objects.

For more information about the type modifier, please visit https://graphql.org/learn/schema/lists-and-non-null.

5. Define resolvers to specify how you want to resolve the value for the `posts` field in the `Query` type and the `author` field in the `Post` type:

```js
// src/app.ts
var resolvers = {
  Query: {
    posts: (root, args, context, info) => posts
  },

  Post: {
    author: root => authors.find(author => author.id === root.
    authorId)
  }
}
```

Notice how the GraphQL schema language has helped us to decouple the resolvers from the object types and they are simply defined in a single JavaScript object. The resolvers in the JavaScript object are **magically** connected with the object types, as long as the property names for our resolvers map the field names in the type definitions. Hence, this JavaScript object is called the resolver map. Before defining resolvers, we must also define the top-level property names (`Query`, `Post`) in the resolver map to match the object types (`Author`, `Post`, `Query`) in the type definitions. But we don't need to define any specific resolvers for the `Author` type in this resolver map because the values for the fields (`id`, `name`) in `Author` are resolved by the default resolvers automatically.

Another point to note is that the values for the fields (`id`, `title`) in the `Post` type are also resolved by the default ones. If you don't like using property names to define resolvers, you can use resolver functions instead, as long as the function names correspond with field names in the type definitions. For example, the resolvers for the author field can be re-written as follows:

```js
Post: {
  author (root) {
    return authors.find(author => author.id === root.authorId)
  }
}
```

6. Pass the GraphQL type definitions and resolvers to `makeExecutableSchema` to create a `GraphQLSchema` instance from GraphQL schema language as follows:

```js
// src/app.ts
const executableSchema = makeExecutableSchema({
  typeDefs,
  resolvers
})
```

7. Run the app on the `dev` environment for development:

```
$ npm run dev
```

You should see the following JSON response on your browser at `localhost:5000` or on any `GET` route:

```json
{"message":"GraphQL API is ready!"}
```

8. Open a separate terminal and send the `posts` GraphQL query with `curl`:

```
$ curl --request POST \
  --header ‘content-type: application/json’ \
  --url http://localhost:5000/ \
  --data ‘{“query”:”query { posts { id, title, author { name
} } }”}’
```

```
```

You should get the following JSON response on the separate terminal:


```json
{"data":{"posts":[{"id":1,"title":"Post
1","author":{"name":"Jane"}},{"id":2,"title":"Post
2","author":{"name":"Jane"}},{"id":3,"title":"Post
3","author":{"name":"John"}},{"id":4,"title":"Post
4","author":{"name":"Molly"}}]}}
```


Send the `post` GraphQL query with `2` as the value for the `id` parameter via `curl` on the separate terminal as follows:

```
$ curl --request POST \
  --header 'content-type: application/json' \
  --url http://localhost:5000/ \
  --data '{"query":"query { post (id: 2) { id, title, author
{ name } } }"}'
```

You should get the following JSON response on the separate terminal:


```json
{"data":{"post":{"id":2,"title":"Post 2","author"
:{"name":"Jane"}}}}
```


There you go. That is how easily we can build a GraphQL API with GraphQL schema language and GraphQL Tools. It is worth knowing the long and painful way a GraphQL schema and resolvers are created before adopting the shorthand method. Once you have this basic concrete knowledge established, you should be able to query the data like a piece of cake! But still, you will find it difficult to test your GraphQL APIs during development by using cURL. For that, you will just need a **GraphQL IDE** – a graphical and interactive IDE for testing GraphQL APIs, such as Kong Insomnia (https://insomnia.rest/) and Altair GraphQL Client (https://altairgraphql.dev/). Kong Insomnia is not just an IDE for testing REST APIs, but also an IDE for testing GraphQL APIs. You just have to install one of these IDEs on your local machine, launch it, and throw in your GraphQL queries whenever you need to test your GraphQL APIs.

Even though we only have covered a few of GraphQL types in this section: scalar type, object type, query type, and the type modifier. There are a few other types, such as the `mutation` type, `enumeration` type, `union` and `input` types, and `interface`, please check them out at https://graphql.org/learn/schema/. Right now, let's venture further into how you can use a database such as MongoDB with GraphQL. So let's find out how you can integrate GraphQL with MongoDB in the next topic!

You can find the example apps for this topic in `/4.graphql/1.vanilla/` in the GitHub repository of this book.

Creating GraphQL Servers with MongoDB and Node.js HTTP API

So far, you have created GraphQL schema all in a single file and have used static data. But your schema is going to grow over time when you need to rely on a professional database system like MongoDB for managing your data. Keeping all schema in one file isn't ideal in the long term, especially for large projects. And your schema and code will get messy and cluttered by keeping them in the same file. So in this topic, besides looking into how to incorporate a database with your GraphQL server, we will also look into how to split your schema into separate files and then merge them altogether into a single schema for the GraphQL engine to execute it. We will be using MongoDB as the database system in this exploration.

Creating a GraphQL Server for Nuxt: Node.js HTTP API, GraphQL Tools, MongoDB

Just like in the previous topics and chapters, we will reuse the skills and knowledge that you have learned from here so far. We will reuse the Node.js HTTP server and turn it into a GraphQL server with GraphQL.js. We will reuse the skills on MongoDB that you have learned in *Chapter 6, Managing Data with Nitro Server Engine in Nuxt*, in which you learned to insert multiple user documents with a BSON timestamp type in the `users` collection. So we are going to reuse the same database from *Chapter* 6 to store and query the user documents but with a GraphQL schema on top of it. We will create this user GraphQL schema in a separate file as well as the "hello world" schema that you have just learned in the previous topic. You will see how exciting it is to split them into files and then merge them together beautifully with the help of GraphQL Tools. So let's find out in the following steps:

1. Create the following folders and files in the `/src/` folder as follows:

    ```
    src
    ├── app.ts
    ├── utils
    └── schema
        ├── app.ts
        ├── types
        └── resolvers
    ```

2. Create the following folders and files in the `/utils/`, `/types/`, and `/resolvers/` folders as follows:

- The `/utils/` folder:

    ```
    utils
    ├── normalize-body.ts
    ├── mongo.ts
    └── gql
        └── resolvers.ts
    ```

- The `/types/` folder:

    ```
    types
    ├── hello.ts
    └── user.ts
    ```

- The `/resolvers/` folder:

    ```
    resolvers
    ├── hello.ts
    └── user.ts
    ```

3. Install `mongodb` via `npm` in your project:

    ```
    ```

```
$ npm i mongodb
```

4. Add the MongoDB connection details in a `.env` file as follows:

```
// .env
# Set db env variables:
VITE_DB_HOST=mongodb://127.0.0.1:27017
VITE_DB_DBNAME=advanced-nuxtjs-course

# Set app env variables:
VITE_APP_HOST=localhost
VITE_APP_PORT=5000
VITE_CROSS_ORIGIN=http://localhost:3000
```

5. Use the MongoDB connection details from the `.env` file to create a `connect` function, a `close` function, and an `ObjectId` constant in `/src/utils/mongo.ts`:

```js
// src/utils/mongo.ts
import { MongoClient, ObjectId as objectId } from ‘mongodb’

const url = import.meta.env.VITE_DB_HOST
const dbName = import.meta.env.VITE_DB_DBNAME

export async function connect () {
  const client = new MongoClient(url)

  await client.connect()
  console.log(‘🚀 Connected successfully to MongoDB server’)

  const db = client.db(dbName)
  return { client, db }
}

export function close (client) {
  client.close()
  console.log(‘🚀 Disconnected from MongoDB server’)
}

export const ObjectId = objectId
```

Notice that the preceding exported functions and the constant are the same as those you have created in *Chapter 6, Managing Data with Nitro Server Engine in Nuxt*, and in *Chapter 7, Managing Data with Node.js Apps for Nuxt*.

6. Create a **`getItem`** async function for fetching a single document from the database in **`/src/utils/gql/resolvers.ts`**:

````
```js
// src/utils/gql/resolvers.ts
import { connect, close, ObjectId } from ‘@/utils/mongo’

export async function getItem (collectionName, root, args) {
  const { client, db } = await connect()
  const collection = db.collection(collectionName)

  const result = await collection.findOne({
    $or: [
      { slug: args.slug },
      { _id: ObjectId(args._id) }
    ]
  })

  close(client)
  return result
}
```
````

In the preceding code, we use the **`findOne`** method to find a document by a slug or a MongoDB document ID. The parameters of slug and MongoDB document ID are derived from the **`args`** argument.

7. Create a **`getItems`** async function for fetching multiple documents from the database in **`/src/utils/gql/resolvers.ts`**:

````
```js
// src/utils/gql/resolvers.ts
import { connect, close, ObjectId } from ‘@/utils/mongo’
...
export async function getItems (collectionName, root, args) {
  const limit = args.limit ? args.limit : 12
  const skip = args.skip ? args.skip : 0

  const { client, db } = await connect()
  const collection = db.collection(collectionName)
````
````

~~~
    let query = {}
    const docs = await collection.find(query)
      .limit(limit)
      .skip(skip)
      .toArray()

    close(client)
    return docs
  }
  ```
~~~

In the preceding code, we use the `find` method to find documents with a limit and an offset to skip documents. The parameters of `limit` and `skip` are derived from the `args` argument.

8. Create a `countItems` async function for counting documents of a collection in the database in `/src/utils/gql/resolvers.ts`:

~~~
  ```js
  // src/utils/gql/resolvers.ts
  import { connect, close, ObjectId } from '@/utils/mongo'
  ...
  export async function countItems (collectionName, root, args) {
    const { client, db } = await connect()
    const collection = db.collection(collectionName)

    let query = {}
    const total = await collection.countDocuments(query)

    close(client)
    return total
  }
  ```
~~~

9. Create a `Query` type in `/src/schema/types/hello.ts` with a `hello` field for the client to query:

~~~
  ```js
  // src/schema/types/hello.ts
  export default `
    type Query {
      hello: String
    }
~~~

```
`
```

10. Create a `Query` type and a `User` type in `/src/schema/types/user.ts` with the following fields:

```js
// src/schema/types/user.ts
export default `
  type Query {
    user (
      slug: String,
      _id: String
    ): User

    users (
      limit: Int,
      skip: Int
    ): [User]

    total: Int
  }

  type User {
    name: String
    slug: String
    email: String
    createdAt: String
    _id: String
  }
`
```

11. Create a resolver in `/src/schema/resolvers/hello.ts` for the `hello` field in the hello `Query` type:

```js
// src/schema/resolvers/hello.ts
export default {
  Query: {
    hello: () => 'Hello world!'
  }
}
```

12. Create resolvers in `/src/schema/resolvers/user.ts` for the `user`, `users`, and `total` fields in the user `Query` type:

```js
// src/schema/resolvers/user.ts
import { getItem, getItems, countItems } from '@/utils/gql/
resolvers'

export default {
  Query: {
    user: async (root, args) => await getItem('users', root,
    args),
    users: async (root, args) => await getItems('users',
    root, args),
    total: async (root, args) => await countItems('users',
    root, args)
  }
}
```

13. Create a resolver in `/src/schema/resolvers/user.ts` for the `createdAt` field in the `User` type:

```js
// src/schema/resolvers/user.ts
...
export default {
  Query: {
    ...
  },

  User: {
    createdAt: root => {
      if (
        typeof root.createdAt === 'object' &&
        root.createdAt.constructor.name === 'Timestamp'
      ) {
        return root.createdAt.getHighBits() * 1000
      }
      return root.createdAt
    }
  }
}
```

The preceding resolver is used to convert a BSON timestamp created from **`new Timestamp()`** to a UNIX timestamp for the **`createdAt`** field, which accepts a **`String`** type only. For example, you would get the following value for the BSON timestamp:

```
`new Timestamp({ t: 1692466633, i: 1 })`
```

The BSON timestamp value is an object and it conflicts with the **`String`** type of the **`createdAt`** field, so we just need to convert it to **`1692466633000`**.

14. Import all the preceding types and resolvers and merge them with **`mergeTypeDefs`** and **`mergeResolvers`** from **`@graphql-tools`** in **`/src/schema/index.ts`**:

````
```js
// src/schema/index.ts
import { mergeTypeDefs, mergeResolvers } from
'@graphql-tools/merge'

import helloType from '@/schema/types/hello'
import userType from '@/schema/types/user'
import userResolvers from '@/schema/resolvers/user'
import helloResolvers from '@/schema/resolvers/hello'

const typeDefs = mergeTypeDefs([helloType, userType])
const resolvers = mergeResolvers([helloResolvers,
userResolvers])

export {
  typeDefs,
  resolvers
}
```
````

In the preceding code, we manually import types and resolvers and merge them. But it is repetitive to do so because types and resolvers are going to grow over time. So it is better to import them automatically with **`globEager`**, loops, and push them into arrays as follows:

````
```js
// src/schema/index.ts
import { mergeTypeDefs, mergeResolvers } from
'@graphql-tools/merge'
````
````

~~~
const typesArray = []
const resolversArray = []

const globTypes = import.meta.globEager('./types/**')
const globResolvers = import.meta.globEager('./resolvers/**')

Object.entries(globTypes).forEach(([path, type]) =>
  typesArray.push(type.default)
)
Object.entries(globResolvers).forEach(([path, resolver]) =>
  resolversArray.push(resolver.default)
)

const typeDefs = mergeTypeDefs(typesArray)
const resolvers = mergeResolvers(resolversArray)

export {
  typeDefs,
  resolvers
}
```
~~~

15. Import the merged types and resolvers to create the required executable GraphQL schema with **`makeExecutableSchema`** in **`/src/app.ts`**:

~~~
```js
// src/app.ts
...
import { makeExecutableSchema } from '@graphql-tools/schema'
import { typeDefs, resolvers } from '@/schema'

const schema = makeExecutableSchema({
  typeDefs,
  resolvers
})
```
~~~

16. Enable CORS in the **`requestListener`** async function for a remote client to access our GraphQL server:

~~~
```js
// src/app.ts
...
const requestListener: http.RequestListener = async (req,
~~~

```
res) => {
  res.setHeader('Access-Control-Allow-Origin', '*')
  res.setHeader('Access-Control-Allow-Methods', 'POST')
  res.setHeader('Access-Control-Allow-Headers',
'X-Requested-With, Content-Type')
  res.setHeader('Access-Control-Allow-Credentials', true)
  res.setHeader('Content-Type', 'application/json')
  res.statusCode = 200

  if (req.method === 'OPTIONS') {
    res.end()
  } else {
    ...
  }
}
```

Notice that we don't want to run the main code if the incoming HTTP request method is `OPTIONS`. So wrap our code in an if-else condition block.

17. Run the app on the `dev` environment for development:

```
$ npm run dev
```

You should see the following JSON response on your browser at `localhost:5000` or on any `GET` route:

```json
{"message":"GraphQL API is ready!"}
```

18. Launch Kong Insomnia and send a GraphQL query to the GraphQL server for a test, for example:

```
query {
  users(limit: 2) {
    _id
    email
    name
    slug
    createdAt
```

```
  }
}
```

You should get the following JSON response on Insomnia:

```json
{
  “data”: {
    “users”: [
      {
        “_id”: “64e0fdc9e3939a03c2dac6f2”,
        “email”: “john@example.com”,
        “name”: “John”,
        “slug”: “john”,
        “createdAt”: “1692466633000”
      },
      {
        “_id”: “64e0fdc9e3939a03c2dac6f3”,
        “email”: “jane@example.com”,
        “name”: “Jane”,
        “slug”: “jane”,
        “createdAt”: “1692466633000”
      }
    ]
  }
}
```

19. Create a `.env` file in your Nuxt project root with the following variables and values for the app and the cross-origin API:

```
// .env
APP_BASE_URL=http://localhost:3000
API_BASE_URL=http://localhost:5000
```

Note that `localhost:3000` is your Nuxt app, while `localhost:5000` is the cross-origin GraphQL API.

20. Use `useF3tch` in the `<script>` block to send the GraphQL query to fetch the list of users from the cross-origin API:

````
```js
// pages/users.vue
<script setup>
const users = ref()
  const query = `
    query {
      users {
        _id
        name
        slug
        email
        createdAt
      }
    }
  `
  const { data , error } = await useF3tch('/', {
    method: 'POST',
    body: { query }
  })

  if (data.value) {
    users.value = data.value.users
  }
</script>
```
````

21. Display the data of each user in the `<template>` block:

````
```html
// pages/users.vue
<template>
  <div v-if="users">
    <h1>Users</h1>
    <ul>
      <li v-for="user in users" v-bind:key="user._id">
        {{ user.name }}
      </li>
    </ul>
  </div>
</template>
```
````

22. Run the Nuxt app on the `` `dev` `` environment:

    ```
    ```
    $ npm run dev
    ```
    ```

You should see all the users are fetched from the cross-origin API and displayed successfully on your browser at `` `localhost:3000/users` ``.

There you go. You can see how we have uncluttered the code in `` `/src/app.ts` `` by moving GraphQL types and resolvers out into separate files in `` `/src/schema` ``. We only have to import and merge them, and then create the root schema to pass it to the GraghQL instance in `` `/src/app.ts` ``. You can also see that we can auto-import multiple GraphQL types and resolvers and merge them into related arrays in `` `/src/schema/index.ts` ``. So you don't need to touch the `` `/src/app.ts` `` and `` `/src/schema/index.ts` `` files again basically once they are done; you just need to develop your schema inside the `` `/type/` `` and `` `/resolvers/` `` directories. You can also see that we have reused the code from *Chapter 7, Managing Data with Node.js Apps for Nuxt*, to enable CORS for our Nuxt app to send GraphQL queries. Sending GraphQL queries from the Nuxt app is also extremely straightforward. It is the same as those queries you would dump onto a GraphQL IDE like Kong Insomnia to test your GraphQL APIs for development.

GraphQL is beautiful. It places the power on the client side. It makes the ordinary and traditional data management system exciting and fun. It also makes the development experience and process joyful and playful. You can see all the joy, fun, and excitement in this topic with MongoDB. But you may ask, what about those database systems that are older than MongoDB like MySQL? What if you have existing and established projects that are deeply coupled with the old generation content management systems like WordPress? How can we make them fun and exciting? The short answer is yes, you can do that. You can achieve that easily with what you have already learned so far and reusing code that you have already written. So let's find out how you can use GraphQL with WordPress to manage data for your Nuxt app in the next topic!

You can find the example apps for this topic in **`` `/4.graphql/2.mongodb/ and /1.nuxt/3.cross-domains/3.connect-graphql/1.mongodb/` ``** in the GitHub repository of this book.

Creating GraphQL Servers with WordPress and Node.js HTTP API

Just like the previous topic, Creating GraphQL Servers with MongoDB and Node.js HTTP API, we will reuse the Node.js HTTP GraphQL server that you have learned to create so far. We will also reuse the skills on WordPress REST API that you have learned in *Chapter 8, Managing Database with PHP Apps for Nuxt*, in which you learned to develop custom headless WordPress REST APIs for the Nuxt app. So we are going to reuse the same database from *Chapter* 8 to store and query the `` `page` `` and `` `project` `` post-type pages. Since we have created the WordPress REST APIs, we can leave them as they are. We just need to create a GraphQL server to fetch data from the headless WordPress REST APIs, and our Nuxt app will fetch data from the GraphQL server by sending GraphQL queries. In other words, this GraphQL server is a bridge between the WordPress REST APIs and the Nuxt app. So let's find out how to build this GraphQL bridge with WordPress for Nuxt apps!

Creating a GraphQL Server for Nuxt: Node.js HTTP API, GraphQL Tools, WordPress

Just like the previous topic, we will separate GraphQL types and resolvers for the `` `page` `` and `` `project` `` post-type pages. However, since the `` `page` `` and `` `project` `` post-type pages have the same fields as the `` `post` `` post-type pages, we will abstract these fields into a separate file so that they can be shared between different post-type pages. Then we will merge them together beautifully with the help of GraphQL Tools just as in the previous topic, *Creating GraphQL Servers with MongoDB and Node.js* HTTP API. So let's find out in the following steps:

1. Create the following folders and files in the `` `/src/` `` folder as follows:

````
```

src
├── app.ts
├── composables
├── utils
└── schema
    ├── app.ts
    ├── fields
````
````

```
    ├── types
    └── resolvers
```

2. Create the following folders and files in the `/composables/`, `/utils/`, `/fields/`, `/types/`, and `/resolvers/` folders as follows:

- The `/composables/` folder:

```
composables
└── use-f3tch.ts
```

- The `/utils/` folder:

```
utils
├── normalize-body.ts
└── gql
    └── resolvers.ts
```

- The `/fields/` folder:

```
fields
└── post.ts
```

- The `/types/` folder:

```
types
├── page.ts
└── project.ts
```

- The `/resolvers/` folder:

```
resolvers
├── page.ts
└── project.ts
```

````
```
````

3. Add the WordPress API base URL in a `` `.env` `` file as follows:

````
```
# Set api env variables:
VITE_API_BASE_URL=http://localhost:4000

# Set app env variables:
VITE_APP_HOST=localhost
VITE_APP_PORT=5000
VITE_CROSS_ORIGIN=http://localhost:3000
```
````

4. Use the Node.js Fetch API to create an async function for fetching data from the WordPress REST API in `` `/src/composables/use-f3tch.ts` ``:

````
```js
// src/composables/use-f3tch.ts
export default async (path, options = {}) => {
  let data = null
  let res = null
  const baseURL = options.baseURL ?? import.meta.env.VITE_
  API_BASE_URL

  if (options.body) {
    options.body = JSON.stringify(options.body)
    options.headers = { ‘Content-Type’: ‘application/json’ }
  }

  try {
    res = await fetch(`${baseURL}${path}`, options)
  } catch (err) {
    throw Error(err)
  }

  data = await res.json()
  if (!res.ok) {
    const error = new Error(`${res.statusText} ${res.url}`)
    error.statusCode = res.status
    error.statusText = res.statusText
    error.message = data.message
    throw error
  }
````

~~~
    data = data.data ?? data
    return { data }
  }
  ```
~~~

In the preceding custom fetch function, we use the try-catch blocks to catch any error from data fetching. If an error is caught, we use the if-condition block to throw a custom error object with the **`Error`** object. If the data is fetched successfully, then we return it. Also, if a **`data`** key is set from the fetched data, then we want to return data that is stored in this key. For more information about the Node.js Fetch API (all known as Node.js Undici), please visit https://undici.nodejs.org/.

5. Create a **`getItem`** async function for fetching a single page (or post) data from the WordPress API in **`/src/utils/gql/resolvers.ts`**:

~~~
```js
// src/utils/gql/resolvers.ts
import useF3tch from '@/composables/use-f3tch'

export async function getItem (namespace, root, args) {
  const { data, error } = await useF3tch(`${namespace}${args.
  slug}`)
  return data
}
```
~~~

In the preceding code, we use our custom **`useF3tch`** function to fetch the page by a slug. And the parameter of the slug is derived from the **`args`** argument.

6. Create a **`getItems`** async function for fetching the data of multiple pages from the WordPress API in **`/src/utils/gql/resolvers.ts`**:

~~~
```js
// src/utils/gql/resolvers.ts
import useF3tch from '@/composables/use-f3tch'
...
export async function getItems (namespace, root, args) {
  const limit = args.limit ? args.limit : 6
  const currentPage = args.page > 0 ? args.page : 1

  const query = {
    page_number: currentPage,
    posts_per_page: limit
~~~

```
  }

  const { data, error } = await useF3tch(`${namespace}`, {
    method: 'POST',
    body: query
  })

  const nodes = data.items
  const totalPages = data.total_pages
}
```

In the preceding code, we use our custom **`useF3tch`** function to fetch pages with a limit and an offset to skip pages. The parameters of **`limit`** and **`skip`** are derived from the **`args`** argument. After the data is fetched successfully, we manipulate it for pagination and edges before returning the data as follows:

```js
// src/utils/gql/resolvers.ts
...
export async function getItems (namespace, root, args) {
  ...
  const nextPage = currentPage + 1
  const previousPage = currentPage - 1
  const hasPreviousPage = previousPage > 0
  const hasNextPage = nextPage <= totalPages

  const edges = nodes.map((edge) => {
    return {
      node: edge,
      cursor: edge.ID
    }
  })

  return {
    edges,
    pageInfo: {
        currentPage,
        previousPage,
        nextPage,
        hasPreviousPage,
        hasNextPage,
        totalPages
    },
  }
```

````
}
```
````

7. Create a **`countItems`** async function for working out the total number of pages of a post type in the database in **`/src/utils/gql/resolvers.ts`**:

````
```js
// src/utils/gql/resolvers.ts
import useF3tch from '@/composables/use-f3tch'
...
export async function countItems (namespace, root, args) {
  const query = {
    count_only: true
  }

  const { data: total, error } = await useF3tch(`$
  {namespace}`, {
    method: 'POST',
    body: query
  })

  return total
}
```
````

8. Create the post fields and set their types in **`/src/schema/fields/post.ts`**:

````
```js
// src/schema/fields/post.ts
export default `
  ID: String
  post_title: String
  post_name: String
  post_excerpt: String
  post_content: String
  post_date: String
  post_type: String
  post_author: String
  featured_image: String
  head: HtmlHead
`
```
````
````

In WordPress, the `page` and `project` post types, or any other custom post types have identical fields, so we can abstract these fields into a separate file so that they can be shared among the GraphQL types in our GraphQL server.

9. Create a `Query` type and a `Page` type in `/src/schema/types/page.ts` with the fields from `/src/schema/fields/post.ts`:

```js
// src/schema/types/page.ts
import post from '@/schema/fields/post'

export default `
  type Query {
    page (
      slug: String,
    ): Page
  }

  type Page {
    ${post}
  }
`
```

10. Create a `Query` type, a `Project` type, a `ProjectConnection` type, and a `ProjectEdge` type in `/src/schema/types/project.ts` with the fields from `/src/schema/fields/post.ts`:

```js
// src/schema/types/project.ts
import post from '@/schema/fields/post'

export default `
  type Query {
    projects (
      limit: Int,
      page: Int
    ): ProjectConnection

    project (
      slug: String,
    ): Project
  }

  type Project {
```

````
    ${post}
  }

  type ProjectConnection {
    edges: [ProjectEdge]
    pageInfo: PageInfo
    total: Int
  }

  type ProjectEdge {
    node: Project
    cursor: String
  }
`
```
````

In the preceding code, the `ProjectConnection` and `ProjectEdge` types are used to help us to paginate through pages. Each fetched project data is attached to the `node` field in the `ProjectConnection` type. All populated project nodes are attached to the `edges` field in the `ProjectEdge` type. Lastly, the pagination information is attached to the `pageInfo` field in the `ProjectConnection` type. For more information about pagination and edges, please visit https://graphql.org/learn/pagination/#pagination-and-edges.

11. Create a `PageInfo` type in `/src/schema/types/page-info.ts` with the following fields:

````
```js
// src/schema/types/page-info.ts
export default `
  type PageInfo {
    # Required fields for cursor-based pagination:
    hasPreviousPage: Boolean
    hasNextPage: Boolean
    startCursor: String
    endCursor: String

    # Required fields for offset-based pagination:
    previousPage: String
    nextPage: String
    currentPage: String
    totalPages: String
  }
`
```
````
````

There are two popular types of pagination – cursor-based pagination and offset-based pagination. The `PageInfo` type in the preceding code contains the required fields for making these types of pagination. We will be using the offset-based pagination to paginate our WordPress pages. For more information about cursor-based pagination and offset-based pagination, please visit https://www.apollographql.com/docs/react/pagination/cursor-based and https://www.apollographql.com/docs/react/pagination/offset-based.

12. Create a resolver in `/src/schema/resolvers/page.ts` for the `page` field in the page `Query` type:

```js
// src/schema/resolvers/page.ts
import { getItem } from '@/utils/gql/resolvers'

export default {
  Query: {
    page: async (root, args) => await getItem('/wp-json/api/v1/page/', root, args),
  }
}
```

13. Create resolvers in `/src/schema/resolvers/project.ts` for the `project`, `projects`, and `total` fields in the project `Query` type:

```js
// src/schema/resolvers/project.ts
import { getItem, getItems, countItems } from '@/utils/gql/resolvers'

export default {
  Query: {
    project: async (root, args) => await getItem('/wp-json/api/v1/project/', root, args),
    projects: async (root, args) => await getItems('/wp-json/api/v1/projects/', root, args)
  },

  ProjectConnection: {
    total: async (root, args) => await countItems('/wp-json/api/v1/projects/', root, args)
  }
}
```

Notice that the preceding resolver in `ProjectConnection` is used to resolve the value for the `total` field.

14. Auto-import all the preceding types and resolvers and merge them with `mergeTypeDefs` and `mergeResolvers` from **@graphql-tools** in `/src/schema/index.ts` with `globEager`, loops, and arrays as follows:

    ```js
    // src/schema/index.ts
    import { mergeTypeDefs, mergeResolvers } from
    '@graphql-tools/merge'

    const typesArray = []
    const resolversArray = []

    const globTypes = import.meta.globEager('./types/**')
    const globResolvers = import.meta.globEager('./resolvers/**')

    Object.entries(globTypes).forEach(([path, type]) =>
      typesArray.push(type.default)
    )
    Object.entries(globResolvers).forEach(([path, resolver]) =>
      resolversArray.push(resolver.default)
    )

    const typeDefs = mergeTypeDefs(typesArray)
    const resolvers = mergeResolvers(resolversArray)

    export {
      typeDefs,
      resolvers
    }
    ```

15. Import the merged types and resolvers to create the required executable GraphQL schema with `makeExecutableSchema` in `/src/app.ts`:

    ```js
    // src/app.ts
    ...
    import { makeExecutableSchema } from '@graphql-tools/schema'
    import { typeDefs, resolvers } from '@/schema'
    ```

```
const schema = makeExecutableSchema({
  typeDefs,
  resolvers
})
```

16. Enable CORS in the `requestListener` async function for a remote client to access our GraphQL server:

```js
// src/app.ts
...
const requestListener: http.RequestListener = async (req,
res) => {
  res.setHeader('Access-Control-Allow-Origin', '*')
  res.setHeader('Access-Control-Allow-Methods', 'POST')
  res.setHeader('Access-Control-Allow-Headers',
'X-Requested-With, Content-Type')
  res.setHeader('Access-Control-Allow-Credentials', true)
  res.setHeader('Content-Type', 'application/json')
  res.statusCode = 200

  if (req.method === 'OPTIONS') {
    res.end()
  } else {
    ...
  }
}
```

17. Run the app on the `dev` environment for development:

```
$ npm run dev
```

You should see the following JSON response on your browser at `localhost:5000` or on any `GET` route:

```json
{"message":"GraphQL API is ready!"}
```

18. Launch Kong Insomnia and send a GraphQL query to the GraphQL server for a test, for example:

```
query {
  page(slug: “projects”) {
    ID
    post_title
  }
}
```

You should get the following JSON response on Kong Insomnia:

```json
{
  “data”: {
    “page”: {
      “ID”: “34”,
      “post_title”: “Projects”
    }
  }
}
```

Now, let’s try to fetch multiple pages by using the following GraphQL:

```
query {
  projects(page: 1) {
    total
    edges {
      node {
        ID
        post_title
      }
    }
    pageInfo {
      currentPage
      previousPage
      nextPage
      totalPages
    }
  }
```

```
}
```

You should get the following JSON response on Kong Insomnia:

```json
{
  “data”: {
    “projects”: {
      “total”: 12,
      “edges”: [
        {
          “node”: {
            “ID”: “32”,
            “post_title”: “Sample 12”
          }
        },
        {
          “node”: {
            “ID”: “31”,
            “post_title”: “Sample 11”
          }
        },
        ...
      ],
      “pageInfo”: {
        “currentPage”: “1”,
        “previousPage”: “0”,
        “nextPage”: “2”,
        “totalPages”: “2”
      }
    }
  }
}
```

19. Create a `.env` file in your Nuxt project root with the following variables and values for the app and the cross-origin API:

```
// .env
APP_BASE_URL=http://localhost:3000
API_BASE_URL=http://localhost:5000
```

Note that `localhost:3000` is your Nuxt app, while `localhost:5000` is the cross-origin GraphQL API.

20. Use `useF3tch` in the `<script>` block to send the GraphQL query to fetch the list of projects from the cross-origin API:

```js
// pages/projects.vue
<script setup>
const posts = ref()
const query = `
  query {
    projects {
      edges {
        node {
          ID
          post_name
          post_title
        }
      }
    }
  }
`
const { data , error } = await useF3tch(‘/’, {
  method: ‘POST’,
  body: { query }
})

if (data.value) {
  posts.value = data.value.projects.edges
}
</script>
```

21. Display the data of each project in the `<template>` block:

```html
// pages/projects.vue
<template>
  <div v-if=”posts”>
    <h1>Projects</h1>
    <ul>
      <li v-for=”{ node: post } in posts” v-bind:key=”post.
      ID”>
        {{ post.post_title }}
```

```
        </li>
      </ul>
    </div>
  </template>
```

22. Run the Nuxt app on the `dev` environment:

```
$ npm run dev
```

You should see projects are fetched from the cross-origin API and displayed successfully on your browser at `localhost:3000/projects`.

There you go. You can see how easy it is to create this GraphQL bridge with WordPress for our Nuxt app. Most of the code and steps in this topic are similar to the previous topic, the only big difference the `use-f3tch.ts` composable is added in this GraphQL server for fetching data from the WordPress REST APIs. There are some small differences, such as abstracting the shared fields and implementing the GraphQL connection with nodes and edges for making an offset-based pagination.

In this topic, we only have demonstrated how to abstract the `post` fields, but in a real and large WordPress project, you would abstract more shareable fields in separate files in the `/fields/` directory, instead of repeating the same exact fields in different custom GraphQL object types. The `PageInfo` object type that you have created also can be used for making cursor-based pagination if you want to implement this kind of pagination instead, for other database systems such as MongoDB. The `use-f3tch.ts` composable you have created with the Node.js Fetch API also can be used in Nuxt projects if you prefer that, instead of using the Nuxt Fetch APIs (such as `$fetch`, `useFetch`, and `useLazyFetch`), which are based on UnJS `ofetch` (https://github.com/unjs/ofetch). So, if you need an established CMS like WordPress with GraphQL to manage data for your Nuxt apps, instead of building one from scratch, you have the answer that you have just learned from this topic!

You can find the example apps for this topic in `/4.graphql/3.wordpress/` and `/1.nuxt/3.cross-domains/3.connect-graphql/2.wordpress/` in the GitHub repository of this book.

Conclusion

In this chapter, you have learned about GraphQL and its query, schema, object types, and resolvers. You have understood GraphQL schema and GraphQL default resolvers by creating GraphQL servers and GraphQL APIs. You have learned to use GraphQL schema language to create schema and GraphQL queries to query data. You have reused the HMR Node.js HTTP server that you have learned in the past and have turned it into GraphQL servers with GraphQL.js and GraphQL Tools. You have managed to split your GraphQL object types, resolvers, and fields into separate files and then merge them all together with the help of GraphQL Tools. Also, you have incorporated MongoDB into your GraphQL server and have bridged GraphQL with WordPress REST APIs to serve data for your Nuxt apps. Lastly, you have used the Node.js Fetch API to create a custom HTTP fetch composable for fetching data from the WordPress REST APIs.

In the next chapter, which is the last chapter of this book, you will learn to create static-generated (SSG) sites with Nuxt and WordPress; fetch data and stream assets from WordPress into your Nuxt project for making SSG sites; take your Nuxt app further with testing, deployment, other Nuxt modules, such as Nuxt GTA an Nuxt-Auth, and other Nuxt APIs, such as composable APIs, utilities APIs, and component APIs (for example,`` `<Teleport>` ``). Finally, you will look into options, such as using Quasar and Vite SSR alone or Vite SSR plugins, for building Vue SSR and SSG apps.

CHAPTER 10

Creating SSG Sites with Nuxt and WordPress and Going Further

Introduction

Welcome to *Chapter 10*. In this last chapter, you will create static-generated (SSG) sites with Nuxt and WordPress. You will use Node.js APIs to fetch data and stream assets from WordPress into your Nuxt project for making SSG sites. You will find out what you can do with your Nuxt app on testing, linting, and deployment, as well as taking it further with other Nuxt modules, such as Nuxt GTA, and other Nuxt APIs (composables, utilities, and components) such as the `` `<Teleport>` `` component. Lastly, we will look into options, such as using Quasar, Gridsome, VuePress, Vue SSR, Vite SSR, Vite SSR plugins, and Vite SSG plugins, for building Vue SSR and SSG apps.

Structure

The topics that will be covered in this chapter are as follows:

- Fetching Data from WordPress for Static Sites
- Streaming Assets from WordPress for Static Sites
- Going Further and Knowing Your Options

Fetching Data from WordPress for Static Sites

Nuxt is not just a framework for creating SSR Vue apps, but it is also a framework for creating SSG apps. It generates static pages out of the box for us without any configuration. Static sites (or SSG apps) can be a great solution if you don't need server-side scripting to process and serve your site. You can get your static site hosted at any static hosting server, which definitely can save the cost of hosting for your business. So let's find out how you can leverage this feature from Nuxt to create static sites!

Fetching Data and Generating SSG Sites

To create our static site and to speed up the process, we will re-use the knowledge and skills from *Chapter 3, Managing Assets and Adding UI Frameworks*, in which you learn to server dynamic assets, and from *Chapter 8, Managing Database with PHP Apps for Nuxt*, in which you learn to manage data and metadata with WordPress for populating the body content and head meta of pages in the Nuxt app. So you should be familiar with the steps you are going to follow to generate static pages with Nuxt. So let's recap and find out as follows:

1. Create a `.env.production` in the project root with the base URL of the Nuxt app and WordPress APIs as follows:

````
```
// .env.production
APP_BASE_URL=http://localhost:3000
API_BASE_URL=http://localhost:4000
```
````

2. Add `.env.production` to the `generate` script command with `--dotenv` in `/package.json` as follows:

````
```json
// package.json
"scripts": {
  "build": "nuxt build --dotenv .env.production",
  "dev": "nuxt dev",
  "generate": "nuxt generate --dotenv .env.production",
  "preview": "nuxt preview",
  "postinstall": "nuxt prepare"
````
````

````
    },
    ```
````

Note that you can add `.env.production` to the `build` script command if you want to run your Nuxt app as an SSR app.

3. Ensure you have the following code in `/composables/use-asset.ts` as before for requiring assets:

````
    ```js
    // composables/use-asset.ts
    export default src => {
      if (!src) {
        return
      }

      const array = src.split(‘/’)
      const filename = [...array].pop()
      const images = import.meta.globEager(‘/assets/images/*.
      {jpg,jpeg,png,svg}’)
      const image = images[`/assets/images/${filename}`]
      if (image !== undefined) {
        return image.default
      }
      console.log(`${filename} doesn’t exist locally!`)

      if (src.startsWith(‘http://’) || src.
      startsWith(‘https://’)) {
        return src
      }
      return
  }
    ```
````

Notice that we want to log the image that doesn't exist locally in the `/assets/` directory. If the required image doesn't exist, then we will get it from the remote API, if the full URL path of the image is provided in the string.

4. Fetch projects with an offset in the `<script>` block in `/components/projects/items-with-pager.vue` for the project index and pagination pages:

````
    ```js
    // components/projects/items-with-pager.vue
    <script setup>
````

```
const route = useRoute()
const number = route.params.number
const query = {
  posts_per_page: 6,
  page_number: number === undefined ? 1 : parseInt(number)
}
const { data, refresh, error } = await useF3tch(‘/wp-json/
api/v1/projects/’, {
  method: ‘POST’,
  body: query
})
refresh()
</script>
```

5. Display the fetched projects on the `<template>` block in **`/components/projects/items-with-pager.vue`** for the project index and pagination pages:

```html
// components/projects/items-with-pager.vue
<template>
  <div v-if="data">
    <ul>
      <li v-if="data.prev_page">
        <NuxtLink :to="'/projects/pages/' + data.prev_page">
          Previous
        </NuxtLink>
      </li>
      <li>
        <p v-if="data.current_page && data.total_pages">
          {{ data.current_page }} of {{ data.total_pages }}
        </p>
      </li>
      <li v-if="data.next_page">
        <NuxtLink :to="'/projects/pages/' + data.next_page">
          Next
        </NuxtLink>
      </li>
    </ul>
    <ul>
      <li v-for="post in data.items" :key="post.ID">
        <h3>
          <NuxtLink :to="`/projects/${post.post_name}`">
            {{ post.post_title }}
          </NuxtLink>
```

```
          </h3>
          <div
            v-html="post.excerpt"
          />
          <img
            :alt="post.post_title"
            :src="useAsset(post.thumbnail)"
          />
        </li>
      </ul>
    </div>
  </template>
```

6. Import the preceding `<projects-items-with-pager>` component as before in `/pages/projects/index.vue` for the project index page:

```js
// pages/projects/index.vue
<template>
  <projects-items-with-pager />
</template>
```

7. Import the preceding `<projects-items-with-pager>` component as before in `/pages/projects/pages/[number].vue` for the project pagination pages:

```js
// pages/projects/pages/[number].vue
<template>
  <projects-items-with-pager />
</template>
```

8. Fetch a single project data in the `<script>` block in `/pages/projects/[slug].vue`:

```js
// pages/projects/[slug].vue
<script setup>
const route = useRoute()
const slug = route.params.slug
const { data: post, error } = await useF3tch(`/wp-json/api/
```

````
v1/project/${slug}`)
    </script>
    ```
````

After the data is fetched, we want to make sure there is data in **`post`** before setting the local head meta and overriding the default head meta with **`useHead`**:

````
```js
// pages/projects/[slug].vue
...
if (post.value) {
  const head = unref(post).head
  useHead({
    title: head.title,
    meta: [
      {
        name: ‘description’,
        content: head.description
      },
      {
        name: ‘keywords’,
        content: head.keywords
      },
      {
        property: ‘og:title’,
        content: head.og.title
      },
      {
        property: ‘og:description’,
        content: head.og.description
      },
      {
        property: ‘og:image’,
        content: head.og.image
      }
    ],
  })
}
```
````

9. Display the fetched single project data on the **`&lt;template&gt;`** block in **`/pages/projects/[slug].vue`**:

````
```html
// pages/projects/[slug].vue
````

```
<template>
  <div v-if="post">
    <h2>
      {{ post.post_title }}
    </h2>
    <div
      v-html="post.post_content"
    />

    <h3>
      Post Carousels
    </h3>
    <ul>
      <li v-for="carousel in post.carousels" v-bind:key="carou-
sel.id">
        <h3 v-if="carousel.title">
          {{ carousel.title }}
        </h3>
        <div
          v-if="carousel.description"
          v-html="carousel.description"
        />

        <ul>
          <li v-for="asset in carousel.assets" v-bind:key="as-
set.id">
            <img
              :alt="asset.title || null"
              :src="useAsset(asset.sizes.medium.url)"
            />
          </li>
        </ul>
      </li>
    </ul>

    <h3>
      Post Assets
    </h3>
    <ul>
      <li v-for="asset in post.assets" v-bind:key="asset.id">
        <img
          :alt="asset.title || null"
          :src="useAsset(asset.sizes.medium.url)"
        />
      </li>
    </ul>
  </div>
```

````
</template>
```
````

10. Fetch the project index data in the **`<script>`** block in **`/pages/projects.vue`**:

````
```js
// pages/projects.vue
<script setup>
const route = useRoute()
const { data: post, error } = await useF3tch(`/wp-json/api/
v1/page/projects`)
</script>
```
````

After the data is fetched, we want to make sure there is data in **`post`** before setting the local head meta and overriding the default head meta with **`useHead`**:

````
```js
// pages/projects.vue
...
if (post.value) {
  const head = unref(post).head
  useHead({
    title: head.title,
    meta: [
      {
        name: 'description',
        content: head.description
      },
      {
        property: 'og:title',
        content: head.og.title
      },
      {
        property: 'og:description',
        content: head.og.description
      },
      {
        property: 'og:image',
        content: head.og.image
      }
    ],
  })
}
```
````
````

11. Add the **`<NuxtPage>`** component in the **`<template>`** block for displaying the child component in **`/pages/projects.vue`**:

```html
// pages/projects.vue
<template>
  <div v-if="!error">
    <h2 v-if="!route.params.slug">
      Projects
    </h2>
    <NuxtPage :page-key="route.path" />
  </div>
</template>
```

12. Fetch the home page data in the **`<script>`** block in **`/pages/index.vue`**:

```js
// pages/index.vue
<script setup>
const { data: post } = await useF3tch(`/wp-json/api/v1/page/
home`)
</script>
```

After the data is fetched, we want to make sure there is data in **`post`** before setting the local head meta and overriding the default head meta with **`useHead`**:

```js
// pages/index.vue
...
if (post.value) {
  const head = unref(post).head
  useHead({
    title: head.title,
    meta: [
      {
        name: 'description',
        content: head.description
      },
      {
        name: 'keywords',
        content: head.keywords
      },
```

````
        {
          property: 'og:title',
          content: head.og.title
        },
        {
          property: 'og:description',
          content: head.og.description
        },
        {
          property: 'og:image',
          content: head.og.image
        }
      ],
    })
  }
  ```
````

13. Add the **`Hello World`** message on the **`<template>`** block in **`/pages/index.vue`**:

````
```html
// pages/index.vue
<template>
  <p>
    Hello World!
  </p>
</template>
```
````

14. Fetch the site info data in the **`<script>`** block in **`/app.vue`**:

````
```js
// app.vue
<script setup>
const { data, error } = await useF3tch(`/wp-json/api/v1/
siteinfo`)
</script>
```
````

After the data is fetched, make sure no error before setting the default head meta with **`useHead`**:

````
```js
// app.vue
````

```
...
if (!error.value) {
  const siteinfo = unref(data)
  siteinfo.url = import.meta.env.VITE_APP_BASE_URL

  useHead({
    title: '',
    meta: [
      {
        name: 'description',
        content: siteinfo.description
      },
      {
        name: 'keywords',
        content: siteinfo.keywords
      },
      {
        property: 'og:type',
        content: siteinfo.open_graph.og_type
      },
      {
        property: 'og:url',
        content: siteinfo.url
      },
      {
        property: 'og:title',
        content: siteinfo.title
      },
      {
        property: 'og:description',
        content: siteinfo.description
      },
      {
        property: 'og:image',
        content: siteinfo.open_graph.og_image
      },
      {
        property: 'og:image:width',
        content: siteinfo.open_graph.og_image_width
      },
      {
        property: 'og:image:height',
        content: siteinfo.open_graph.og_image_height
      },
      {
        property: 'fb:app_id',
        content: siteinfo.open_graph.fb_app_id
```

```
        }
      ],
    })
  }
```

15. Add the `<NuxtPage>` component in the `<template>` block for loading pages from the `/pages/` directory in `/app.vue`:

    ```html
    // app.vue
    <template>
      <div v-if="!error">
        <site-header />
        <nav-main />
        <NuxtPage />
      </div>
    </template>
    ```

16. Run the app on the `generate` script command for generating static pages:

    ```
    $ npm run generate
    ```

You should see the following output on your terminal with the logs of images that don't exist locally in the `/assets/` directory:

```
...
i ✓ built in 776ms
✓ Server built in 791ms
✓ Generated public .output/public
i Initializing prerenderer
i Prerendering 5 initial routes with crawler
  ├─ /200.html (72ms)
  ├─ /404.html (72ms)
  ├─ /contact (149ms)
  ├─ /contact/_payload.json (2ms)
  ├─ / (179ms)
  ├─ /_payload.json (1ms)
```

```
R0007183-150x150.jpg doesn’t exist locally!
R0009791-150x150.jpg doesn’t exist locally!
R0007866-150x150.jpg doesn’t exist locally!
R0000261-150x150.jpg doesn’t exist locally!
R0009300-150x150.jpg doesn’t exist locally!
R0003515-150x150.jpg doesn’t exist locally!
...
```

17. Run the app on the `preview` script command to view the built static site on your browser locally:

```
$ npm run preview
```

You should see the following the **Hello World** message appears on the home page of your browser at `localhost:5000`. If you navigate to `localhost:3000/projects` and open up the Console tab on your browser, you should see the following logs of images that don't exist locally in the `/assets/` directory:

```
R0007183-150x150.jpg doesn’t exist locally!
R0009791-150x150.jpg doesn’t exist locally!
R0007866-150x150.jpg doesn’t exist locally!
R0000261-150x150.jpg doesn’t exist locally!
R0009300-150x150.jpg doesn’t exist locally!
R0003515-150x150.jpg doesn’t exist locally!
```

Again, if you navigate to a single project page, for example, `localhost:3000/projects/sample-12` and open up the Console tab on your browser, you should see the following logs of images that don't exist locally in the `/assets/` directory:

```
R0003303.jpg doesn’t exist locally!
R0000166.jpg doesn’t exist locally!
R0007856.jpg doesn’t exist locally!
R0002116.jpg doesn’t exist locally!
R0009300.jpg doesn’t exist locally!
R0003515.jpg doesn’t exist locally!
R0001844.jpg doesn’t exist locally!
```

You have managed to create a static site with Nuxt by re-using the knowledge and skills that you have already learned in the earlier chapters of this book. You should see a `dist` folder generated by Nuxt in your project root. If you inspect this folder, you should see all pages are generated into separate folders with `.html` and `.json` files, in which you find the pre-rendered HTML, metadata, and content of each page. You also should see a `200.html` and a `404.html` files generated for you by Nuxt at the root of the `/dist/` folder. Sweet!

However, as you can see, the logs of images don't exist locally, so this static site isn't perfect yet, because you still rely on WordPress to serve the asset of each page for you remotely. This is not ideal for a static site as we still have to couple with WordPress, which requires a server that supports PHP, such as Apache. Ideally, we want our static site completely standalone independently. Of course, we cannot manually place the asset of each page in the local `/assets/` directory. Hence, we need to pull the remote assets automatically into the `/assets/` directory when generating the static pages. How can we do that? Let's find out in the next topic!

You can find the example apps for this topic in `/1.nuxt/3.cross-domains/2.connect-php/1.wordpress/` in the GitHub repository of this book.

Streaming Assets from WordPress for Static Sites

Assets, whether they are images or videos, are an essential part of a good-looking website. The static site we generated in the previous topic is missing this essential part locally. Nuxt can't generate these remote assets for you, because it assumes you are developing the app with assets stored in the local `/assets/` directory. Nuxt also expects you to develop the server-side business in the local `/server/` directory. So it can't pull the remote assets into the `/assets/` directory for you when generating the static pages. Hence, we need to help Nuxt in this part and that is where Node.js comes in. Let's find out!

Streaming Assets and Generating SSG Sites

Node.js can stream a remote asset and create a copy for us anywhere we want to, in our case, the `/assets/` directory in our Nuxt project. Once we have the assets created automatically in the `/assets/` directory, Nuxt can use them to generate static pages. Only that our static can be fully **static** and standalone independently. So let's find out what you need to do for that to happen in the following steps:

1. Create a `use-stream.ts` file in the `/composables/` directory:

```
├── ...
└── composables
    ├── ...
    └── use-stream.ts
```

2. Add `STREAM=true` to the `.env.production` file to tell your Nuxt app to stream resources from the remote API as follows:

```
// .env.production
APP_BASE_URL=http://localhost:3000
API_BASE_URL=http://localhost:4000

STREAM=true
```

Or, better, pass the environment variables through Vite directly as follows:

```
// .env.production
...
VITE_APP_BASE_URL=http://localhost:3000
VITE_API_BASE_URL=http://localhost:4000

VITE_STREAM=true
```

If you are using the Vite way to set environment variables, then you don't need to configure them again in `/nuxt.config.ts`. You can access them later from Vite directly on any page and component.

3. Refactor the `useAsset` composable to stream the remote asset with a `useStream` composable in `/composables/use-asset.ts`:

```js
// composables/use-asset.ts
export default (src, relativePath) => {
  if (!src) {
    return
```

```
    }

    const array = src.split('/')
    const filename = [...array].pop()
    const images = import.meta.globEager('/assets/images/*.
    {jpg,jpeg,png,svg}')
    const image = images[`/assets/images/${filename}`]
    if (image !== undefined) {
      return image.default
    }
    console.log(`${filename} doesn't exist locally!`)

    const apiBaseUrl = import.meta.env.VITE_API_BASE_URL
    const isStream = import.meta.env.VITE_STREAM
    if (relativePath) {
      src = `${apiBaseUrl}${relativePath}${filename}`
    }
    if (import.meta.env.SSR && isStream === 'true') {
      useStream(src, filename)
    }
    if (src.startsWith('http://') || src.
    startsWith('https://')) {
      return src
    }
    return
  }
```

In the preceding refactored code, the function accepts two arguments: **`src`** and **`relativePath`**. So if the value of **`relativePath`** is provided, then we construct the string value of **`src`** with **`apiBaseUrl`**, **`relativePath`**, and **`filename`**. For example, you can provide **`R0003303.jpg`** as the value for **`src`**, and **`/contents/uploads/`** as the value for **`relativePath`**. Then they will be used to construct a new value for **`src`** as follows:

```
http://localhost:4000/contents/uploads/R0003303.jpg
```

The preceding string value is then passed to the **`useStream`** composable with the value of **`filename`**. Note that we use **`import.meta.env.SSR`** in the if-condition block to ensure that the **`useStream`** composable is used on the server side only. Also, notice how we access the environment variables directly from Vite using **`import.meta.env`**:

```js
const apiBaseUrl = import.meta.env.VITE_API_BASE_URL
const isStream = import.meta.env.VITE_STREAM
```

4. Create the **`useStream`** composable with **`stream`** and **`fs`** modules from Node.js in **`/composables/use-stream.ts`** as follows:

```js
// composables/use-stream.ts
import stream from ‘node:stream’
import fs from ‘fs’

export default async (src, filename) => {
  const desc = fs.createWriteStream(‘./assets/images/’
   + filename)

  stream.Readable
    .fromWeb((await fetch(src)).body)
    .pipe(desc)
}
```

In the preceding code, we get the info of **`src`** and **`filename`** from the **`useAsset`** composable, then use the Node.js Fetch and Stream APIs to fetch and create resources from the remote server. Alternatively, you can install and use **Axios** (https://github.com/axios/axios) to do the same thing:

```js
...
const { data } = await axios({
  url: src,
  method: ‘GET’,
  responseType: ‘stream’
})
data.pipe(desc)
```

For more information about the Node.js Stream API, please visit https://nodejs.org/api/stream.html.

5. Run the app on the **`generate`** script command for streaming assets first for the static pages:

```
$ npm run generate
```

You should see the following output on your terminal with the logs of images that don't exist locally in the **`/assets/`** directory:

```
...
i ✓ built in 776ms
✓ Server built in 791ms
✓ Generated public .output/public
i Initializing prerenderer
i Prerendering 5 initial routes with crawler
  ├─ /200.html (72ms)
  ├─ /404.html (72ms)
  ├─ /contact (149ms)
  ├─ /contact/_payload.json (2ms)
  ├─ / (179ms)
  ├─ /_payload.json (1ms)
R0007183-150x150.jpg doesn't exist locally!
R0009791-150x150.jpg doesn't exist locally!
R0007866-150x150.jpg doesn't exist locally!
R0000261-150x150.jpg doesn't exist locally!
R0009300-150x150.jpg doesn't exist locally!
R0003515-150x150.jpg doesn't exist locally!
...
```

In the preceding process, when the log is printed on the terminal, the **`useStream`** composable is triggered to stream the remote asset and create a local copy in the local **`/assets/`** directory.

6. Run the app on the **`generate`** script command **one more time** to generate static pages:

```
$ npm run generate
```

You should see the following output on your terminal **without** the logs anymore:

```
...
i ✓ built in 802ms
✓ Server built in 815ms
✓ Generated public .output/public
i Initializing prerenderer
i Prerendering 5 initial routes with crawler
  ├─ /200.html (100ms)
  ├─ /404.html (100ms)
  ├─ /contact (224ms)
  ├─ /contact/_payload.json (1ms)
  ├─ / (295ms)
  ├─ /projects (314ms)
  ├─ /_payload.json (2ms)
  ├─ /projects/_payload.json (1ms)
  ├─ /projects/sample-12 (200ms)
  ├─ /projects/sample-10 (216ms)
...
```

7. Run the app on the `preview` script command to view the built static site on your browser locally:

```
$ npm run preview
```

You should see the following the "**Hello World**" message appears on the home page on your browser at `localhost:5000`. If you navigate to `localhost:3000/projects` or a single project page, `localhost:3000/projects/sample-12`, you will no longer see the log that says the image doesn't exist locally.

There you go. A static site that is fully standing alone – just with a little help from Node.js. You just have to refactor the existing `useAsset` composable and create a `useStream` to stream and create a copy of the asset with the Node.js Fetch, Stream, and File System APIs. If you inspect the `/assets/` directory, you should see all images created inside the `/images/` sub-directory. That is perfect! A perfection indeed, isn't it? Thanks to Node.js.

With static sites, we no longer need a Node.js server, or a server to run PHP and WordPress. We can move anywhere and get them hosted in a static hosting server, which can save you lots of money in the long term – only if your site is meant to be static and doesn't need the server process. Before moving your static site to a production server, you should always check the static pages locally whether are really static and independent. For that, you can use a server, for example, Apache server, to create a port in your local machine that can be accessed publicly on your browser, for example, an `` `8000` `` port. Then dump all the static pages into an independent folder outside your Nuxt project and configure your server to point the `` `8000` `` port to this folder. After that, you can access your static site on your browser at `` `localhost:8000` ``. Once you have done checking and testing, and you are finally happy with it, the static site can be uploaded to the live production server.

You can find the example apps for this topic in `` `/1.nuxt/3.cross-domains/2.connect-php/1.wordpress/` `` in the GitHub repository of this book.

Going Further and Knowing Your Options

It has been quite a journey. You've gone from learning the directory structure of Nuxt to adding pages, routes, stores, and composables, to managing data with Nitro in Nuxt, to Node.js HTTP servers, PHP, WordPress, MongoDB, RethinkDB, MySQL, Redis, GraphQL, and to creating static sites with Node.js Fetch, Stream, and File System APIs. But before closing this chapter and bidding farewell, we should look at testing and deploying your Nuxt apps, checking out other Nuxt modules and APIs that we didn't cover in this book but are there for you to leverage, and then lastly, besides Nuxt, you should know that there are other SSR and SSG options and we are going to look into them in the following sections.

Testing Your Nuxt Apps

Testing in Nuxt 3 is still in development. The APIs and behaviors for testing your Nuxt.js applications may change in the near future. So testing will not be included in this book. However, you can check out the following test runners that are officially supported in Nuxt 3:

- Jest (https://jestjs.io/)
- Vitest (https://github.com/vitest-dev/vitest)

Also, you are encouraged to use **JavaScript Standard Style** (https://standardjs.com/) to lint your JavaScript code. You can install it globally or locally to test and fix the errors you might make in your code. For example, if you want to install it locally that applies to a specific Nuxt project only, you can add install it via `npm` as a development dependency and create the following command scripts in the `package.json` file as follows:

````
```json
// package.json
{
  ...
  "scripts": {
    ...
    "test": "standard src/**/*.{js,ts}",
    "fix": "standard --fix src/**/*.{js,ts}"
  },
  ...
  "devDependencies": {
    "standard": "^17.0.0"
  }
}
```
````

You can find an example app for the preceding configurations in `/2.native/3.mongodb/` in the GitHub repository of this book. For more info about testing in Nuxt 3, please check it out at https://nuxt.com/docs/getting-started/testing.

Deploying Your Nuxt Apps

Of course, you will need to deploy your Nuxt app when it is completely developed and ready for production. You can deploy to a Node.js server (ideally) for SSR Nuxt apps, a static hosting server such as GitHub Pages (https://pages.github.com/) for SSG Nuxt apps, a serverless platform for SSG Nuxt apps (again) that don't need any server-side processing or an edge CDN server.

If you are deploying to a Node.js server for an SSR Nuxt app, you can simply build it locally with the `build` command script and deploy the generated `.output` folder to the server. And then use `node` to execute your SSR app from your terminal as follows:

````
```
$ node .output/server/index.mjs
```
````

However, your app will "**die**" when you close your terminal. If you want to "**survive**" that, you will need to use **PM2** (https://pm2.keymetrics.io/), a daemon process manager, to help you manage and keep your apps always online 24/7. For example:

~~~~
```
$ cd /var/www/[path-to-your-nuxt-app]/
$ pm2 start npm --name "my-nuxt-app" -- start
```
~~~~

Of course, you need to install PM2 on your Node.js server before you can run the preceding `pm2` command:

~~~~
```
$ npm i pm2 -g
```
~~~~

And most importantly, you have the `start` command script set in the `package.json` file:

~~~~
```json
// package.json
{
  ...
  "scripts": {
    ...
    "start": "./.output/server/index.mjs"
  }
}
```
~~~~

You might need to install the package dependencies of your SSR app on the Node.js server if you have set any of them in the "**dependencies**" key in the `package.json` file. For more information about deploying Nuxt 3 apps, please check it out at https://nuxt.com/docs/getting-started/deployment.

Knowing Other Nuxt Modules and APIs

Nuxt 3 has a list of useful Nuxt modules, created by the Nuxt team and community, that you can install and integrate with your Nuxt app automatically. We only have used Nuxt Content in *Chapter 6, Managing Data with Nitro Server Engine in Nuxt*, for managing our data with Markdown documents, Whereas we have integrated many other libraries and software manually, such as Pinia in *Chapter 5, Managing States and Stores*, for managing stores. You can use a Nuxt module,

`@pinia/nuxt` (https://nuxt.com/modules/pinia), to integrate with Pinia if you want to. There are a few Nuxt modules that are worth looking into:

- **gtag** (https://nuxt.com/modules/gtag) for using Google Analytics 4 (https://developers.google.com/analytics/devguides/collection/ga4?hl=en) to track user activities.
- **Unocss** (https://nuxt.com/modules/unocss) for using UnoCSS (https://unocss.dev/) to style your app HTML with utility-first CSS. Note that UnoCSS can be considered as the next generation of Windi CSS (https://windicss.org/) that we used in *Chapter* 3, *Managing Assets and Adding* UI *Frameworks*. You can consider this Nuxt module if you want to migrate from Windi CSS.
- **swiper** (https://nuxt.com/modules/swiper) for using Swiper.js (https://swiperjs.com/) to create desktop and mobile-friendly touch sliders.
- **vee-validate** (https://nuxt.com/modules/vee-validate) for using VeeValidate (https://vee-validate.logaretm.com/v4/) to validate forms.
- **authjs** (https://nuxt.com/modules/authjs) for using Auth.js (https://authjs.dev/) to authenticate user logins.

The preceding Nuxt modules are probably the basic "**helpers**" you would need to develop a website that is packed with modern CSS styles, image/ video carousal/ sliders, forms such as a contact form, and users to log in to access certain protected pages. You can check out the rest of Nuxt modules to suit your needs at https://nuxt.com/modules. However, bear in mind that bloating a project/ website with tons of external dependencies or Nuxt modules isn't good for future long-term maintenance. You might be stuck at a dependency forever if it is unfortunately deprecated or outdated and that can jeopardize your website. So, you are encouraged to integrate any library and software manually if you can, just like you have learned in this book, unless something that cannot be achieved without the help of a Nuxt module. For example, the `useCooki3` composable that you have learned to create in *Chapter* 5, *Managing States and Stores*, for setting, updating, and removing cookies in the shopping cart system, if you can develop it without any other libraries and dependencies, then do it on your own as it can give you more control and keep your project lightweight. It is easier to debug and fix when bugs pop out.

Besides Nuxt modules, Nuxt APIs are Nuxt internals that you can benefit from. We have used some Nuxt composable heavily in the earlier chapters, such as `useFetch`, `useHead`, `useRoute`, `useRouter`, and `useRuntimeConfig`. We even have built a custom composable, `useF3tch`, on top of `useFetch`, since *Chapter* 4, *Fetching Data and Handling Errors*, for fetching data and modifying the default Nuxt error object. We also have used some Nuxt utils a lot in this book, such as `` `createError` ``, `` `definePageMeta` ``, and `` `showError` ``. Moreover, we have used some Nuxt components heavily in the previous chapters, such as `` `<NuxtPage>` ``, `` `<NuxtLayout>` ``, and `` `<NuxtLink>` ``. There are many more Nuxt APIs available than this book can cover! However, there are a few Nuxt APIs that are worth knowing that they exist and might be helpful for you at some point in the future:

- **Nuxt Composables**:
  - `` `useRequestEvent` `` (https://nuxt.com/docs/api/composables/use-request-event)
  - `` `useRequestHeaders` `` (https://nuxt.com/docs/api/composables/use-request-headers)
  - `` `useRequestURL` `` (https://nuxt.com/docs/api/composables/use-request-url)
  - `` `useSeoMeta` `` (https://nuxt.com/docs/api/composables/use-seo-meta)
  - `` `useServerSeoMeta` ``(https://nuxt.com/docs/api/composables/use-server-seo-meta)
- **Nuxt Utils**:
  - `` `$fetch` `` (https://nuxt.com/docs/api/utils/dollarfetch)
  - `` `onBeforeRouteLeave` `` (https://nuxt.com/docs/api/utils/on-before-route-leave)
  - `` `onBeforeRouteUpdate` `` (https://nuxt.com/docs/api/utils/on-before-route-update)
  - `` `refreshNuxtData` `` (https://nuxt.com/docs/api/utils/refresh-nuxt-data)
- **Nuxt Components**:
  - `` `<ClientOnly>` `` (https://nuxt.com/docs/api/components/client-only)
  - `` `<Teleport>` `` (https://nuxt.com/docs/api/components/teleports)
  - `` `<NuxtImg>` `` (https://nuxt.com/docs/api/components/nuxt-img)
  - `` `<NuxtPicture>` `` (https://nuxt.com/docs/api/components/nuxt-picture)

For more information about the preceding Nuxt APIs and the rest of them, please visit https://nuxt.com/docs/api. Of course, just like Nuxt modules, if there is something you can create and manage on your own, you are always encouraged to do so, even though Nuxt APIs are more reliable than Nuxt modules. But, for example, since we now can use Node.js Fetch API out of the box already, we can make use of it instead if we need to, rather than using Nuxt's `` `$fetch` `` or `` `useFetch` ``, which are based on UnJS `ofetch` (https://github.com/unjs/ofetch). Using our own custom composables and functions always gives us more controls and is easier to debug. Also, they are more plug-able if we want to use them outside Nuxt, such as in a Node.js HTTP or Express app.

Knowing Other SSR and SSG Options

If you are building a serious and large web app, any kind of SPA is not a good solution, especially if you are concerned about SEO. You would want to see all the HTML tags and data of your SPA rendered on the browser, just like the traditional SSR web app, such as WordPress and Node.js apps (for example, an Express app). A hybrid app such as Nuxt is the best of both worlds. But to create a Vue SSR app, we don't necessarily need to use Nuxt. We can create Vue SSR apps with Vite SSR and Node.js HTTP server.

Creating a Vue SSR app is possible just because of the `` `renderToString` `` API from Vue that renders our app into an HTML string. We only need a Node.js server-side server (it also can be an Express app) to handle the rendered HTML string. But we also need Vite to perform HMR and load ESM modules for development, and build our SSR app for production. For example, some snippets of a Vue SSR:

- The entry file for the server side:

````
```js
// entry-server.ts
import { renderToString } from ‘vue/server-renderer’
import { createApp } from ‘./main’

const app = createApp()
async function render(url) {
  const appHtml = await renderToString(app)
  return appHtml
}

export { render }
```
````

- The entry file for the client side:

````
```js
````
````

```
// entry-client.ts
import { createApp } from './main.js'

createApp().mount('#app')
```

- The main Vue app that is shared between the server and client:

```js
// main.ts
import { createSSRApp } from 'vue'
import App from './App.vue'

export function createApp () {
  return createSSRApp(App)
}
```

Of course, this is a low-level approach and you need to do the setup for handling the rendered HTML string from Vue. Nuxt is a high-level framework and it takes care of the chores for us with many other APIs out of the box, such as `useFetch`. But being able to build a Vue SSR app from the bottom-up is rewarding and we have much more control over the app. For more information about Vue SSR and Vite SSR, please visit https://vuejs.org/guide/scaling-up/ssr.html and https://vitejs.dev/guide/ssr.html.

If you are interested in building a low-level Vue SSR, as well as Vue SPA, you can check out Advanced Vue.js Web Development (https://github.com/lautiamkok/Advanced-Vue.js-Web-Development) by the same author of this book. If you want to go for **Nuxt 2**, or you are working on existing Nuxt projects that are on Nuxt 2 and prefer to stay that way, please check out *Hands-on Nuxt.js Web Development* (https://www.packtpub.com/product/hands-on-nuxt-js-web-development/9781789952698), which is written by the same author as well.

However, you might have wondered: what is the alternative to Nuxt for high-level server-side rendering? **Quasar**. Quasar allows you to target SPA, SSR, PWA, mobile app, desktop app, and browser extension (however, no SSG support internally). You can find out more about this high-level solution at https://quasar.dev/. Besides Nuxt, Quasar, Vue SSR, and Vite SSR, you also can use a Vite community plugin such as `vite-ssr` (https://github.com/frandiox/vite-ssr) for creating Vue 3 SSR apps. Creating a Vue SSR app with Vite and Node.js HTTP API from the bottom-up is perhaps rewarding, but we can use the **`vite-ssr`** plugin can do the same thing by simplifying our process as follows:

````
```js
// main.ts
import App from ‘./App’
import routes from ‘./routes’
import viteSSR from ‘vite-ssr’

export default viteSSR(
  App,
  { routes },
  (context) => {
  ...
  }
)
```
````

That's right, with the **`vite-ssr`** plugin, we only need one single entry file by default, as opposed to three files if we use Vue SSR and Vite SSR alone. For more information about this Vite SSR plugin, please visit https://github.com/frandiox/vite-ssr.

On the other hand, if you are looking for Nuxt alternatives for building SSG apps, you have the following options:

- **Gridsome**

Gridsome is an alternative to Nuxt if you want to take Vue further for building SSG websites and apps with GraphQL as a centralized data layer. You can use any headless CMSs (such as WordPress), APIs, or Markdown files for data sourcing. However, the current stable version (https://gridsome.org/) of Gridsome does not support Vue 3, nor does the next generation (https://next.gridsome.org/) of Gridsome. So you will have to stick to Vue 2 and Options API if you go for Gridsome.

GraphQL data layer is the main attractive key feature of Gridsome. If you are interested in using GraphQL, Hands-on Nuxt.js Web Development has also covered this exciting technology for querying data. However, the advantage of Gridsome is that it comes with GraphQL support by default. So you don't have to install this data layer technology manually. The only you need is to pick up GraphQL and bring in your own data. But if you don't want to use GraphQL, then Gridsome is not the right option for you to venture further.

- **VuePress**

VuePress is a good choice if you want to take Vue further for building SSG sites with a markdown-centered project structure. In VuePress, you write your site contents in Markdown documents in which you have the frontmatter data inserted. The advantage of using VuePress is that it comes with Markdown support by default. You don't have to create the Markdown data layer yourself. However, the current version (https://vuepress.vuejs.org/) of VuePress does not support Vue 3, only the next version (https://v2.vuepress.vuejs.org/) does, which is version 2.

In VuePress 2, you will have APIs like `usePageData`, `usePageFrontmatter`, `usePageHead`, `useSiteData`, and so on, that come from VuePress by default and you can use them in `<script setup>` blocks. For more about these Composition APIs from VuePress 2, please visit https://v2.vuepress.vuejs.org/reference/client-api.html#composition-api. However, bear in mind that VuePress 2 is still a beta, so it should not be used for production yet.

VuePress in nature is a popular choice for building documentation sites. If you need a Vue-powered framework for creating a documentation site, VuePress is worth venturing into. But you can use VuePress for other purposes if it suits you. You can check out a good example of a personal site that runs VuePress at https://davidangel.net/. Also, check out Awesome VuePress (https://github.com/vuepress/awesome-vuepress) for things related to VuePress, such as plugins and themes for your VuePress sites.

- **VitePress**

Like VuePress, VitePress (https://vitepress.vuejs.org/) is well-suited for building documentation sites. VitePress is built on top of Vue 3 and Vite. So you can use Composition API in VitePress. It also comes with some composition methods (https://vitepress.vuejs.org/guide/api.html#helper-methods) of its own like `useData`, `useRoute`, `useRouter`, and `withBase` that you can use in `<script setup>` blocks out of the box. Because it uses Vite, it has a faster dev server start and hot updates just like the standard Vue apps you have created on top of Vite in the previous chapters.

VitePress is production-ready, but it is still very new. And that you should expect some changes in the coming minor releases on the configuration and theming API. So use it with caution. Compared to VuePress, VitePress is more minimalist, while VuePress is more complex. For example, there are more predefined variables in the frontmatter in VuePress. VuePress has a large ecosystem and its community is bigger. Also, VitePress targets the browsers that support native ES module imports only. So these are some basic things to consider when venturing into VitePress, which has the Vue 3 support out of the box.

- **Other SSG Options**

You can use one of the preceding options that suits you for a static-site generation. Otherwise, you can use a community plugin, `` `vite-ssg` `` (https://github.com/antfu/vite-ssg), for pre-rendering your Vue 3 app. How to use `` `vite-ssg` `` is similar to how we use `` `vite-ssr` ``:

````
```js
// src/main.js
import { ViteSSG } from 'vite-ssg'
import App from './App.vue'

export const createApp = ViteSSG(
  App,
  { routes },
  ({ app, router, routes, isClient, initialState }) => {
    ...
  }
)
```
````

Last, but not least, it is worth mentioning that you also can use Vite alone for pre-rendering the Vue 3 SSG app. For more information about this option, please visit https://vitejs.dev/guide/ssr.html#pre-rendering-ssg.

As you can see, Nuxt is still evolving. Even though testing isn't quite there yet, Nuxt is evolving fast. It is indeed. You may find it hard to catch up or even to migrate if started off with Nuxt 2. However, Nuxt evolves with Vue. Nuxt goes where Vue goes. If testing is important for you in your project, or if you feel adventurous and want to explore possibilities or solutions outside Nuxt, you always can start with a low-level and lightweight approach with Vue and other options that this last topic has informed you. But bear in mind that Nuxt is a high-lever Vue framework. It has done all the chores for you to create SSR and SSG Vue apps out of the box. And, most importantly, Nuxt has a strong and large community! It is loved and enjoyed by many.

Conclusion

Congratulations! You have completed this Book, which attempts to show you what you can do and create with Nuxt alone, or in conjunction with other amazing technologies, frameworks, and tools in the past chapters. Let's take a last look at the prominent ones you have learned from this book:

- Vite
- Windi CSS
- Less CSS
- Pinia
- Redis
- MongoDB
- RethinkDB
- MySQL
- Socket.IO
- GraphQL
- GraphQL Tools
- WordPress
- Node.js HTTP API
- Node.js Fetch API
- Node.js Stream API
- Node.js File System API

Indeed, it has been quite a journey, hoping that it has been an inspiring journey and that you will be adopting Nuxt and the preceding awesome technologies, frameworks, and tools in your projects wherever they fit, taking them further to benefit yourself and the community. Be inspiring and inspired. Keep coding and enjoy it!

Index

Symbols

A

B

C

D

E

F

G

H